Evangelical Catholics

KEITH A. FOURNIER

THOMAS NELSON PUBLISHERS

NASHVILLE

Published in Nashville, Tennessee, by Thomas Nelson, Inc., and distributed in Canada by Lawson Falle, Ltd., Cambridge, Ontario.

Unless otherwise noted, scripture quotations are from the NEW AMERICAN BIBLE, Copyright © 1987, by Thomas Nelson Publishers. Other translations used are the NEW KING JAMES VERSION of the Bible, Copyright © 1983, 1982, 1980, 1979, by Thomas Nelson Publishers; the HOLY BIBLE, NEW INTERNATIONAL VERSION, Copyright © 1984, 1978, 1973, by the Zondervan Corporation; THE HOLY BIBLE, REVISED STANDARD VERSION, Copyright © 1965, by the Zondervan Corporation; THE JERUSALEM BIBLE, Copyright © 1966 by Darton, Longman & Todd Ltd. and Doubleday & Company, Inc.

Library of Congress Cataloging-in-Publication Data

Fournier, Keith A., 1954–
    Evangelical Catholics / Keith A. Fournier.
      p.   cm.
    Includes bibliographical references.
    ISBN 0-8407-7196-7
    1. Evangelistic work—Philosophy. 2. Catholic Church—Doctrines.
3. Catholic Church—Membership. 4. Catholic Church—Relations-
-Evangelicalism. 5. Evangelicalism—Relations—Catholic Church.
6. Fournier, Keith A., 1954-   . I. Title.
BX2347.4.F68   1990
269′.2′08822—dc20   90-43529
                                        CIP

Printed in the United States of America
1 2 3 4 5 6 7 — 95 94 93 92 91 90

Contents

DEDICATION

This book is lovingly and admiringly dedicated to two men whom I count it a privilege to call my friends. They are both great evangelical Christians and deeply rooted in their respective church tradition and heritage. Their courage, prophetic insight, and holy example have inspired and fueled my own conviction that the time has come for evangelical believers of all Christian communions to recognize the urgency of these times and rise to call one another brother.

To my brothers:

Father Michael Scanlan, T.O.R., and Chuck Colson

Foreword

By CHARLES COLSON

A few years ago I was invited to Franciscan University of Steubenville, in Ohio, to receive the Poverello award. I had been to many Christian campuses and had had an opportunity to meet with students from many denominations, but this was my first visit to a Catholic university. At first glance the campus looked like any other. But as I walked across the grounds, I felt a sense of purposefulness often missing from college campuses. Students were involved in evangelistic outreach and community service; they were hungry for academic and spiritual growth; perhaps most exciting of all, many had knit themselves together into small households of commitment and accountability.

While on campus, I met one truly outstanding able young man, the Dean of Evangelism and the University's legal counsel, Keith Fournier. Like myself, Keith had pursued a career in law and later coupled it with a ministry of evangelistic outreach. When he arrived in Steubenville as an undergraduate some years ago, the school was on the verge of spiritual and academic collapse. Drugs, sexual promiscuity, and hopelessness were epidemic. There was even talk of closing the campus. Keith and his mentor, the University's President, Father Mike Scanlan, committed themselves to encouraging true discipleship among the students. And God proved faithful.

The changes at Steubenville have been miraculous. They can only be attributed to a great movement of the Holy Spirit among people completely committed to Christian living within the Catholic Church. Evangelical Catholics.

Only in recent years have the terms *evangelical* and *Catholic* been joined. And those who claim both—like Keith Fournier—are often misunderstood by their brothers and sisters in the faith, be they Catholic or Protestant. This isn't surprising. The pain and distrust between Catholics and Protestants goes back centuries. The church has often been plagued by wars within her walls, crippling her in her battle against the encroaching armies of secularism.

But at root, those who are called of God, whether Catholic or Protestant, are part of the same Body. What they share is a belief in the basics: the virgin birth, the deity of Christ, His bodily resurrection, His imminent return, and the authority of His infallible Word. They also share the same mission: presenting Christ as Savior and Lord to a needy world. Those who hold to these truths and act on this commission are evangelical Christians.

Soviet dissident Aleksandr Solzhenitsyn once said that our efforts at reconciliation are far too slow—the world is perishing a hundred times more quickly. It's high time that all of us who are Christians come together regardless of the difference of our confessions and our traditions and make common cause to bring Christian values to bear in our society. When the barbarians are scaling the walls, there is no time for petty quarreling in the camp.

Keith Fournier stands in the breach—truly orthodox in his adherence to Catholic doctrine and fully evangelical in his relationship to Christ and His creation. Keith's ministry is one of healing. Without compromising or diluting his faith, without any false ecumenism, he calls all of us as Christians to our common heritage and mission. He is building alliances against our mutual enemy. This book is going to make an immense contribution to that cause.

I've found very few people with more gifts and talents being used for the glory of the Lord than Keith Fournier. I am proud to count him among my dearest friends. I pray that his book will be read by Catholics and Protestants alike, that it will be a bridge across many of the historic divisions in the church that have weakened our stand in today's culture.

If, like myself, you count yourself a Protestant in the Reformed tradition, you may be surprised to discover yourself more at home with Keith's thinking than with that of many of your Protestant brothers and sisters. If you are an orthodox Catholic, you may find you are truly part of the evangelical camp.

We have much to forgive, much to relearn. But *Evangelical Catholics* can help us do both so we can band together against the rising tides of secularism which threaten to engulf us.

May God grant healing to His church.

Acknowledgments

I will never forget the morning in 1988 when I awoke in my hotel room to find anti-Catholic literature stuffed under my door. I was surprised and saddened to see this kind of thing happen at the National Religious Broadcasters Convention. But after sorting through my reactions to this literature in a conversation with the Lord, I decided to stay at the Convention and make the most of the opportunity. After all, I knew the incident did not reflect the sentiments of most of the Convention's participants.

That morning numerous seminars were offered. The one I chose was called "How to Get Your Manuscript Published." Writing had been a strong desire of mine for some time so it was a natural choice.

When I arrived in the seminar room, it was overflowing with aspiring Christian authors. Most of the major evangelical Protestant publishing houses were represented. Each representative presented their company's history, philosophy, and needs. Each did an excellent job. They then invited questions from the floor. I listened with keen interest while several authors shared their concepts and struggles with these publishing moguls. Finally, after about forty minutes I moved to the microphone and asked what I now believe was an insensitive question: "Do any of you publish manuscripts by authors from ancient churches?"

A hush swept the room. The expressions on the faces of the panel seemed to range from shock to indignation. One member finally retorted, "We are all members of ancient churches. What do you mean?"

I answered, "Well, I am a Catholic. In fact, I am an evangelical Catholic. To me, these are not contradictory terms but complementary. . . . I believe the word evangelical is an adjective, not a noun, and it's the proper domain of Christians of all traditions."

Each panel member then began to tell me how I could go about submitting to their company. I still felt nervousness in the room. Their explanations were followed by an awkward silence broken only by a strong voice from the Thomas Nelson table, "I'd like to talk to you after the session." I promptly sat down, somewhat befuddled, but intrigued by the invitation.

After the seminar was over, I met Bruce Barbour, publisher of Thomas Nelson. He shared with me his interest in my comments, and we initiated that day what has become a friendship I truly cherish. He also asked for an outline of my book, which has evolved into the book you are now reading.

As this book has developed, what I have found in Bruce, in Bill Watkins, my editor, and in Thomas Nelson, is, in fact, an example of the kind of mutuality of respect this book is calling for. It has been a real joy to discover a company which recognizes the evangelical mandate given to all Christians in this challenging time in history and which is willing to take risks for the sake of the Kingdom. I am deeply grateful.

So it is with great appreciation that I wish to acknowledge the hard work and assistance of two wonderful people in the long process of developing this book: Mary Sansone and Bill Watkins.

Mary is a devout Catholic Christian who has served as my graduate assistant and has become a treasured friend. She represents to me the best of what the Lord is sending out from Franciscan University of Steubenville. She is in love with the Lord Jesus Christ completely and given to His holy church. I am grateful for her many long hours of dedicated listening, arguing, affirming, and editing.

Bill, senior editor of Thomas Nelson Publishers, is a devout evangelical Protestant Christian. He considers himself a "Protestant Thomist" (a contradiction in terms?). His sensitivity, intelligence, hard work, and kindness will always be appreciated. He represents the best to me of a publishing house deeply committed to Jesus Christ, the Evangel, and to excellence in His service.

PART I

Evangelical Moments

CHAPTER 1

Evangelical Catholic: A Contradiction in Terms?

I am a Christian.

I am a Catholic Christian.

I am an evangelical Catholic Christian.

To many who read all three claims, they are either contradictory or can only stand together in certain limited configurations. Nevertheless, it is my contention and my experience that not only can I be all three, but each is necessary to define my relationship with Jesus Christ and with His church as well as my role in the church's ongoing mission to bring all men and women to salvation in Jesus Christ.

I am not alone. An evangelical wave is sweeping Christian churches of every tradition, including my own. And it is leaving in its wake renewed and committed believers who are striving to reevangelize their churches and evangelize the nations.

But, for the most part, these believers are doing their work apart from one another. Long-standing historical rifts, deep-seated doctrinal misunderstandings, even spiritual pride have all played devastating roles in keeping them from working together to penetrate the contemporary darkness with the light of the gospel. Without denying their important and genuine distinctives in doctrine and practice, evangelical Christians of all traditions must join forces if they have any hope of fulfilling the church's Great Commission, spoken through our common Savior and Lord, Jesus Christ:

> Then Jesus approached and said to them, "All power in
> heaven and on earth has been given to me. Go, therefore, and
> make disciples of all nations, baptizing them in the name of
> the Father, and of the Son, and of the Holy Spirit, teaching
> them to observe all that I have commanded you. And behold,
> I am with you always, until the end of the age." (Matt. 28:18–
> 20)

I am one of these believers, committed to Christ and His
Commission. And I believe with every fiber of my being that we
stand on the threshold of an unprecedented opportunity to reach
the world for our Lord. All that stands in our way is ourselves.
Christ promised the church victory over all the powers of hell
(Matt. 16:18), but He also warned us that a house divided against
itself will not stand (Matt. 12:25). The church today is a house
divided. The Family of families is suffering the destructive effects
of divorce. Catholics, Protestants, and Orthodox all have the same
Christ and Commission, but they are pursuing Him and His work
as separated brothers and sisters. Consequently, when the world
looks for the Family founded on and functioning by unifying love,
they see the Family filled with members who deeply distrust each
other, label each other, fight against each other, and accuse each
other. Satan must be pleased. Certainly God is not.

On the other hand, the more I travel, read, and listen, I
discover pockets of believers who have not allowed their differences
to divide their efforts. Many of these movements have sprung up
among the laity, but some others have been birthed by professional
church leaders. All saw the light of day when they lifted their heads
above the fog of divisiveness and caught the glittering rays of unity
founded on a common agenda—penetrating society with the gospel
of Christ. And this was made possible, oddly enough, by retaining
rather than rejecting their doctrinal and ecclesiastical distinctives.
We Christians have differences—important, critical differences.
But we have far more in common both in beliefs and in mission.
These believers have built on their commonalities without denying
their differences.

This is a book about commonalities and differences, unity
and divisiveness, true ecumenism and false ecumenism. This book
is a call, even a plea, to all Christians to pound their weapons into

ploughs and to use them to tenderly plant and fertilize the seeds of the gospel throughout the world and to nurture their growth in the life-giving power of the Holy Spirit. We can—and must—do this together. This book is an apologetic for this agenda and a plea to embrace it.

My defense begins here, by explaining how I can legitimately claim that I am an evangelical Catholic Christian. My defense begins with the personal because that is where Christ begins. He builds His church and wins the world one person at a time. Yes, He's concerned with community, but communities are founded on individuals. He begins with Amanda, John, Hillary, Steven—not with Europe, Japan, Ohio, or San Francisco.

WHY I AM A CHRISTIAN

Acts 11:26 tells us that first-century believers were first called Christians in ancient Antioch. *Christian* simply means "follower of Christ." The word was coined to describe those who claimed to have a personal relationship with Jesus the Messiah and were committed to serving Him.

I am a Christian. As I will explain in more detail in Chapters 2 and 3, I have personally placed my trust in Jesus Christ as my Savior and Lord; I have committed my life to following Him. I do not follow perfectly. Like all disciples, I am a learner, and I am lesser than my Master. But I am still a Christian, a Christ follower. *Christian* is the noun that defines who I am in relationship to the triune, living God.

As a Christian, I am also deeply rooted in the doctrinal essentials of the Christian faith. Though first revealed in the person of Jesus Christ and later proclaimed in the sacred Scripture, these essentials were reformulated and reaffirmed throughout church history in numerous creeds. One of the earliest was the Apostles' Creed:

> I believe in God, the Father almighty, creator of heaven and earth;
> And in Jesus Christ, his only Son, our Lord; who was conceived by the Holy Spirit, born of the Virgin Mary,

suffered under Pontius Pilate, was crucified, died, and was buried. He descended into hell; the third day he arose again from the dead; He ascended into heaven, and sits at the right hand of God, the Father almighty; from thence He shall come to judge the living and the dead.
I believe in the Holy Spirit, the holy catholic Church, the communion of saints, the forgiveness of sins, the resurrection of the body, and the life everlasting. Amen.

The Apostles' Creed reflects early credal formulas, but it is not of apostolic origin. Because of that some Christians refuse to accept it. It probably emerged from the earliest expressions of faith professed by the catechumens (those preparing for baptism) in the second century. Similar professions were used throughout the West, but this formulation had become the standard throughout the West by the ninth century.

Another ancient but later creed is known as the Nicene Creed:

We believe in one God, the Father, the Almighty, Maker of heaven and earth, of all that is, seen and unseen.
We believe in one Lord, Jesus Christ, the only Son of God, eternally begotten of the Father, God from God, Light from Light, true God from true God, begotten, not made, one in Being with the Father. Through him all things were made. For us men and for our salvation he came down from heaven: by the power of the Holy Spirit he was born of the Virgin Mary, and became man. For our sake he was crucified under Pontius Pilate; he suffered, died, and was buried. On the third day he rose again in fulfillment of the Scriptures; he ascended into heaven and is seated at the right hand of the Father. He will come again in glory to judge the living and the dead, and his kingdom will have no end.
We believe in the Holy Spirit, the Lord, the giver of life, who proceeds from the Father and the Son. With the Father and the Son he is worshiped and glorified. He has spoken through the Prophets. We believe in one holy catholic and apostolic Church. We acknowledge one baptism for the forgiveness of sins. We look for the resurrection of the dead, and life in the world to come. Amen.

Since the fifth century, the Nicene Creed (Creed of Nicaea-

Constantinople) has been the only creed used in the liturgy of the
Eastern churches. It consists of early baptismal creeds used in Jerusalem and enactments of two early church councils (Nicaea in 325,
and Constantinople in 381). It is particularly strong in its trinitarian
emphasis because of the councils' efforts at combating Arianism, a
heresy which denied the Trinity.

I embrace these creeds as accurate statements of the historic
Christian faith. I believe them not only in my mind but also in my
heart. They set forth what the Scriptures reveal and what the
church proclaims. They plant me squarely in the rich soil of two
thousand years of Christian belief.

WHY I AM A CATHOLIC CHRISTIAN

I am a Catholic Christian. This is not a contradiction in
terms. Over the years I have discovered that non-Catholic Christians struggle with this claim. Unfortunately, they have lost all historical connections. They either do not know or choose to forget
that Catholic as a description of Christians has firm connections to
even the earliest centuries of the church.

For years, well-intended "evangelical" Christians have
sought to "save" me. Thank God for their fervor and zeal. I will
always need deeper conversion. But as I will explain in Chapters 2
and 3 and provide additional support in Chapter 6, I have been
saved, I am being saved, and I hope with the eye of faith to be
saved.

In a sense, *Catholic* is my first name and *Christian* my last.
Literally, the word *catholic* means universal or all-inclusive. An
early bishop, Ignatius of Antioch, wrote a letter to Christians in
Smyrna right before his martyrdom in A.D. 110. I remember the
delight I felt when I discovered this letter and many other "post"
New Testament writings during my semester at a Bible college. In
it he wrote: "Where the bishop is present, there let the congrega-
tion gather, just as where Jesus Christ is, there is the Catholic
Church."[1] Not only does this letter, and many similar texts, demonstrate an early episcopal form of church government, but it shows
that the term *Catholic* was used when referring to all Christian people. The church is intended to be Catholic and to include all be-

lievers under its umbrella. Too many of us frequently forget that critical fact.

By the second century, errant doctrines began to creep into the church, and splits began over vital issues such as the divinity of Christ. The bishops of the early united Christian church began to use the word *Catholic* to distinguish the church of Christians who held to the true gospel from groups like the Montanists (second century) and the Arians (fourth century) who had varied from it. In other words, by this early date *Catholic* was being used like a first name. We can even see this in the *Confessions,* a Christian classic written between A.D. 397 and 401 by the early Bishop of Hippo, Saint Aurelius Augustine. In this great work, Augustine recalls how his mother, Monica, revealed her heartfelt prayer to him before she died: "I did have one reason for wanting to live a little longer: to see you become a Catholic Christian before I died."[2]

Throughout Christian history what was once intended to be an all-inclusive (catholic) body of disciples of the Lord Jesus Christ has been fractured over and over, threatening to sever us from our historical and doctrinal roots. I'll deal with this in Chapter 9. But such divisions were never part of the Lord's intention. Who's to blame is not for me to decide—it seems as if there's enough blame to go around to all of us. Instead, I want to focus my call to Christians on Jesus' greatest desire for His church: *unity clothed in love* (John 13:34–35; 15:12–17; 17:11, 20–26). If we are to be effective in winning nonbelievers to Christ, we must have room for one another in our hearts and in our mission.

I am not advocating a false nondenominationalism which denies distinctives of doctrine or practice. These differences are very real and very important. But there is a world to be won to Jesus, and it is time that all who bear the name Christian get on with the task.

In their marvelous document entitled the "Decree on Ecumenism," the Bishops of the Catholic Church show the respect which must properly be afforded to all Christians:

". . . All those justified by faith through baptism are incorporated into Christ. They therefore have a right to be honored by the title Christian, and are properly regarded as brothers in the Lord by the Sons of the Catholic Church."[3]

So should it be among Christians of all traditions—mutuality of respect, commonality of mission, and commitment to dialogue. We desperately need such traits to permeate our ranks if we are to carry out effectively the evangelical mission the darkness of our age demands. I will discuss this need and how to fulfill it as the book unfolds, especially in Chapters 10 through 12, but now let me take you back to the personal. What makes me a *Catholic* Christian?

First, I am a Catholic Christian who can point to various times of conversion in my life, "evangelical moments" as I call them. This is consonant with my understanding of conversion. I believe in a church that is "one, holy, Catholic, and apostolic" and will one day be restored. I believe in a church rooted in a two-thousand-year history of progress and mistakes. I believe in a church which continues to display the wonder of the Incarnation by revealing the Lord's love in "flesh and blood," a church which is not the Kingdom but merely a "seed of the Kingdom," as the Fathers of the Second Vatican Council so clearly stated. I reject "triumphalism" whether old or new, "spiritual" or political.

Second, I believe the Bible is the Book of the church, not that the church is the church of the Book. That understanding, rather than lessening my love for the sacred Scriptures, deepens it and gives it clarity, consistency, and dynamism. Jesus came to establish a church, a new people who would inherit all the promises of Israel and become the messenger of salvation. The Bible is a gift to that church and a measuring stick (canon) for all her actions.

Third, I believe that Jesus literally meant what He said about the consecrated bread and wine of the Eucharist, and that that is a tremendous gift to the church—indeed, a source of life to all who will believe. I believe it would be ingenuine for believers who do not agree on the real presence of Christ in the Eucharist to join this sacrament of unity. But I long for the day when it will be possible for all Christians to share this sacred meal either here or in the wedding feast of heaven, which it symbolizes.

Fourth, I am a sacramentalist. I believe that God reveals Himself in sign and symbol, spirit and mud. I remember learning as a boy that a sacrament was an outward sign instituted by God to give grace. I believe as well in sacramentals which reveal the love and mercy of a wonderful God.

Fifth, I believe that belonging to Christ must affect our

whole lives and give rise to an incarnational world view, a genuinely Christian culture, and an integrated piety.

Sixth, I am thoroughly convinced that the church of Christ must be both hierarchical and charismatic, institutional and dynamic, and that she is indeed the "universal sign (sacrament) of Salvation"[4] still revealing Christ's presence in the world. Therefore I have submitted myself to the teaching office of the church and its leadership.

I could continue my list, but it would lead to another book. These six points, however, are enough to show why I define myself as a Catholic Christian. But I want to emphasize that they have no significance apart from my Christian life. Jesus Christ, the Evangel, is the source and summit of it all. He is my life and redemption. Membership in my church—for that matter, membership in any Christian church—is not a ticket to heaven. Saint Augustine in his *City of God* warned his fellow Catholics that baptism and membership in the church would not assure salvation,[5] but could offer great assistance in the Christian life. The Catholic Bishops of the Second Vatican Council echoed Augustine's warning:

> He is not saved, however, who, though he is part of the body of the Church, does not persevere in charity. He remains indeed in the bosom of the Church, but, as it were, only in a 'bodily' manner, and not 'in his heart.' All the sons of the Church should remember that their exalted status is to be attributed not to their own merits but to the special grace of Christ. If they fail moreover to respond to that grace in thought, word, and deed, not only will they not be saved but they will be the more severely judged.[6]

The challenge I have as a Catholic Christian is the same as it is for any Christian: to bring people to Jesus Christ, to a personal decision to accept Him as Savior and Lord, to bring them to personal repentance and conversion. But for me, that is only the beginning. That salvation must be sustained, nourished, and deepened. It must also lead to personal transformation and holiness through implantation into Christ's Body, the church. The church is not an option, an extra we can accept or reject. It is the ark, the ship of God, and her mission is to help rescue and restore the drowning.

This has always been her primary mission. The Church exists to evangelize, a mission entrusted to her by her Head, Master, and Lord, the Evangel Himself, Jesus Christ.

WHY I AM AN *EVANGELICAL* CATHOLIC CHRISTIAN

Defining myself as a Christian is not a problem for most people. When I use the word, its meaning is generally understood. When I add to that the term *Catholic*, however, many Protestants raise their eyebrows, flinch, or even get upset. *Christian* and *Catholic*, they think, don't combine well. But when I add *evangelical* to these terms, sparks fly—and not just among Protestants. Many of my Catholic brethren also believe I have attached a term that contradicts my understanding of what it means to be a Catholic Christian. For them, *evangelical* is a label, a synonym for a small sect of "fundamentalist" or "Bible-pounding" Protestants who are ardently anti-Catholic. If this were what *evangelical* meant, I would not use it to define myself. But if you would step back with me to gain a clearer vision of this term, you would see that not only can I use *evangelical* to describe myself, but I must. It should be—and indeed is—a most proper description for all Christians, be they Protestant, Orthodox, or Catholic.

SOME HISTORY

For many years, we have been told that *evangelical* is a noun that refers to a select group of Christian believers. For instance, *The Encyclopedia of Religion* defines the term *evangelicalism* as usually referring "to a largely Protestant movement that emphasizes 1) the Bible as authoritative and reliable and 2) eternal salvation as possible only by regeneration."[7] In many circles, the words *Protestant* and *evangelical* have become synonyms, and in others *evangelicalism* has been defined as a "term within Protestantism that has been applied to several groups and has had various emphases since the 16th century Protestant Reformation."[8] Flowing from such a narrow usage, the word is most frequently used to describe a small segment of Christianity of post-Reformation, and more specifically, an Anglo-American phenomenon concerned mostly with personal piety. Yet even a cursory glance at history shows that evangelical Protestant Christians have often championed social reform.

Evangelicals in Great Britain, such as William Wilberforce (1759–1833), greatly contributed to the effort to eradicate slavery. Charles Finney (1792–1875) used the gifts that made him a dynamic and effective evangelist to reach out to the poor and needy, establish schools, and organize private charities both in England and in America.[9] These evangelical Christians epitomized a fervent incarnational worldview that stressed not only personal conversion but its necessary social implications.

Over time, however, certain brands of evangelicalism evolved which placed great emphasis on the personal need for Christ and far less on social responsibility. Such church leaders as D. L. Moody (1837–1899) championed this perspective. As a result, we were led to an even more narrow understanding of the word *evangelical*—one that stressed personal victory over sin, personal holiness, and personal salvation in Christ.[10] Before long, the groundwork was laid for an apparent dichotomy between the spiritual and the temporal, a problem which is still being felt in many evangelical circles today.

Furthermore, reactions against certain abuses of Scripture often led to confusion over the role of the charismatic, or spiritual, gifts and their validity. Still other reactions against a "creeping modernism" led to a litmus test for faith which caused even further splintering of what was initially seen as the evangelical movement within Protestant Christianity. Disagreements over the Second Coming of Christ, understandings of "dispensations," and approaches to Scripture separated the movement even more between those who identified with the term *fundamentalist* and those who adopted the term *evangelical*.

The final break between these two groups seems to have accompanied the 1957 decision of the Billy Graham Crusade organizers to accept the help of certain so-called "liberal church leaders" to promote Graham's New York crusade.[11] Because of this, the great evangelist was anathematized by some Protestant Christians. Fortunately for the church at large, his evangelical leadership has not only weathered the storm but become much stronger and more respected than ever.

As the modern-day evangelical Protestant movement has

spread, it has produced widespread and international impact leading to such ecumenical conferences as Lausanne. Yet it has brought with it a definition of *evangelical* that confines it to small circles of Protestant Christians which all too often include anti-Catholics in their ranks. The term has evolved far from its roots and original historical context. It is time for a radical redefinition of the word, a return to its traditional sense, a return to its roots.

EVANGELICAL *IS AN ADJECTIVE*

The root of *evangelical (euaggelion)* literally means "good news" or "gospel,"[12] and the term *evangelical* has been used to refer to the essential message of the gospel—salvation by faith in the death of Jesus Christ. In its action verb form *(euaggelizo)* it means "to proclaim the good news."[13] So the word in its most basic sense covers both the message and the proclamation of the Christian faith. Today, the term *kerygma* is used most when referring to the oral proclamation of the gospel and the word *euaggelion* to the written message;[14] however, both designations are properly contained in the root word *evangel*. An evangelical Christian then is one who believes the good news about Christ and proclaims it. In other words, an evangelical Christian *is* a Christian. Adding evangelical almost results in redundancy. It's like talking about buildings that lack structure or ordering Italian pizza without sauce. If it's a building, it has structure. If it's an Italian pizza, it has sauce. You don't get one without the other. Likewise, if someone is a Christian, he or she is an *evangelical* Christian. You can't have a Christ follower without having a person who believes the gospel and shares it.

That great dean of evangelization, Dr. Carl F. H. Henry, agrees. An evangelical, he says, is "one who believes in the Evangel. The Good News is that the Holy Spirit gives spiritual life to all who repent and receive divine salvation proffered in the incarnate, crucified, and risen Redeemer."[15]

So in the truest sense of the term, I am an evangelical Christian. And since I am also Catholic, I am an evangelical Catholic Christian—without contradiction in terms, logic, theology, or history.

Evangelical is an adjective, not a noun. Injustice and divisiveness have been spawned in the church, in part, because of the misuse of this grand term. We need to reclaim and restore its proper meaning and use. In its intriguing article "Evangelical Spirituality," *The Westminster Dictionary of Christian Spirituality* perhaps comes closest to grasping the adjectival usage of the term when speaking of William Wilberforce:

> The main ingredients of evangelical spirituality have always been early rising, prayer, and Bible study. Wilberforce spent two hours each day, before breakfast, praying and studying the Bible, rebuked himself when the time became shortened. . . . Evangelicals kept a diary, not as a means of reordering events, but of self-examination of the recent past and adjustment of the future; it was the evangelical equivalent of the confessional.[16]

The *Dictionary* goes on to cite other elements of evangelical spirituality such as family prayer: "Family prayers were expected to take place in every evangelical household, the head of the household calling his family and servants together every morning and evening and reading a portion of the Scripture before the prayers."[17]

What this paints is a portrait of a type of Christian who fervently believes in his or her Lord, lives that out in patterns of daily personal and communal life, and is compelled by the Evangel to proclaim the truth about Jesus to others. I am that kind of Christian, and I hope to become even more so in the years I have left. I know I am not alone.

But I'm sure many of you are still uncomfortable with my claim of being an evangelical Catholic Christian. You may prefer that I call myself a Catholic Evangelical. But for the sake of accuracy and in the hopes of fruitful controversy, I must reject this designation. I certainly admire some of its proponents, notably pastor Richard John Neuhaus and Thomas Howard, now an evangelical Catholic himself. In Howard's brilliant work *Evangelical Is Not Enough*, he wrote:

> "The Catholic evangelicals," if we may describe them that way, are most eager to see the ancient Church roused and animated, speaking with a vigorous witness faithful to the gospel life. On the other hand, they yearn to see evangelicalism, so energetic in so many ways, rooted once

again in the mystery and authority of the Church understood as one, holy, Catholic, and apostolic.[18]

When he wrote this book, he was on a spiritual journey which eventually led to Rome and his entrance into the Catholic Church. But unlike Thomas Howard, I am a Catholic, both by upbringing and by choice. For me and many other Catholic Christians like me (in fact, for all Catholics who are truly Christians), *evangelical* is the adjective, *Catholic* is the noun.

THE INVITATION

For the rest of this book, I invite you to come with me on a journey. It will begin on a beach in Southern California with my coming face-to-face with the Savior and His claims on my life. In between, we will learn how much binds us together as we re-examine our common faith and heritage. It will end with our standing together, facing the world with all its challenges, dangers, and opportunities . . . a world that runs from the light . . . but a world that will be drawn by the promise of the gospel if its proclaimers rejoin forces and re-embrace their common faith and common mission in genuine love and compassion.

I invite you on a journey that will lead us home.

CHAPTER **2**

Over the Rainbow

I opened the letter. It was postmarked Jerusalem, Israel, and dated April 1972. It had been several years since I had heard from my long-time friend, Fred.

Fred had been my closest friend since the fifth grade. When he met me, I was a new kid in a new town, and I was deeply afraid of rejection. He reached out to me at a point of real need in my life.

We searched for truth together, each of us somehow believing that what we needed were roots, but neither of us knowing where to find them. Eventually, Fred learned that he needed to find his meaning, purpose, and Jewish heritage in Israel, the land of his forefathers. I still missed him and had wondered many times if he had made it to Jerusalem. Periodically, he sent unusual updates to my parents' house. For instance, once he sent pieces of a broken stained-glass window from a cathedral in France.

Fred was a romantic, a poet, a young man who felt deeply. When we parted company, I felt a great loss.

Now I was thousands of miles away, standing alone on a beach in Santa Cruz, California, tired, frightened, and without a place to stay. By this time I had traveled across the U.S. in my search for meaning, purpose, and truth. But I had come up empty.

Fred's letter began:

Dear Keith,

As I sit on the Mount of Olives I read these words: "How can a young man keep his way pure? By living according to your word. I seek you with all my heart. Do not let me stray from your commands. I have hidden your word in my heart that I might not sin against you. Praise be to you, O Lord. Teach me your decrees. With my lips I recount all the laws that come from your mouth. I rejoice in following your statutes as one rejoices in great riches. I meditate on your precepts and consider your ways. I delight in your decrees. I will not neglect your word." (Ps. 119:9–16)

Some of these words were vaguely familiar to me. I remembered reading them in the insert of the large family Bible, the one with a picture of Pope Pius inside, that Mom and Dad kept on the shelf in our parlor. Following these words of Scripture was Fred's moving description of his encounter with Yeshua, the Messiah. I was challenged, realizing that even though I had been Catholic, and supposedly Christian, all of my life, I did not know this Jesus the way my friend did. Jesus had come alive for Fred, but for me, He was still a theory out of my past.

I thought about all of this as I felt the warm sand beneath my feet and tried to ignore the intense hunger pangs rippling through my stomach and the fears clawing at my soul. I was at the end of a cross-country journey that had begun when I left my home in Massachusetts at the age of seventeen. Of course, the preparations for my journey had begun much earlier. Don't get me wrong. I had not left with enough money, adequate transportation, or any confirmed hotel accommodations. In fact, from day to day I didn't know where I would be, how I would get by, or where I would sleep. But I did know that it was a trip I had to take. That sense of destiny, of determination, began building very early in my life.

UPROOTED

I grew up in Dorchester, Massachusetts, an inner-city section of Boston with an intensely Catholic culture. The church and the Christ she proclaimed were my life. Even as a young child, I enjoyed a peace flowing from a Catholic family life—a life rooted in the church. When I was in first grade, I can still recall being asked by a stranger, "Where are you from, kid?" My response was, "Saint Matthews." The parish, the church, and the faith that it stood for were my culture and my greatest source of identity. Over the years, I have heard horror stories about the experiences others had with parochial education, but I was a Catholic kid who experienced it only as a blessing.

My first-grade teacher was a nun named Sister William Patricia. She told me that I could talk to Jesus anytime and that, in addition to the prayers I was learning, I could speak to Him "from my heart." So I did. Often I knelt in front of my favorite statue of the Sacred Heart of Jesus, pouring my heart out to Him. To some people, this might have appeared idolatrous, but I was praying to the One whom the statue represented, Jesus the Christ, not to the statue itself.

The beautiful church adjacent to my school held daily mass in the main upstairs sanctuary as well as in the sanctuary downstairs. I frequently sneaked upstairs and sat alone, looking at the beautiful stained-glass windows and enjoying the fragrance of the votive candles as it filled the air. I admired the Stations of the Cross on the church walls which recounted the different stages of Jesus' courageous climb up the mountain of Calvary. I knew Him then and I loved Him. For me, even as a child, these times of private devotion were "evangelical moments."

As soon as I was able, which was around the third grade, I served dutifully as an altar boy at the altar of sacrifice. Even though I didn't understand the Latin spoken in the Catholic liturgy of that time, I knew that I was a part of something miraculous. Even then, I had a metaphysical appreciation of the presence of the all-holy God. I believed what I had been taught: At the moment of consecration, I stood at the foot of the cross, in some miraculous way becoming a part of the timeless event of Jesus' crucifixion on Calvary. Sadly, I would later wander from the cross, but the memories of those "evangelical moments" would linger, albeit buried beneath the grave of my fears and confusion.

As I completed the fourth grade, my family experienced a personal tragedy that rocked us with the devastation of a terrible earthquake. Our oil burner exploded, causing our house to go up in flames. I'll never forget the experience.

We had come home from school as usual and left our shoes on the landing. The smell of chicken cacciatore filled the house. We sat down to eat and to be entertained by my father's wonderful humor. But within minutes the security of routine, home cooking, and a carefree father would be consumed in flames.

Suddenly, we heard the woman who lived in an apartment below cry, "Fire!" My father looked at us sternly and directed us to leave the house immediately, stopping to take nothing. He then ran downstairs and I followed him. As he opened the basement door, flames singed his eyebrows and hair. Again he directed me to leave. He went into the bottom apartment and helped a mother and her children escape. I ran outside into the night. Heavy rain quickly drenched me as I watched the crowd that had gathered to watch my family's life burn away. The deep loss and fear of that moment were indescribable. The trauma would influence my life for years to come.

I finally got into a car for shelter in time to watch one last explosion bring the roof in and seriously injure two firemen. I looked across the street and saw my mother sobbing.

Things would never be the same. Along with the destruction of that wooden structure collapsed the structure of my family's faith. That which had bound us together, had given us our very identity, fell in ruins. Although it took a few years for the devastation to show through our lives, we eventually stopped praying and going to mass regularly, and we stopped believing in Christianity almost entirely.

Our misfortune happened on the heels of the Second Vatican Council in the Catholic Church (1964), which unfortunately became a significant source of confusion for Catholics worldwide. My family, along with many others, became secularized. For us, to be "Catholic" became more of a cultural statement and less of a religious one. In time, I stopped going to mass altogether. I relied on my own devices and the world's values to "make it" in life. Those values soon left me spiritually bankrupt but not intellectually or culturally inactive.

By the ripe old age of fourteen, I must have appeared to many as a successful junior high school student in a quaint, southern New England town. But looks can be deceiving. Inside, I was a cauldron of anger born of disillusionment, fear, and insecurity. Much of that anger released itself in rebellion. I edited the first underground newspaper in my school—a politically radical paper we called *Metamorphosis*, which, ironically, was just what I was looking for. A transformation. But I didn't know how to find it. Because I expressed my discontent in creative ways, I was encouraged by well-meaning teachers. They, however, didn't see the pain and desperation behind it all.

SEARCHING

Although my anger was fueled by the fire that had destroyed my home, my search for meaning and purpose came about another way—quite innocently, in fact. It began with a highly inquisitive mind. While other boys were playing baseball at the age of thirteen, I was away from the baseball field asking existential questions:

Why am I?
Who made me?
Why are there poverty and injustice in the world?
If there is a God, why do people suffer?

I hungered for answers to these and many other questions, and in my open-mindedness, I wanted to give every philosophy a fighting chance to provide those answers. So at thirteen I turned eastward, as so many other young people were doing. I began reading the works of Herman Hesse as I sought to understand the *Bhagavad-Gita,* a book of Hindu scriptures.

Fred had also hungered for answers as a young boy. Though he joined with me in most of my pursuits, he still focused much of his energy on art. He wrote inspiring poetry, painted murals, even composed some music. In all that he did, he showed himself to be a dreamer in search of meaning. He was deeply intrigued by my childhood Catholic faith. Jesus Christ and all things related to the Christian faith fascinated him. Even though he had a religious home life, his Jewish upbringing had not satisfied his spiritual hunger. So he kept looking—looking for more answers to what seemed an unending list of questions.

Thus, our search began together. Though we were younger than most of the pilgrims on the countercultural journey of the sixties, we, like them, embraced it all. Our search encompassed religion, politics, and philosophy. We read the great spiritual classics from both Western and Eastern traditions and dabbled in every New Age religious group available at the time. And there were plenty; they were springing up in Boston like weeds. We attended scientology lectures and listened to that version of how to find true meaning in life. We danced with Hare Krishnas on the Boston Common and tried to converse with them about the *Upanishads.*

We even visited some of the darker elements of the growing new religions, including a group called "The Process," who years later would be clearly identified as satanic.

My parents, like many during the sixties and early seventies, were confused about my behavior. They didn't know what to do with me, so they responded with well-intended tolerance.

But despite all my early searching I found no answers to my questions. No matter what system of thought I probed, it did not fill the emptiness in my soul. Paradoxically, no matter where my searching took me, I stayed fascinated with Jesus—the One who claimed to be *the* way, *the* truth, and *the* life. I frequently felt pulled back to this Jesus who had offered Himself on the cross, this Jesus of whom I had learned as a child, the Jesus who was meek and humble of heart.

Spiritual journeys were not all that preoccupied me, however. I became consumed with the plight of the poor and oppressed, a concern that was molded for a while by the "new Marxists." They attempted to recruit me and my friends, playing not only on our social concern but also on our anger over the war in Vietnam. Inspired by two friends of mine who lived in a "political collective" in Boston and gave me Marxist literature to convert me, I became fascinated with Che Guevara and other so-called revolutionaries, people who sought to overthrow an "oppressive" system for the sake of freedom. Soon I wanted to be like them. And for a season, I was. In 1969, I linked arms with a virtual sea of quasi-revolutionaries and, armed with a desire to stop war and expose injustice, marched on Washington, D.C. During these days of political enthusiasm, I also handed out leaflets against the Chicago Eight's trial, convinced they were victims of an oppressive system.

Fortunately, I eventually saw that in spite of their rhetoric, most of these "new revolutionaries" were as self-centered as the "them" they railed against. Like the alleged oppressors, these "liberators" were preoccupied with self-advancement and self-love. I concluded they were paper revolutionaries, so I abandoned my fling with radical politics. My searching, on the other hand, intensified.

At the age of sixteen, I had accumulated enough credits to graduate from high school, but under Massachusetts state law, I was unable to because of my age. So I dropped out, convinced that

I would not be another cog in the "establishment wheel." I wanted to make a difference. In my egocentric adolescence, I decided to become an individual about whom books are written. I began by leaving home.

It was the early seventies. Eastern philosophy was making incredible inroads into Western thought. Bookstores were giving more and more shelf space to what we now know as the New Age Movement. Self-professed gurus were finding followers among the hippies, musicians, and artists scattered throughout the country. Their mystical ideologies were attractive, but they only added to the already confusing array of choices.

It was a time when many young people were experimenting with drugs in their search for significance. Songs by such groups as Jefferson Airplane, Cream, Buffalo Springfield, Ten Years After, and the Beatles had heralded mind-altering drugs as the doorway to personal peace and happiness. Many took the songs at their word, tasted the forbidden fruit, and soon discovered that it delivered a nightmare rather than a blissful dream.

I was seventeen, a high school dropout, a fallen Catholic, a pursuer of the elusive dream—the dream that would open the world of answers to me. And I was sure that I could capture this dream if I left Massachusetts and hit the open road. So, like many other young people at this time, I enlisted a traveling companion—Stuart Baker. Stuart, like Fred and me, was a seeker. Stuart, however, was much more interested in feeling than thinking. He was daring, heroic, and reckless. Deeply into the music of the time, he lived his life song to song in a fast-paced, frantic stream of consciousness. He had already hitchhiked across the country the previous summer and lived in Hollywood Hills. He so often shared his wild experiences that I was ripe when he invited me to join him again in a new adventure.

So we set out as pilgrims, hoping to find our personal Promised Lands. Our search was not unlike Dorothy's in *The Wizard of Oz*, a favorite film of mine. Maybe we too would find our answers "somewhere over the rainbow." My clothing for the journey was the typical uniform of the day—an army jacket, a T-shirt, bell-bottomed jeans, and "Earth shoes." The rest of my meager belongings were a toothbrush, a hair brush, and a change of underwear and socks. Everything fit into my backpack. My transportation was my feet. My emotional and spiritual preparation for the journey, next to none. I was totally unprepared for what I encountered.

Stuart and I left Boston and traveled through the Midwest, sleeping in rest areas, cars, and church hostels. We camped on the plains of Kansas and stayed in a cheap hotel in Denver with other guests of the crawling variety. We saw the stark beauty of Arizona's deserts, and after several months we finally arrived in what we hoped would be our Promised Land—Los Angeles.

On the road, we ran into many young seekers like ourselves—people who also sensed that there was more to life than just school and career. What more, none of us knew for sure; we only knew that it was supposed to be better than what we had or had been offered. But because we couldn't define the "more," any road that promised "more" got our attention. Drugs . . . sex . . . alcohol . . . Transcendental meditation . . . revolution . . . social activism . . . no road was left untried. Of course, all of us didn't try every road. But it seemed that none of us were finding anything more than dead ends. As the journey kept producing little to nothing, our optimism waned while pessimism and hopelessness grew.

Although Stuart and I found lodging in a variety of places, many times we had no *safe* place to sleep. Fear often kept us awake. Sometimes our fear came as the result of experiencing the unfamiliar. For example, since I had spent my early childhood in the inner city of Dorchester, Massachusetts, I was not used to the sound of coyotes. One evening as I slept outside on the plains of Kansas, I heard coyote cries shatter the silence of the night. I nearly crawled out of my skin in fear. At other times, our fears were anchored to real dangers. Once when we were hitchhiking, we traveled for two days with a man we thought was a fellow pilgrim. Tired of what he called his "banal life," he was headed for the coast. We spent two days traveling, partying, and discussing what we were going to do once we arrived in Los Angeles. He was going to drive us the whole way. We and our tired feet were thrilled.

Stuart had a pair of bongo drums, and as we sped down the open highway, we turned up the radio to a decibel level unfit for human ears while he beat a mesmerizing rhythmic pattern to the music. For a while, the music and bongos dulled our fear.

But this dream situation didn't last long. One evening we pulled into a remote rest area to sleep. Because the weather was so pleasant, we decided to sleep under the stars. As the night wore on, however, the stars disappeared and the sky opened with a fierce downpour. I remember waking and finding myself at the curbside, soaked with run-off water. The sky was pitch black because the moonlight was gone. And so was our ride. Our driver had abandoned us. He had even taken our few belongings with him. We were wet, cold, hungry, and broke—a state with which we had grown all too familiar.

When we ate, which sometimes happened only once every several days, our meals often consisted of day-old bread and water. A meal that included meat and almost anything green, except for mold, was a treat we relished.

When we weren't sleeping, fearing for our lives, chasing an elusive meal, or working a little to get some money, we read. Two books that caught my attention were with me wherever I went. In my top left jean-jacket pocket was the "little red book," *Quotations from Chairman Mao Tse-tung*, which I had received from a well-intentioned friend, who in his own search for truth had become a dedicated Maoist and revolutionary. He had joined the Students for a Democratic Society and even belonged to its militant faction, the Weathermen Underground. For him, truth involved the violent overthrow of the American government. I had dinner with him on several occasions at a political collective in Boston. There my friend Stuart and I listened to this group's plans to promote violent activities for the sake of the revolution. The walls of their apartment were covered with large portraits of Che Guevara and Mao Tse-tung. The little red book was my friend's gift to me, a gift he hoped would lead to my conversion to his system of thought.

In my right pocket was a New Testament given to me by other friends, a pentecostal couple from Sharon, Massachusetts—a little town where I lived from the fifth grade through my sophomore year of high school. They opened their home on Friday evenings to anyone who needed a place to get warm. During those gatherings, they read from the Gospels and talked about Jesus to anyone who would listen. Many Friday nights I found myself going to their home for warmth, potato chips, and Coke with a group of many other young people. Thank God for their courage and evangelical fervor. I would look back later and understand that those evenings were "evangelical moments" for me. Though I did not know it at the time, the love I saw in their eyes was the love of Jesus Christ. Yet I was like a Teflon pan—their proclamation never seemed to stick.

FINDING THE WAY

Finally, after months of traveling, I sat on that beach in Santa Cruz, California, and faced the emptiness I had been unable to fill. I looked back on my journey, realizing that it had not turned out as I had expected. Instead of the Promised Land, I had found hunger, sleeplessness, disappointment, disillusionment, despair, and fear.

Through all of this, and always at the most frightening times, certain words rolled through my mind:

Who made you?
God made you.
Why did God make you?
To know, love, and serve Him in this world, and be happy with Him in the next.

These were the words of the Baltimore Catechism I had learned as a child. They stuck in my mind. Why? I wasn't sure. And I never really knew what to do with them. Until that moment on the beach.

In the midst of my confusion and fear, the Baltimore Catechism and Fred's letter of his startling conversion to Jesus Christ penetrated my awful fog. His letter was on fire with the good news, telling me what the catechism had taught me: God is real, He loves me, and He understands me more than I understand myself. Fred's letter also told me what I needed to do: Tell God that I love Him, confess my sin to Him, admit my weakness to Him, and ask for His forgiveness. If I simply invited "Yeshua," Jesus, God's Son, into my heart to be my Savior, He would renew my life. In Him I would find the meaning, purpose, and truth I had been so desperately searching for. Although I had heard these claims many times before and I thought I had embraced them, I realized at that moment that my heart had never really made a commitment to Christ.

How clear it all was now! The hand of the Lord had been upon my whole life—even during my early teen years of questioning, even during my brief encounter with radical politics, even during my honeymoon with the "counterculture" of the sixties, even during my long, arduous, despairing trek across the U.S. He had spared me from so much destruction, while allowing me to get lost in the fog of my idealism and egocentricity so that I would be ready to see Him more clearly and accept Him more readily. My recollection of all of this, evoked by the words in Fred's letter, culminated in a deep longing and heartfelt cry to God. I had tried everything but Him. He was my last hope to find the truth. The urgency of this "evangelical moment" swept through my soul.

"Lord, I want to believe," I cried out. "If You are real, please come to me and save me. I confess my sin, and I ask Your forgiveness. I invite You, Lord Jesus Christ, to be my Savior."

It was the most important "evangelical moment" of my life. On that day, on that beach in 1972, I encountered the Evangel, the Good News, the God who became flesh, Jesus Christ. I stood at the foot of the cross. I found the Answer—the One from whom all the other answers to my questions would flow. My spiritual and intellectual journey wasn't over, but for the first time it was guided by faith rather than by a false drive for self-discovery. For the first time my life was changing—from the inside out.

That internal change impacted my external life right away. I knew that my decision for Christ required a change of lifestyle—a change that immediately affected my relationship to Stuart and my current housing situation.

Stuart would be difficult to talk to because he had never understood my spiritual journey. Although he was culturally Jewish, he had no real faith in the God of Abraham, Isaac, and Jacob. So I didn't know how he would respond to my newfound faith.

Our living situation was another matter entirely. When Stuart and I first arrived in Santa Cruz, we slept for days in the basement of a local church until a small advertisement on a church bulletin board caught our eyes: "One young man needed in return for room and board." We didn't need to know any more than that. We applied for the job and got it.

It was wonderful to have a warm bed and good meals, all for a little daily labor. We were so exhausted, it took us about a week to recover from our cross-country travel, but when we did, I sensed something strange in that house. The man who hired us was more than a bit unusual. He sent us out daily to pick wild spearmint, bay leaves, and other herbs that he used in his "potions." It all seemed quite funny to me until calls from all over the States began to come in the middle of the night. Callers were looking for wealth and success and magical solutions to their problems in this man's potions. Stuart also picked up on the oddity of all this, but both of us were so tired of traveling and grateful for a place to settle that we didn't challenge any of it.

But now—sitting there on the beach, fresh in the Lord—I knew that I couldn't keep silent. I had to confront the lies I was living, the owner of the house who I now knew was deceived, and my own fears and insecurities about my newly rediscovered faith. My initial evangelistic challenge was to share my faith with this man of potions.

To say the least, my outreach attempt was shoved back in my face. And that wasn't all that got attacked. Late one evening, I entered the house and found him sitting at the kitchen table either drunk or high on drugs. He wanted to know why I was reading the Bible so often. I told him that I had given my life to Jesus Christ and wanted to get back to my childhood faith.

"What?" he shouted angrily. Then he lunged across the table and tried to grab my throat to choke me. As he came at me, the only thing I could think to do was scream a Scripture verse I had read that same day. In the heat of the moment, I even misquoted it. At the top of my lungs, I yelled, "Greater is He that is in me than he that is in you!"[1]

My employer cursed me with vile profanity, stopped his assault, and stumbled out of the kitchen. What an evangelistic encounter!

Later I learned that he was heavily involved in the occult. I didn't know it at the time, but even the symbol on his hat was a pentagram, a satanic symbol. I also discovered that earlier his emotional problems had been serious enough to require institutional treatment.

As traumatic and frightening as that experience was, I felt the power of God surging within me. This time it would stick.

The next morning I confronted my friend Stuart. I told him

about my disillusionment and discouragement with Marxism, the political left, and the false spiritualities we had encountered. I spoke to him about my childhood Christian faith and my return to faith in Christ. But he wasn't interested. He believed there was more of life for him to experience before he would consider settling into one "system of belief." Stuart was not engaged in a spiritual journey. His search was of another kind.[2]

I felt bad about Stuart, but I knew I had to break away and build on what God had begun in me. So I took the little income I had earned from doing odd jobs around that house, called my parents, boarded a bus, and began the long trek back across the country. But this time, the only book in my army jacket was the Good Book.

CHAPTER 3

There's No Place Like Home

Not unlike Dorothy in *The Wizard of Oz*, I discovered the emptiness of what I thought would be my Oz and the futility of my journey on the Yellow Brick Road. I longed to go home. But it would take much more than clicking the heels of my ruby slippers and saying out loud, "There's no place like home." It would take a Greyhound bus ticket, a willingness to say goodbye to my friend Stuart, and another step in faith.

Just before my trek across the U.S., my parents had moved from Boston to a small city in Florida called Lakeland. Upon my return, I had no sooner walked in their door when I began blurting out my experience of meeting Jesus Christ as my Savior. With good intentions but not much tact, I tried to "save" them. They responded much differently than I had imagined they would.

"Son," my father replied, "if you're going to get religious, for goodness sake, please stay Catholic!"

My mother agreed. As time passed, my parents grew to better understand my love for the Lord. But at that point, it was more important to them that I stay Catholic.

FRIENDLY SUPPORT

I enjoyed spending time with my parents, but before long, my need for genuine Christian support and for people who could help me study the Bible outweighed my desire to stay home. Ever since that day on the Santa Cruz beach, I hungered to know the Word of God. I spent hours poring over chapter after chapter, never failing to find words of strength and encouragement. Nevertheless,

I wanted more. I wanted to study the Scriptures more deeply and to discuss different perspectives on what they taught. So I began searching for a quality Bible study—one that would help meet my growing need. Strangely enough, I found one in an unexpected corner of my past.

When I left to cross the country, Chuck, a friend of mine from Boston, had moved with my family to Florida. He played lead guitar in a rock band. Everyone called him "Spider" because of the black widow spider tattooed on his arm that moved when he played guitar. How he got that tattoo is a story in itself. It began as a dare one evening. We were at Chuck's home in North Attleboro, Massachusetts. We challenged each other to make a physical statement about our independence from the "establishment." The statement had to come in the form of either a tattoo or an earring. After sealing our pact with a handshake, we climbed into Chuck's green '64 Chevy and traveled to Rhode Island. I watched Chuck get a tattoo. That was enough to convince me to pierce my ear!

Thankfully, my momentary madness healed quickly; it's not even noticeable anymore. Chuck hasn't been so fortunate. Today he pastors a Presbyterian church in Indiana and edits a marvelous periodical on spirituality for pastors called *The Country Parson*. The spider still moves when he flexes his bicep—an ode to a time past.

But during our rebellious adolescent years, Chuck, like me, wandered from his Christian upbringing, swept up in the craziness and confusion of the age.

When I returned to Florida to "convert" my parents, I looked up Chuck, who was living only one town away from my parents. I found his trailer and knocked on the door. While waiting for him to answer, I heard the words of a song I had heard before. The song was "Welcome Back," and the lyrics did not fit the Chuck I had left.

> You thought you could turn away and
>   no one could see through your eyes.
> But I can see that you know better
>   now.
> You never were the untruthful kind,
> And I'm so happy now to welcome you
>   back.
> Welcome back to Jesus.

"Come in. Door's open," came the familiar voice.

But when I walked in, I saw a very different Chuck. His hair was much shorter and he looked happy. A stark contrast, indeed. When I had last seen Chuck, his deep black, curly hair cascaded past his shoulders. He had been fond of "muscleman" sleeveless T-shirts. And when he didn't wear those, he wore short-sleeved T-shirts with a package of cigarettes rolled under one sleeve. No matter what shirt he wore, however, he defiantly exposed the spider on his arm. But in the Chuck I now saw, the defiance was gone. He was a new man.

"What happened to you, Chuck?" I asked. "You look so different."

"I've become a Christian, Keith."

"You're kidding! Me too."

We embraced each other and laughed as we spent the rest of the day recalling our different yet similar journeys. When I encountered Chuck that day, I now know that I also encountered Jesus Christ who now lived within him. This was another evangelical moment. And it led to the beginning of a wonderful summer—the summer of my conversion honeymoon.

Chuck and I, along with two other men who had a deep faith in Christ, rented a home and began studying the Bible together. One man was a member of the Assemblies of God church, one was a Southern Baptist, Chuck was Presbyterian, and I, of course, was a fallen-away Catholic. And all of us were now deeply Christian, in love with Jesus, and committed to knowing His Word.

THE SPIRIT AND STUDY

We soon heard of a prayer meeting being held at night in a small private home. We decided to attend. At our first meeting we saw people excited and worshiping God and heard them speaking in a language we couldn't decipher. My curiosity got the best of me. I asked the leader of the group to explain what was happening. He opened his Bible and took me through the Acts of the Apostles, showing me that I was witnessing the very manifestations of spiritual gifts that had occurred in the early church.

I fell to my knees. If there was "more of God" to be had, I wanted Him. So I prayed and received an abundance. The power of the Holy Spirit was manifested in me more deeply than I had ever experienced before. The participants at the prayer meeting called this the "baptism of the Holy Spirit." For me, it was another evangelical moment.

In later theological reflection I realized I had experienced a deepening of what had already begun on that beach in California—indeed, what had begun in me as a child at baptism and had grown stronger as I became a confirmed Catholic. Without a doubt, something special happened to me that night: the Holy Spirit began to lead me in a new way. In the wider context of my life, this event was yet another sign of God's involvement.

Soon after this prayer meeting, I discovered a Bible college in my area. My passion for studying the Scriptures had been steadily increasing, and I knew that I needed to learn more. So I enrolled in the college, thinking it would be the best way to study the Scriptures intensively. As it turned out, I was one of only a handful of Catholics who had ever enrolled there, although there were plenty of former Catholics and anti-Catholics among the student body.

During my first semester, I met some wonderful people who were on fire for Jesus Christ and for spreading the good news. With them, I fully embraced my study of the Scriptures and took advantage of every possible opportunity to worship God. I was gradually becoming aware that to belong to Jesus meant to belong to His church, His community of faith. I discovered a wealth of teaching on *koinonia*, a Christian fellowship, in the New Testament letters.

Saint Paul's letters were written mostly to bodies of believers, to communities of believers, not just to individuals. Even those written to individual disciples were filled with instructions for community life. For example, Paul's letter to Timothy was directed not only to his personal life, but to his leadership of the church at Ephesus. Community life was normative for early Christians. To belong to the Head (Jesus) meant to belong to His Body.

I searched for that experience of belonging. I tried many different churches—Baptist, Presbyterian, Assemblies of God, Church of God, Church of God of Prophecy . . . and the list went on. At each church, I experienced the Lord's presence and found people in love with Him, but I somehow knew I was not yet home. That did not stop God from working in my life.

Another evangelical moment occurred during the time of my involvement at an Assemblies of God church. In their zeal for evangelism this community of believers sent bus loads of young people to a particular downtown park during secular rock concerts. These young people walked through the crowds, freely sharing their faith in Christ. I was inspired to join them one Saturday, and I was teamed up with a real dynamo. He was on fire for Christ. He shared that fact freely with anyone who would listen. How? By telling his own conversion story with honesty, humility, and power. For the first two hours, I simply accompanied him, marveling at his courage and learning from his example. Then I went out on my own. Mustering up enough courage and filled with spiritual zeal, I witnessed to the first concert participant I could find. I sensed God's presence as I told this young man how I had placed my faith in Jesus Christ.

Much to my delight, he really listened to my message, and the Holy Spirit began to take over his life. I asked him if he would like to meet the Jesus I knew. His eyes lit up as he nodded yes. During the next moments, I had the privilege of introducing him to Jesus, the Evangel. I simply said, "Jesus, I want you to meet my friend, Rick. He wants you to be his Savior." Rick confessed his sin and invited Jesus Christ into his heart. What an evangelical moment! From that time on I desired nothing more than to bring people to Jesus Christ and eternal life. Personal evangelism became as natural as breathing.

I experienced this and many other evangelical moments during my stint at the Bible college, and I know that many of these moments were possible because of my study of God's Word. Nothing else cuts like a two-edged sword. I will always be grateful for the intense exposure to Scripture I received there. But I eventually became perplexed by the very classes that had once inspired me.

My experience in one class is still vivid. We were discussing the sixth chapter of John's Gospel, where Jesus claims to be "the bread of life." This passage served as the springboard for discussion of the Assemblies of God doctrine of the Last Supper. As the professor explained the Assemblies' perspective, I realized how different it was from my own understanding. In my parochial school and catechism classes, I was taught to believe that the bread and the wine of the Last Supper miraculously become the body and blood of Jesus Christ. For me it was the Eucharist, where Jesus in His flesh and blood were actually present, not simply being remembered by a group of His followers. It was the heart of the Christian life, not just a tangential religious act.

My professor argued that the words of Jesus were figurative. Jesus really did not mean that He would give His flesh to the disciples to eat. "That, after all," he said, "would be tantamount to cannibalism."

His explanation and reasoning amazed me. Up to this point in the course, we had studied the Gospel of John with a literal approach to all of its verses. In others words, in all other instances Jesus meant exactly what He said. I had admired this consistency and clarity. On this day, however, the approach was quite different. My newfound literalist approach to Scripture was disrupted, and I could not accept such a hermeneutical shift of gears. Which way was right? Were Jesus' words to be interpreted within their grammatical-historical framework? Or were they to be treated as allegory with hidden meanings? Somehow, I knew there was more to what we were studying. There was a profound gift and mystery that was not being grasped.

I went up to the professor at the end of class and asked him why the same Jesus who literally meant everything else He said spoke figuratively here. He didn't answer my question. Instead, he gave me a discourse on his understanding of the Lord's Supper. So I also asked him to explain why grape juice is substituted for wine at many Protestant communion services. Once again, he didn't answer my question. Rather, he told me that "new wine" in the Scripture referred to unfermented grape juice. But this didn't square with the biblical accounts. How, for instance, could people get drunk on "unfermented grape juice?" And why would people who knew the quality and power of good wine berate the host of a wedding for allegedly withholding the best of his brew until the end of the celebration (John 2:1–10)? Certainly they weren't complaining about his withholding the best of his grape juice! Needless to say, I was confused. I wanted to know the truth, but I believed the truth was being suppressed. I questioned and questioned, but my hunger for answers went unsatisfied.

TRADITION REDISCOVERED

So I began to delve more deeply into church history. First I read the reformers—men such as Zwingli, Luther, and Calvin. I discovered that their teaching about the Gospel of John and the Lord's Supper was significantly different from what I had heard in class. After poring over their works, I also discovered the church before the 1500s. It was not the church I knew now.

I found that Christianity had a wealth of tradition and that *tradition* was not a bad word. We had recently sung a verse in chapel assembly: "Tradition had me bound but Jesus set me free!" But I was finding both Jesus and freedom *in my tradition*.

The reformers and medieval theologians took me back to the early church fathers: Ignatius, Polycarp, Tertullian, and numerous others. They were wellsprings from which I drank insatiably. Another personal discovery was the Didache, the earliest compilation of post-New Testament writings. It helped me see that very early on Christians had gathered for liturgy. Ignatius of Antioch in his ancient letters showed me that church government was not a later addition to Christian history. Over and over again, the more I unearthed the church's past the greater my appreciation grew for its incredible wealth of worship, wisdom, and biblical understanding. My thinking definitely needed to be reshaped. I knew that I had not yet found my religious home, but I was now centuries closer. Still, I kept on with school, even though its instruction became increasingly unsettling.

One day I received a homiletics assignment that would woo me closer to my religious home. We were told to give an oral report on a great pentecostal hero. After several hours of research and reflection, I decided to speak on Saint Francis of Assisi—also known as Francis Bernardone, the "little poor man"—my favorite saint from my childhood years. I still remembered the sisters' stories of his proclamation of the gospel and the miracles worked through his prayers. So I dug into his life and writings and discovered a man filled with the Holy Spirit and with an evangelical fervor that rivaled that of many of his contemporaries, not to mention many of us today. Studying the renewal movement he inspired, I discovered that all of Europe had been set aflame by one little man so in love with Jesus and so in love with the church that even when he saw inconsistencies within her, he refused to abandon her. He had truly lived his life touching lives with supernatural power and compassion. This for me was another evangelical moment, an encounter with the good news of the church.

To the chagrin of my professor but to the interest of my classmates, I gave my first sermon on this great pentecostal hero.

My college studies also led me to great evangelical Protestants like John Wesley, Charles Finney, and Smith Wigglesworth, and also to such mendicant evangelical Catholics as Dominic. But I found myself most drawn to that little poor man of Assisi, Francis, who while praying before the Cross at San Damiano received a commission from the mouth of the Lord: "Francis, go and rebuild my church which, as you see, is falling down in ruins around you." Francis had seen so much that needed to be rebuilt in the church of his day that on a purely human level, he could have rejected God's call. Yet, he understood the deep mystery: To belong to Christ is to belong to his church. I knew I had to belong, as well. My call and my place were in the church of my childhood. This, too, was an evangelical moment, an encounter with the Lord who still incarnates Himself through His church. I did not, however, return immediately to active participation in the Catholic church.

One morning while at prayer, I opened my Bible to the prophet Isaiah and read about his commission. These words from the pages of the sacred Scriptures came alive: "Then I heard the voice of the Lord saying, 'Whom shall I send and who will go for us?' And I said, 'Here I am. Send me'" (Isa. 6:8). Another evangelical moment. Through this passage I heard the voice of the Lord commissioning me. But what my commission would be was still not totally evident. I believe that part of it, which was also a fervent personal desire, was to see my family come back to faith in Christ. I knew, however, that a major obstacle for them was my attending a Protestant Bible college.

Every time I approached the topic of religion, my parents gave me the same response: "Son, will you please get back to the Church?" Although their question frustrated me, I became increasingly aware that my behavior was a stumbling block to them. Moreover, my constant need for "something more" was ever more strongly drawing me back to my Catholic roots.

WELCOME HOME

One Saturday morning after personal prayer, I borrowed my father's truck and drove through the streets of Lakeland, Florida. I noticed an advertisement for Saint Joseph's Catholic Church, and I felt compelled to find the church. This was a strange feeling. I had not been a practicing Catholic since the fifth grade. I had attended an occasional liturgical service, but that was all. So why such a strong pull on my heart to locate this church? Could it be of the Holy Spirit?

After I passed the sign, I came to a railroad track and was forced to stop because of an oncoming train. Waiting, I looked around, exploring a part of town to which I had never given a second glance. What immediately caught my eye was a Christian bookstore. I pulled in to kill some time. The minute I walked through the door, the first book that caught my eye in a crowded bookrack was *Catholic Pentecostals* by Kevin and Dorothy Ranaghan. *Is there really such a group?* I thought. With my father in mind I bought the book. But as I began to read it, still standing in the bookstore, I was fascinated by story after story of Catholics like me who had returned to a deep faith in Christ, had been empowered by the Spirit, and had never been the same as a result. Now more than ever, I felt led to find Saint Joseph's Catholic Church.

I got back in the truck and started to drive. Minutes later, I found the church. As I walked inside, I recognized the familiar aroma peculiar to older Catholic churches—the votive candles. The candles, the statues, and the tabernacle all reminded me of the wonder of God. I felt drawn into His presence, filled with a sense of mystery and awe. I slowly made my way up the aisle. The closer I came to the altar, the more my heart was filled with an unspeakable Presence, an excitement that made my whole being attentive. Reaching the altar, I fell prostrate and cried out, "O God, I need to find my home in Your church."

I could have lain there for hours, lost in the homecoming, but within seconds the church lights went on. I was startled, torn from the intensity of my petition and worship. I hurriedly stood up and moved toward the exit, all the while realizing that something had happened within me, but too frightened to find out what.

As I began to leave the church, an elderly woman was coming in the door. She invited me to stay for the mass that was about to begin, but I declined her invitation and left. Within a matter of minutes, however, I knew I had to return. So I did.

I sat through the mass and felt everything come alive—the words of the Scriptures, the words of the canon, the words of consecration. Each point of the mass pierced my heart. I wept openly.

Afterward, I approached the priest and told him my whole story—my encounter with Jesus Christ, my new birth, and my empowerment through the Holy Spirit. He smiled and welcomed me home. He told me about another Catholic church in town that held a charismatic prayer meeting. Coincidentally, they were to meet that evening. So I went to mass again that day. How remarkable to attend mass twice in one day after a hiatus of nine years. The name of this Catholic community was Resurrection Church, appropriate for me as I was entering new life there, encountering the power of Jesus' resurrection in a personal way.

After that church's mass, which was another powerful experience, I again shared my story with the priest. My heart was racing when he introduced me to the couple who led the prayer meeting, Chris and Pauline Earl. The Earls were gracious hosts. They took me home that night and gave me dinner, then later drove me to the church hall for the prayer meeting.

When we walked into the back of the church, I saw about twenty-five elderly Catholic men and women with their hands raised, singing "Alleluia." Something inside me immediately clicked. I knew at that moment I was finally home. This was where I belonged. This was the ark. This was the place where God would show me His plan for my life.

In the months that followed, I fell deeply and passionately in love with the Catholic church and was obsessed with learning more about her. I went to the Lakeland Public Library and found more books on the early Fathers, which I pored over day after day. I studied about Saint Polycarp whose heroic martyrdom greatly inspired me. I studied the lives of many other saints as well, but was still moved by the life of Saint Francis of Assisi. My fascination with him led me to write to a Francisan friar about whom I had read in a popular magazine. His name was Father Michael Scanlan.

At that time, he was the rector president of a seminary in

Loretto, Pennsylvania. I sought his advice for my vocational direction. As a Catholic man in love with Christ and His church, I aspired to the priesthood and was attracted to the Francisan spirit. Father Mike's written response marked the beginning of a friendship that grows stronger even to this day.

For a time, I continued discerning my vocational goals and growing deeper in my knowledge and love of God. Once I went to a weekend retreat at which a holy Benedictine abbot, David Gaerets, gave a powerful message on conversion. By the time the weekend retreat ended, he had invited me to visit his Benedictine monastery in Pecos, New Mexico.

Abbot David inspired within me a hunger for genuine Christian community. He had a vision for the renewal of the church that was based on Saint Benedict's model. Saint Benedict planted powerhouse monastic communities in the centers of villages to act like a stone cast into a pond. The heroic life of the Benedictine brothers and sisters rippled out by example into the surrounding villages like concentric circles. Their ministry outside of the monastic walls strengthened the townspeople in their resolve to live fully for God. Considering this order's historic work, Abbot David asked a simple question: "Couldn't Saint Benedict's approach still do the same thing?"

He helped me realize more clearly that to belong to Christ I must be a part of His people, not just in theory and theology, but in fact. I embraced this vision. Young, single, in love with Jesus Christ, and seeking His will for my life, I spent the next year and a half aspiring to the monastic life under the tutelage of Saint Benedict and Abbot David. I studied the Philokalia—the writings of the Eastern church fathers—and further rooted myself in a sacramental and incarnational Catholic Christian worldview. I experienced genuine relationships of brotherly love. Church and family came together for me, and I encountered Christ through His incarnational revelation of Himself in His people. This was yet another evangelical moment—an encounter with Him who is the good news and who manifests Himself through genuine Christian community.

At monastery youth retreats, I proclaimed Christ and the gospel to young visitors and invited them to make a personal commitment to Him. I loved to preach the gospel of grace. I was an evangelical, an aspiring young monk, and my time and ministry at the monastery were some of the most wonderful months of my life. But I soon came to see that I was not called to remain single for the Lord and the Church, although I was convinced of the dignity and holiness of this extraordinary vocation, chosen by the apostle Paul and so many other believers throughout Christian history.

When I finally left the monastery, I wanted to complete my college education. I had my high school diploma, even though I had left school for my cross-country journey before graduation. I had also taken the opportunity to complete the freshman year at the College of Santa Fe as a Benedictine seminarian. But now I wanted to earn a college degree. Most of all, I wanted to keep studying the Scriptures in an environment where my faith would be nurtured, not attacked. I had received my notice of acceptance and a grant of scholarship monies to Boston College. To a Boston-bred Catholic that meant a lot. So I returned home to Boston to enroll. At the time, it appeared to me that the campus lacked a strong, faith-nurturing environment. I am sure many people there were strongly committed to the Christian faith, but the environment of the school was quite secular. And what a culture shock that was after a year and a half in a monastic community. It was too much for me. I couldn't stay. But where could I go instead?

During my stay in the monastery, Father Michael Scanlan and I had corresponded several times, and at one point he had even come to visit me. Before I left the monastery, he moved from Loretto and accepted a position as president of the College of Steubenville. Confused about where to attend college, I called Father Michael on the phone.

"Father Mike, I want to go to school where my faith will be strengthened. Is there any more room at the College of Steubenville?" "Keith," he replied, "there's always room for you—take the next plane."

I felt the little poor man of Assisi beckoning me to "rebuild the church." Following the lead of the Holy Spirit, I moved to Steubenville, Ohio.

When I arrived at the college, it was in desperate shape. There was one Franciscan priest, Father Mike, with a mighty vision, but not much else. Two dorms were empty, many of the faculty were demoralized, many of them were not even committed to a Christian worldview, and students were scarce.

But God has worked miracles over the years. What was once a dwindling, dying college is now a powerhouse for God, with the largest student enrollment in its history. The now Franciscan University of Steubenville also continues to bear fruit in many outreach ministries. Thousands of Christians participate each year in the school's evangelization training or in one of the school's many conferences. I was privileged to be called to stand with Father Mike and become a part of the Steubenville miracle.

Within the university itself, God has opened doors for me to proclaim and preach the gospel, both as dean of students and currently as dean of evangelization. Along with this responsibility has come the opportunity to present the good news over radio and television. With Father Mike and a holy layman, Tom Kneier, I have also had a role in building the "Servants of Christ the King," a lay Catholic community committed to proclaiming the gospel of Christ and living a radical Christian life within the heart of the Catholic Church. This community is fully Catholic, fully "evangelical," fully alive in the Holy Spirit, and fully committed to mission.

I have had many opportunities to be Christ's witness, and I am grateful for each chance. My evangelical conviction rests on my identity as a Christian, as one called to follow in the footsteps of Jesus, as one called to preach about the "the Evangel." I am a Catholic Christian tied to two thousand years of Christian history, believing in an incarnational God who constantly makes known His will through a church that is very human as well as divine; a church full of problems, yet full of power; a church that is sacramental and incarnational, showing the truths of the faith through sign and symbol and inviting all who will come to hear the good news about Jesus Christ. The church is not God's Kingdom, but she is a seed of the Kingdom, growing into a mighty oak and spreading her limbs and fragrant aroma throughout the earth as she draws nourishment from her King.

Furthermore, my identity as a Catholic Christian is necessarily evangelical. I am "evangelical" because I am on fire to proclaim the good news of Jesus Christ. As I said earlier, the word *evangelical* must not be reserved for one small segment of Christians. Rather, it should be the proud adjectival description of all Christian people.

Dr. Carl Henry, one of the foremost deans of evangelical

history, in a recent talk entitled "The Christian Scholar's Task," defined an evangelical as "one who affirms the good news that God forgives sin and gives new life to sinners on the ground of the substitutionary death of Christ and His bodily resurrection."[1] He was quick to add that the message to be proclaimed must be scripturally controlled and scripturally authenticated. Just such a proclamation is being made at an evangelical Roman Catholic college, which is in the midst of a revival.

CHAPTER 4

Classical Revival at a Catholic College

In the late sixties and early seventies, the College of Steubenville suffered from the disease that afflicted many church-based schools—*secularization*, the purging of God and a God-grounded ethic from, at least, the public arena of life. Alcohol, drugs, sexual immorality, and depression—symptoms that so often accompany this illness—were rampant. Though the situation at Steubenville was not that different from many other colleges, a search committee recognized the need for action and assembled to find a captain to steer what appeared to be a sinking ship. In 1974, they chose Father Michael Scanlan.

After a trip to Assisi to rekindle the Franciscan fervor in his own spirit, Father Mike stepped upon the campus of the College of Steubenville. What he met at the college was a board of trustees whose hearts had been prepared by the Lord to cautiously relinquish control of their plan for the college and make room for God's plan of the renewal of Christian and Catholic values—the values of the college's founders—which would disrupt and upset the existing campus lifestyle. The rather tenuous but open acceptance of Father Mike's nomination for the college presidency was the first step in a series of slow yet steady efforts, under the direction of the Holy Spirit, to begin the restructuring and revival of the Steubenville campus.

Though the board of trustees accepted his new leadership, many of the faculty and students did not. That was not surprising. Secularization had infected the entire campus, and it would not be easily cured. Father Mike saw its damaging effects throughout the faculty and student body.

Some among the students were using alcohol and drugs to

ease their depression. One-night stands and other forms of promiscuity were common attempts to find love in their love-starved environment. Many admitted that they had no friends on campus, no one with whom they could talk or share their lives, no one with whom they were close, no one they could love or who would really love them in return. The attempted suicides, though not unusual for college campuses, were a serious, visible sign of the student body's brokenness and woundedness.

The faculty was not much better off. The demoralization of many professors dramatically illustrated their loneliness and despair. Some had even spurned their Catholic roots so thoroughly that their classroom lectures and other public expressions heralded a worldview and ethical perspective antithetical to Christian orthodoxy. A few had even gone as far as advocating alien ideologies devoid of any concept of any God, much less a Christian one. In describing these early years, Father Michael, in his published talk "Making and Keeping Catholic Colleges Catholic," states:

> In our own situation, we went through some very difficult
> situations, which resulted in separating people from the
> university. One involved a faculty member promoting atheistic
> Marxism. We went through a separation process with a faculty
> member who was promoting secular humanism and the
> *Humanist Manifesto*. There was a former faculty member who
> promoted feminism courses and lesbianism as a priority over a
> Christian commitment. There were lecturers in theology
> promoting exegesis and relativism in ways that obscured the
> truths of revelation. I am talking about individual situations
> that are no longer present at the university. There was also a
> former student personnel administrator who regularly
> promoted skepticism regarding eternal values and absolute
> truth. In drama, there was a struggle with a director who
> believed that art for art's sake was the ultimate value rather
> than a commitment that came under serving the glory of
> God.[1]

Secularization showed up in still other ways. Though the college was a Catholic school, faculty and student attendance at even Sunday liturgies was virtually nonexistent. The school's financial condition and physical state were as poor as its student life.

Enrollment was dropping sharply. Two dorms were empty, the cafeteria was seldom occupied, and an extraordinary outburst of vandalism was destroying the appearance of the campus.

The college was a war zone with spiritual ruin visible everywhere. Father Mike's mission was clear, and he went at it armed with divine wisdom and love, a vision of the truth, the strength and conviction to bolster the vision, and the willingness to undergo persecution to carry it out.

Father Michael spent the early months of his first year as president getting to know the students—talking seriously with them; relaxing with them by playing tennis, football, basketball, and volleyball; eating in the cafeteria with them; learning about their lives. (To this day he still pastors in the same manner.) Although he saw blatant sin and ill-fated escapism, he realized that these were symptoms of deep emptiness and loneliness inflicted by the cancer of secularization, and it moved him to compassion. He worked to cure the disease, not to shame or destroy its victims.

As far as the faculty members were concerned, Father Michael spent a good deal of time getting to know them, dialoguing with them about their views, and praying for their spiritual revival. Although some strongly opposed his efforts, others welcomed him, wooed by his genuine concern for their personal lives, not just their public pronouncements.

I arrived on the scene in the initial stages of Father Michael's work of renewal, and I embarked on a new stage in my personal walk of faith.

I will never forget my arrival in Steubenville, Ohio, in 1975. As I rounded the bends of West Virginia Route 2, I saw the smokestacks of the Weirton Steel Mill protruding into a dingy gray skyline. I felt somewhat unsettled as I recalled some of the beautiful landscapes that I have enjoyed living in over the years. I was raised amidst the beauty and strength of the New England countryside. And I had just spent a year-and-a-half sixty-nine hundred feet up in the mountains of New Mexico, nestled in the Sangri de Cristo (Blood of Christ) Mountain Range. As I pursued the monastic life there, the countryside offered me peace and strength. To say the least, I was not prepared for the geography, the climate, or for that matter, much else that I found in Steubenville.

I was unsettled, but somehow it didn't really matter. I was

here for a purpose: to complete my education in an environment of faith. I had long since decided that the most precious thing to me was Jesus Christ. I wanted to give my whole life to Him in service, and I didn't want to be in an academic setting that would threaten my commitment. Little did I know, however, the challenges ahead or how much my faith would be tried and refined by them.

What I found shocked me. The College of Steubenville was barren; enrollment was at an all-time low. An air of despair hovered in the minds and hearts of many. But not in Michael Scanlan. In him I saw hope, vision, conviction, and the fire of God's Holy Spirit. Proverbs 29:18 says, "Where there is no revelation, the people cast off restraint; but blessed is he who keeps the law" (NIV). Or, as another translation puts it, "Where there is no vision, the people perish." There was no lack of vision in Father Mike.

When I arrived on the Steubenville campus, one of the first things I noticed was an etching in the administration building of Saint Francis carrying a stone. I didn't know then that the etching would later become the symbol of a great movement of God to raise up a mighty fortress where His name would be praised and adored.

As a young man, Francis of Assisi had a dramatic conversion. He heard the Lord speak to his heart from a cross at San Damiano church, saying, "Francis, go and rebuild [restore, revive] my church, which as you see is falling down around you." Responsive to God's call, Francis Bernardone immediately set out to restore physically the small churches that had fallen into misuse and disrepair. Stone by stone he started to rebuild them. But his focus wasn't merely buildings; he also sought to rebuild souls. He gathered around himself the misfits of his time, the lepers, and the many others society had rejected or ignored. As he followed the Lord, he prayed fervently for revival, and God added to his group others who were on fire for the divine mission. Eventually, Francis came to see that the ruins of which the Lord had spoken were the *living* stones—the living members of His church—not the physical structures they used for worship.

The apostle Peter describes us as living stones in his first letter: "As you come to him the Living Stone rejected by men but chosen by God and precious to him, you also like living stones are being built into a spiritual house to be a holy priesthood offering spiritual sacrifices acceptable to God through Jesus Christ" (1 Pet. 2:4–5).

I thought of this verse and Francis of Assisi many times in the initial years of rebuilding the Steubenville campus. Yes, buildings needed repair, and other physical and financial matters needed attention, but none of these were as important as addressing the deep personal needs of the college's "living stones." Franciscan Michael Scanlan clearly saw this order of priority. Following in the heritage of Saint Francis, he began assembling around him living stones for the work of revival. His formula was simple:

- Prayer
- Repentance
- Conversion
- The power of the Holy Spirit
- Mission

The nature of revival hasn't changed since the first century. When these essential elements are genuinely embraced and lived out, revival occurs. The great Protestant and Catholic revivalists understood and practiced this and saw incredible results wrought by God. The College of Steubenville would experience no less.

JOINING ONE ANOTHER IN PRAYER

As a resident student, I had to move into one of the college dormitories. Space was not a problem, but at Father Michael's suggestion and my request, I moved into Saint Thomas More Hall, which was nearly empty—except for a group committed to all the elements of revival. They called themselves the "Heart of Mary Household." Joined by many lay people from the local area, they had begun meeting for protracted prayer sessions, beseeching God to send His Holy Spirit to resurrect and renew the dry bones of the campus.

Inspired by their efforts, I moved onto the dorm's third floor and began what would become the first student faith household. The Heart of Mary was comprised of volunteers and employees of the university, which was fine and good. But part of Father Michael's vision for the college's renewal was the building of a genuine *koinonia*—a Christian community—of *students*. He belived that one of the greatest impediments to experiencing the faith at many Christian colleges, and for that matter in many Christian churches, was the lack of true fellowship. So he longed to see dormitories where men and women would gather on their respective floors, commit their lives to love the Lord, love one another, and truly become fellowship groups.

Father Mike suggested I seek other young men who were willing to commit themselves to live in the same wing, pray together daily, study the Scriptures, attend the Eucharist, and engage in missionary work together. I embraced his vision and watched God work. In that first household, I was soon surrounded by some wonderful men: Craig Brotz, David Reuter, Rick Peters, John Heit, Dave Anderson, Rich Stepanski, and Frank Kelly. We all had our shortcomings. We were young and didn't know the first thing about building a genuine experience of Christian community and fraternity, but we all loved the Lord and knew how to pray. And how we prayed! Every day. Every night. Without fail. Always expecting God to honor the humble requests of His people.

In time, we joined forces with other committed Christians on campus and in the surrounding area, constantly interceding for the College of Steubenville. As a household, we prayed with those of the Heart of Mary household, who were also growing spiritually stronger by the day. On yet another floor in our massive dormitory were some religious women—Sister Barbara, Sister Anne, and Sister Loretta—who had also experienced a fresh annointing of the Holy Spirit and a call to be a part of His great work on our campus.

God provided other sources of encouragement and inspiration as well. Several priests in Steubenville played an important role in moving me to give myself totally to Jesus Christ. Perhaps the one I remember with the greatest affection is Father Philip Bebie, who has since gone on to be with the Lord. He loved God and had a joy and vibrancy that I had never seen before. He and the other priests taught me much about living a holy, inspired, and radical life for our Lord.

Finally, there were the lay people who gathered in the college chapel on Thursday evenings to pray: Bob and Betty Burns; George and Mary Gable; Dick and Doris Skibicki; George and Lois Fyke; and of course, one of the early leaders, Tom Kneier who later, with his wife Madeline, would become a founder, along with Father Michael, of the Servants of Christ the King Catholic Community.

All of us became a team unified in vision and prayer, continually pleading for the Holy Spirit to move on the campus and revive it to new life. We had no idea what our prayers would bring; we just knew God would answer.

COMMITMENT IN THE FACE OF OPPOSITION

As my household began to see the fruits of our prayers, our life together deepened. We took on a new name, "Heart of Jesus," which better conveyed our desire to discover the depths of Christ and love Him more faithfully. In the process, we grew to know one another, wrinkles and all. We learned to support each other as we struggled through the processes of growing up, pursuing academic study, and adjusting to college life. The greatest challenge we faced, however, was tremendous opposition.

Not everyone at the college accepted the vision of its new president. I will never forget the day when a contingent of students decided to march up to Father Michael's office carrying a coffin to signify their outrage at the state of affairs on campus. I was extremely concerned about him because my loyalty to him, even then, ran deep. When the students mounted the top of the hill leading to Father Michael's office, he came out of the building with a smile on his face. With Christian charity, he then welcomed them into his office to discuss their concerns. They were surprised, to say the least. But they accepted his invitation. Out of that group of students later came campus leaders who helped bring the president's vision into reality.

Another expression of opposition I remember well concerned the efforts to build the second household of faith in another residence hall. A group of pious and devoted young men wanted to have an alternate faith household experience. One of their number, Tony Corasaniti, invited me to come and address them one night on how my household got started. But some in this group didn't welcome my presence. They thought that the very existence and behavior of the Heart of Jesus were saying, "Nobody else is truly Christian." Have you ever been misunderstood like that? When you try to live a devoted, committed Christian life, other believers are often the first ones who wrongly judge you. Fortunately, their opposition was short-lived, and under the leadership of Tony Corasaniti, they would later become known as "Precious Blood," the second faith household on campus. This marked the beginning of a system that gradually became the mainstay of social activity on campus.

REVIVAL

What happened in the dorms also began taking place in the chapel. A small local prayer meeting started to grow as its members, through the power of the Holy Spirit, experienced God's love in genuine repentance and conversion. The Lord's work among them was magnetic. Soon, the prayer meeting swelled in size until it frequently packed the chapel.

Revival was breaking out all over the campus with a power that could not be contained.

By the time I graduated in 1977, two years after my arrival, the spiritual dimension of the College of Steubenville was really beginning to flourish. The prayer meeting that developed in the chapel had become a vibrant, evangelical Catholic, lay community who called themselves the "Community of God's Love." Members of that community, many of whom were alumni, faculty, and staff of the College of Steubenville and had been deeply affected by the revival, began serving voluntarily and assuming leadership positions in the school. Years later, the Community of God's Love became a formal Catholic covenant community now known as the Servants of Christ the King, who continue to be a great resource for the ongoing work of God on the Steubenville campus.

I have watched God build these monuments of faith from the ashes of secularism. The more I saw His transforming work in action, the more inspired and awed I became. Campus ministry began to thrive. Campus prayer meetings grew rapidly both in frequency and size. The lack of attendance at daily mass which had characterized the campus had been replaced by a need for more liturgies to handle the ever-increasing number of worshipers. Students who were meeting the Lord in a new and fresh way were evangelizing and desiring to spread the gospel beyond the local community. And the Lord kept calling faithful laborers—new faculty, staff, and other devoted Franciscan friars—to develop and manage the work He had graciously begun in answer to the prayers of a handful of His people. "Life in the Spirit" seminars began on campus and in the local area. They were basic, seven-week proclamations of God's love, repentance, and forgiveness and calls to prayer, faith, and mature Christian living. They literally transformed lives and enabled the fire to spread from log to log to burn brighter and stronger.

During this time the Community of God's Love became the Servants of God's Love and then the Servants of Christ the King. The name changes reflected a progression—a move from a prayer group to a community of believers committed to a common way of life according to a covenant. And the transformation happened within a clear and committed Catholic context centered on the Eucharist and faithful to the teaching of the Roman Catholic Church.

From its inception this community identified with the revival at the College of Steubenville, sending volunteer workers to help oversee the burgeoning faith household movement. Household by household the work spread throughout the campus, leaving in its wake a reinvigorated, genuinely evangelical Catholic culture. Indeed, the whole framework of life began to take on a new dynamism; it was even reflected in the names each of the student faith households picked to identify their individual charisms and convictions. To this day, all over the campus at what is now called Franciscan University, you can find sweatshirts, T-shirts, banners, and intramural team rosters bearing the names of groups of men and women differing in gifts but walking in the same Spirit. It is not unusual to see a flag football game between "Mustard Seed" and the "Lion of Judah" or a basketball playoff between "Magnificat" and "The Handmaids of the Lord."

A MATURING CHRISTIAN WORLDVIEW

All that has happened on Franciscan University's campus has been carefully guided by the clear apostolic, pastoral, and prudent leadership of Father Michael Scanlan.

Even the school's name change is a result of Father Mike's untiring work. Because of the college's increased enrollment and ability to offer fully-accredited graduate programs, the College of

Steubenville became the University of Steubenville in 1980. Then, by decision of the board of trustees, the name of the university was officially changed to Franciscan University of Steubenville to reflect more clearly the charism and Christian commitment of the school. Franciscan University, in addition to a full array of undergraduate majors, now offers master's degrees in theology, business, and counseling. In short, after more than fifteen years of revival a mature Christian worldview has emerged on campus.

Student government positions are seen as opportunities for service to the Lord, His church, and His people. Clubs and organizations arise regularly to prepare students who will go into the marketplace as missionaries of the future—God's servants in the business world, the political arena, and foreign service, as well as explicit church service. An ideal of Christian family life has been demonstrated through the faculty and the local community and is being taught on campus with the mission of enabling our students, many of whom have suffered the blight of family breakdown, to find healing and restoration so that they can move ahead with a vision of the Christian family as the domestic church.

Academic instruction has matured as it has been touched by the wind of revival. The university has become increasingly known as a center for Christian orthodoxy that heralds a solidly classical, Western, liberal arts education. We have the largest number of theology majors on any Catholic campus in the United States, which is another sign of God's remarkable grace. In the early seventies there was a general recommendation that the college stop teaching theology classes because of the lack of student interest. This happened on other Catholic campuses as well. But our post-revival experience has made us an exception to the norm. We have men and women touched by the Holy Spirit, eager and hungry to learn about the Scriptures, the history of the church, the elements of Christian living, and the doctrines of the faith.

As you may guess, when people grow in their experiential and intellectual knowledge of God, their love for Him increases. The overflow of this love manifests itself in all types of ministries, and at Steubenville many of these outreaches have developed from within the student body. For example, a group of students travel every spring to Florida to evangelize on the beaches. Student music groups perform Christian music at various high schools. Student evangelistic teams engage in local outreach work. And the thriving Works of Mercy program cares for the shut-ins, developmentally handicapped, and elderly in the local area. All of these ministries are the good fruit of classical revivalism.

THE ELEMENTS OF CLASSICAL REVIVAL

These are merely a few of the details of the "Steubenville Miracle." More of the story is recorded in *Let the Fire Fall*, a wonderful book written by my friend and the president of Franciscan University, Father Michael Scanlan. What is important for my purposes here is for you to see that what has occurred at Franciscan University of Steubenville is a telling example of a classical revival and its perpetuation of spiritual renewal. All the elements of revival can be seen on our campus.

PRAYER

A prevailing hunger for depth of prayer and an understanding of the power of intercession and spiritual warfare pervade this campus. You can nearly always find students praying in the eight available Eucharistic chapels or at informal gatherings. Prayer is proclaimed, taught, demonstrated, and expected. Indeed, there is a "reverse peer pressure," as Father John Bertolucci called it, toward heaven and away from worldliness.

REPENTANCE

This prevailing spirit of prayer has led to a penitential lifestyle, not of heaviness or despair, but of true joy. The word *penitential* has been used throughout Christian history to denote those men and women who have grasped that repentance is not a one-time affair, but a call to continual conversion—a call to acknowledge our sin and God's greatness. There is tremendous joy and freedom in surrendering our sinful nature to the healing touch of the Lord.

Francis of Assisi and his spiritual brothers considered themselves a penitential movement and their work a penitential renewal. Their heritage continues on our campus. Twice a week, long lines form for the Sacrament of Reconciliation. Students, faculty, staff, and local community members gather, all seeking freedom from their sins and reconciliation to God. In honest relationships, people acknowledge their faults and responsibilities and set one another free, obeying the admonition, "Hence, declare your sins to one another, and pray for one another, that you may find healing" (James 5:16).

The great seasons of the liturgical year are celebrated with the fervor and vibrancy that characterize a true spirit of revival, not human concoction. Even as I finish this chapter, we find ourselves in the beginning of the Forty Days of Lent. I marvel at the throngs of students who pack the chapel on Ash Wednesday to receive the ashes on their heads as a sign of their call to repent and believe the good news.

CONVERSION

Such prayer and repentance have led to dramatic and continual conversions. For example, I remember one particular man, a Muslim, who had come to do some engineering work in the local Ohio Valley. He stayed on campus for a month and paid room and board in what was called the Renewal Center, but is now the Saint Thomas More dorm. By the time he left, he had met Jesus Christ as a result of the prayers offered up for him. His life has been transformed.

Many lives have been changed by the touch of the fire that has spread from this hill and gone forth to the nations. Conversion is evident in the lives of the young men and women here, many of whom come to the campus precisely because of the unmistakable signs of the presence of God.

In the final analysis, what changes hearts is not what we do, but what God does. Yes, we must allow Him to penetrate our lives. We can shut Him out. But when we open the soul's door, He touches us with the tenderness of His love. Franciscan University is a testimony to that fact. Through prayer, liturgy, and communal support, we have received the overwhelming experience of His infinite, unconditional love.

The preaching from the pulpits, the teaching in the classrooms, the pastoring from the Franciscan friars are all geared toward an understanding of conversion as the continual call of the Christian to become fully complete and mature in Christ, demonstrating through his or her life the fruit of the Spirit: love, joy, peace, patience, kindness, goodness, and self-control (Gal. 5:22–23).

THE POWER OF THE HOLY SPIRIT

And then there's the power. The power of the Holy Spirit is so tangible on this campus that at times it seems as if one could squeeze it from a hypersoaked sponge. Part of that real presence has been a result of the operation of the gifts of the Spirit. They have become and are seen as normative, not as exceptions to His work. In the early stages of Steubenville's revival, the campus was often viewed as a center of charismatic renewal, but that label has dropped away. Our campus is now more accurately described as deeply Christian and fully Catholic.

Our president, Father Michael Scanlan, reminds us that it is *normal* for a Catholic college to believe in Jesus Christ, to follow Him, to be filled with His Spirit, to receive and use the spiritual gifts given for the upbuilding of His church, and to be faithful to the teaching of Scripture as well as to the teaching authority of the Catholic church.

Normal is one of those words we need to recapture. The secularization prevalent in our contemporary age is *abnormal,* not normal. It is the bad fruit of the Fall, not the good fruit of God's desire for His human creatures. It does not bring freedom, joy, and peace; only the power of the Spirit of God breaking forth into the human experience and transforming individuals and communities can bring those evidences of grace into our lives. The power of God's Spirit plays a vital part in our way of life at Franciscan University of Steubenville.

MISSION

On campus, we also have a clear understanding that every believer, every Christian, is called to the work of the Master—*evangelism.* The evangelical task of proclaiming the gospel is not limited to clergy or professional evangelists. It is, in fact, a mandate binding all Christians. Through life and lip, we are called to penetrate this age with the good news of salvation in Christ. By advancing with this message and its transforming power, we can regain lost ground and advance the cause of Christ. No matter what our career or vocation, our primary task is to be the church and do what the church does. We understand this on the Steubenville campus.

WORLDWIDE REVIVAL?

My evangelical Protestant friends reading this book will recognize the blueprint for revival and its occurrence on our campus. How strange it must seem to some of you to hear of a classical revival flourishing in a Roman Catholic context. But what Franciscan University has experienced is certainly not lacking precedent. It is clearly an expression of our common evangelical heritage. As you well know, revival flourishes where Jesus Christ is proclaimed and honored as Lord. It has been this way since the first Pentecost. And it will always occur in any Christian tradition that once again invites Him in and opens itself to the tangible manifestation of His Spirit.

Some of my Catholic friends, however, may object to my use of the word *revival*. Perhaps you associate it with tents, hell-fire preaching, and emotional but superficial commitments to Christ. But you must realize that some great work has come out of tents (and still does every summer on this campus). Furthermore, some of our heroes, such as Saints Dominic and Francis, were responsible for revival movements during their own day. And these were revivals that positively affected church history, even into our century.

Unfortunately, Christians from all traditions often limit revival. Many have even made it an exclusively Protestant concept, while others have narrowed it further, relegating its possible experience to certain segments of Protestantism. How tragic! For what we need is a classical revival to sweep *all* of today's Christian churches and schools. We need genuine, divinely energized revival—the kind that will release the work of the Holy Spirit in the hearts of *all* of God's people. Then can the sleeping giant—the Christian church in all of its beauty, communions, and traditions—rise up and respond to the desperate hunger of our spiritually starved age. But such a sweeping, dynamic revival will not happen in a fragmented Christian community. Of course, it can begin, as it did in Steubenville, with the prayers and spiritually sensitive actions of a handful of dedicated, visionary Christians. It can even start with the prayers of one believer. But as long as we see ourselves as disconnected, even polarized, communities with some of us adhering to "the right faith" while the rest of us are languishing in error, we will never receive the incredibly rich benefits of a worldwide revival. What Steubenville has experienced will be experienced elsewhere, but only in localized doses. A global sweep of God's Spirit throughout His church will elude us.

It doesn't have to be this way. But it will if we don't change in our perceptions of and attitudes toward each other. We must see that we were meant to be one church united under one Head for the purpose of carrying out a two-fold mission: proclaiming the gospel and maturing in Christ. Remember, in our two-thousand-year history our divisions have been recent.

Can we again be one? I believe we can. Is that a dream? Yes. An unachievable one? Not as long as God is Lord of heaven and earth. How can it be achieved? That's the focus of the rest of this book. We must build together on a solid foundation, building on a truly common heritage so as to achieve, in God's strength and wisdom, a true ecumenism—a true respect for the whole church family and a true desire to see evangelical gospel living flourish within all Christian churches and transform nations.

Read on. Join with me to discover what this dream involves and how you can help make it a reality. Our journey will force us to confront some prejudices and some mistakes, and it will help us rediscover our whole family. We have no other option. The Master has commanded us to go into all the world and make disciples of every nation (Matt. 28:19). Whose disciples? His. Not our own.

PART II

Evangelical Family Living

CHAPTER 5

Returning to Our First Love

With the precision and beauty of a finely crafted machine, a sleek, shiny new truck burns up the road, carrying a payload of tightly-bound hay. The camera zooms in on the large letters embedded in the truck's tailgate. The background music gets louder. Then, with a rhythmic, popular beat, vocalists sing out, "The heartbeat of America is today's Chevy trucks."

Chevrolet uses this TV commercial to try to convince us that its product line is our heartthrob. Chevrolets capture our love for automobiles more completely than any other product from any other car manufacturer. If we want our love for cars or trucks fulfilled, we need to buy Chevrolet. Then we'll be happy. Then we'll find driving satisfaction. Then we'll have the vehicle we need for work and play.

But what is the heartthrob of the Christian? What, above all, will give him happiness and satisfaction? What fulfills her life better than anything else? For the Christian it is Jesus Christ. Jesus Christ is the heartbeat of the Christian's life, and he or she knows that all of life's goodness finds its ultimate source and completion and meaning in Him. Delete Him from life, and life dies. Take Him out of Christianity, and all that's left is religious rubble. Christianity *is* Christ. He is her heartbeat, the Christian's heartbeat, the church's heartbeat . . . and whether non-Christians acknowledge Him or not, He is the uninvited guest who knocks on the door of their hearts, asking to be let in so He can give them the superabundance of everlasting life with Him.

LOVING THE INCARNATE WORD

OUR NEED

Since Christ is at the center of our lives as our Lord and Savior, we need to love Him. Let me repeat that: *We need to love Him.* Contrary to the opinion of many, He does not need us or our love. As the second Person of the divine Trinity, He has been in a perfect love bond with the Father and the Holy Spirit from all eternity. He knows, has experienced, and offers to us unconditional acceptance and commitment. He even demonstrated His intense love for us by coming to live among us. Here He breathed our air, felt our pain, healed our hurts, guided our hearts, challenged our minds, died for our wrongs, and rose from the dead to give us new life now and the hope of eternal bliss in the life to come. Even now, He woos us, seeking to draw us to Him so that we can have the fullness of life that we desperately need and long for. He knows how much we need Him. He knows how much He can and wants to meet our need. But the need is on our side, not on His. As God, He needs nothing: "God, who made the world and everything in it, since He is Lord of heaven and earth, does not dwell in temples made with hands. Nor is He worshiped with men's hands, as though He needed anything, since He gives to all life, breath, and all things" (Acts 17:24–25). As God, He wants us to be fulfilled so much that He was even willing to pave the way for us with His own blood: "For God so loved the world that He gave His only begotten Son, that whoever believes in Him should not perish but have everlasting life" (John 3:16).

God, however, will not force us to love Him. Forced love is a contradiction in terms. Love is a choice, and God will not violate our right to choose. Such a violent act would contradict His benevolent nature and our standing as creatures made in His image. So if in loving Him through His Son, Jesus Christ, we will find the ultimate fulfillment of our heart's yearning, we must choose to love Him—or more accurately, we must first choose to *accept* His love, then turn around and give our love to Him. The apostle John says it well: "We love Him because He first loved us" (1 John 4:19). God has reached out to us, spreading His arms and embracing us, even when we were raising our fists in defiance against Him. He first loved us. So now we have the honor and privilege and joy of embracing His love for us and loving Him in return—not out of duty, but out of a deep sense of gratitude for what He has done and out of an awed recognition of who He is.

LOOKING FOR LOVE IN ALL THE WRONG PLACES

It's tragic that many of us move through our Christian walk without really developing a love relationship with Christ. It's not that we don't want it, but we often want it for the wrong reasons or pursue it in the wrong ways. Some of us go to church looking for the Lord out of duty. Perhaps our parents instilled in us a sense of obligation to God, so we try to fulfill it at least once a week. Others of us pray, study the Scriptures, and engage in the other traditional facets of the Christian life out of habit. That's what we have always done, so we keep on doing it. Why? We're not sure. We haven't even asked that question for as long as memory serves. We just keep going through the motions, and our hearts remain unmoved. Some of us intellectualize our way to God. We think that knowing Him means having our facts straight about Him. We can systematize, understand, explain, and defend those propositions, but we don't allow them to penetrate our souls and change our hearts. So our experience of the Tripersonal Lord remains impersonal and cold. Whatever our motivation or approach, our search for a vital relationship with Christ has hit a dead end, and we can't find the detour sign—indeed, many of us don't even know that we're lost.

Without and within our churches, however, are some true seekers. These don't look only out of duty or habit. Neither do they look just with their minds. They know they are lost, and they are looking for the right street. But they still have not found the way to an intimate relationship with Christ. Why? Again, the reasons vary. For example, some of them have developed a distorted view of love. They grew up in an environment where love was conditional. If they didn't behave in just the right ways or believe just the right "truths" or use just the right language—in other words, be just the right person, living up to the stated or unstated expectations of others—then they were shunned. As adults, they may now know that they were not treated well. They may long for real love and genuine, caring acceptance, but they can't recognize either. They miss the obvious signs of love, so healing, restoration, and intimacy in any relationship (much less with God) eludes them. They need inner healing, adjustments in negative patterns of thinking. It takes action to break unhealthy patterns; it takes the action of unconditional love and consistent affirmation. This will help them begin to see the true vistas of human love and finally the unending horizons of God's love for them. But until they are helped to see the truth, they will go on searching and never find.

FINDERS, KEEPERS

Among us, though, are seekers who have found Christ's love and are returning their love to Him. As they grow in their relationship to Him, they become easier to spot. They are the ones who are secure in God's love. They are so secure, in fact, that their faith in the Lord sustains them through the difficult times and provides them with real peace, even when others around them panic. These are the ones who can move through the spiritually dry times without drinking in the temptations of sin. Their thirst is quenched as they drink in their communion with God—the intimate communion for which each of us was created. They, of course, are not problem free. Hurt . . . hassles . . . misunderstandings . . . frustrations . . . anger . . . disappointments . . . all touch and threaten to twist their lives into a jumbled mass of pain. But they cry out to the Lord to find strength, comfort, and peace in Him. And when He reaches out to them, they recognize His healing embrace. They, in turn, rest in the safety of His arms like a baby snuggling up to the soothing, gentle hugs of her mother.

What do they know that many of us do not? How did they find what some of us are still searching for? *They discovered that the street leading to God's love is paved with a personal, one-to-one, unique relationship with Him, a relationship in which we communicate deeply with Him through the Scriptures, prayer, the sacraments, and our relationships with others in the community of faith.* The "finders" have learned that through the grace of that communication, we become open to the power and presence of God. The truth of who He is and what He has done for us becomes crystal clear. And the more vulnerable we become in our communication with Him, the more He unveils Himself to us, plunging us more deeply into intimacy with Him who is our Creator and Redeemer.

"Okay," you may say, "if that's the street, how do I find it?" You find it the same way I did. The same way the students and faculty on the Steubenville campus did. The same way people have found the way for centuries. *By faith.* Not the blind, irrational faith that causes a traveler to board a plane even though he knows the pilot is drunk, but the reasonable faith we exercise each day. The kind of faith that leads us to trust in the stability of a house built by someone who has proven his construction abilities time and time again. The kind of faith that leads us to have confidence in someone who has never failed to keep his promises. The kind of faith that leads us to trust someone who has repeatedly shown that he has our best interests at heart. This kind of faith is crucial to coming to see, understand, and accept God's love. Only this kind of faith will lead us to trust God with all we have and are. Only this kind of faith will lead us to love God with all our hearts, minds, souls, and strength.

If that's true—and it is—how will we know that our faith has brought us our heart's deepest desire: a love relationship with the Lord who is love? Allow me to explain.

We can know in a real, affective, personal way that God loves us. God has created us so that our inmost beings constantly desire to know truth; therefore, we continually search for the Truth, who is Christ. Of course, we don't usually recognize at first that the Truth we seek is Jesus, but when our search leads to Him and we accept Him, we experience the unexplainable peace that comes only from God. This is the peace the great medieval theologian Augustine finally found and then expressed in what has become one of the best-known prayers in church history: "We are created for thee, O God, and our hearts are restless until they rest in thee." The apostle Paul spoke of this peace also: "Dismiss all anxiety from your minds. Present your needs to God in every form of prayer and in petitions full of gratitude. Then God's own peace which is beyond all understanding, will stand guard over your hearts" (Phil. 4:6–7). But Paul's and Augustine's understanding flowed from the One who is the fountain of peace. Jesus Himself said, "Peace I leave with you, My peace I give to you; not as the world gives do I give to you. Let not your heart be troubled, neither let it be afraid" (John 14:27).

OUR HIGHEST PRIORITY

Christ has done so much for us that He deserves, above all, to be our first love. The One who is number one in our lives. The One who should receive our greatest commitment . . . our utmost respect . . . our unwavering loyalty . . . our total obedience . . . our sacrificial devotion. When we realize this and begin to act on it, our faith experience of Him deepens. In the initial stages of our relationship with God, we ask the more objective questions of the faith:

- What is salvation?
- What must I do to be saved?
- Who is a Christian?
- Why should I become one?

But as God keeps breaking into our lives and our love for Him deepens, we begin looking for answers to the questions of a fuller faith experience:

- What can I do to love the Lord?
- What does Jesus mean to me?
- How can I best serve Him?
- How can I grow closer to Him?

Our relationship with Christ must become Person-oriented instead of functionally based. Too many of us live as if Christ were a cosmic vending machine. We drop our prayer requests in the slot above, select the answers we want, and expect them to drop out the opening below. But Jesus has not entered our world to be our want-supplier. Nor has He come just to be the doorway of our entrance into heaven. He is not simply some means to some end. He is the End of, to, and for all creation. He is the Beloved of the Father who has sacrificially given us Himself so we can sacrificially give Him ourselves.

Unless we really begin to see Jesus this way, our Christianity will grow lifeless. We'll become desensitized to the personal Lord loving us, healing us, and giving us life.

LOVING THE WRITTEN WORD

A KEY TO KNOWING CHRIST

But how can we come to see Jesus as a Person to know and love instead of as a thing we use to get our needs and wants? *Through meditation on the Word.* We can turn our eyes to the written Word to read and contemplate the actions of the living Word—"the word who became flesh and dwelt among us" (John 1:14), walking, breathing, thinking love. We can meditate on Jesus the great Lover, the passionate One—giving His last breath on the cross for love.

Within this entire context, Paul's idea of the renewal of the mind becomes significant (Rom. 12:2). As we seek the Lord as a Person, our minds become transformed so that we become increasingly vulnerable to the truth. In turn, the Scriptures come alive for us personally. Everything takes on new meaning as God becomes more real in our everyday lives. And as we open ourselves to more truth, we receive more of Him who is Truth. He, in turn, transforms us from the inside out. Because He loves us, He must change us. As C. S. Lewis so clearly states:

> Love, in its own nature, demands the perfecting of the beloved; that the mere "kindness" which tolerates anything except suffering in its object is, in that respect, at the opposite pole from Love. When we fall in love with a woman, do we cease to care whether she is clean or dirty, fair or foul? Do we not rather then first begin to care? Does any woman regard it as a sign of love in a man that he neither knows nor cares how she is looking? Love may, indeed, love the beloved when her beauty is lost: but not because it is lost. Love may forgive all infirmities and love still in spite of them: but Love cannot cease to will their removal. Love is more sensitive than hatred itself to every blemish in the beloved; his "feeling is more soft and sensible than are the tender horns of cockled snails." Of all powers he forgives most, but he condones least: he is pleased with little, but demands all.[1]

Receiving God's love brings about the new creation that Paul describes: "If anyone is in Christ, he is a new creation. The old order has passed away; now all is new" (2 Cor. 5:17). When we accept Christ, we are immediately changed. God then becomes free to move within us in a new way. As great and wonderful as this initial change is, it is still only a beginning. Our divine Lover wants more from us, and we need to give more to Him. The moment of justification when we become new creations is crucial, but it is equally important to embrace and desire perpetual *metanoia*—perpetual conversion, perpetual newness. God wants to transform us daily into His likeness. With God we have the capability to move from glory to greater glory, from love on one level to love on a higher level. Why should we stop at less when we can experience so much more?

A KEY TO CHRISTIAN MATURITY

One way to grow in our love for Him is to grow in our love for His written Word—the sacred Scriptures. We should not love the Bible above the Lord. In fact, we must always realize that the goal of the Scriptures is to lead us to Christ and to guide us in developing a love relationship with Him. We reverence the Scriptures because they speak to us of Him, and what they tell us is that God loves us. In fact, they are *sacramental*—they communicate in a tangible way the grace and presence of God. For example, we as temples of the Holy Spirit are sacramental. The creation itself, though longing for its full redemption (Rom. 8:19), is also sacramental. How much more, then, this is true of the written Word, which as we read in 2 Timothy 3:16, is literally God-breathed (the definition of the Greek word used for "inspired") and makes Him present to us. That same breath (*ruach* in Hebrew) which was breathed into the first man and gave him life (Gen. 2:7) is now breathed into us each time we break open His Word.

The Scriptures are the inspired Word of God. When we read them, we hear God's voice. When we pray them, we speak God's words back to Him. The Bible's words are God's words—God's words to the world, God's words to us. And it is the Scriptures that help paint the full, majestic portrait of the face of Christ. So much that we need to know about Him is revealed in the sacred Scriptures—the collection of His love letters to His bride, the church. They are so critical to our knowledge of Jesus that Saint Jerome wrote, "Ignorance of Scripture is ignorance of Christ." To really know the living Word, we must discover Him in the pages of the written Word.

A TESTIMONY TO LOVE

As we study the written Word, we see how God faithfully worked with our ancestors and loved them even through their rebellion. We also discover where we come from, where we are going, and why. The Bible tells us about our heritage, and it also describes our future. We are people of the covenant, "a chosen race, a royal priesthood, a holy nation, a people He claims for His own, to proclaim the glorious works of the one who called us from darkness into His marvelous light" (1 Pet. 2:9). The Bible holds within it the ways that God has worked with us and how we have been grafted onto the vine of salvation.

In the Old Testament, we read how patient God was with our fathers. Time and again He called our parents back to relationship with Him. He worked with our father, Abraham, and made a covenant with him and his descendants. As Christians, we are those descendants, Abraham's spiritual children, so we stand in that covenant.

Furthermore, in the Old Testament prophets we read of God calling our ancestors back to that first love with Him—the love they kept losing. In Hosea, we see the love relationship between Hosea and Gomer, his adulterous wife. Gomer's unfaithfulness to Hosea becomes a parallel for Israel's unfaithfulness to God. But even as unfaithful as our ancestors were (and we often are), God set forth a tender promise in one of the most beautiful passages in all of Scripture: "How could I give you up . . . or deliver you up, O Israel? . . . My heart is overwhelmed, my pity is stirred. I will not give vent to my blazing anger, I will not destroy Ephraim again; For I am God and not man, the Holy One present among you; I will not let the flames consume you. . . . I will heal their faithlessness. I will love them freely for my anger has turned from them" (Hos. 11:8–9, 14:4).

Turning to the New Testament, we find all of the promises of old fulfilled in a divine Person, Jesus Christ. As Paul writes in 2 Corinthians 1:20, "All of the promises of the Bible find their yes in Christ." God's promises were perfectly fulfilled when Jesus

Christ became the incarnated *Logos,* and they will be ultimately demonstrated and revealed in the *Parousia,* His glorious Second Coming. The Kingdom He promised, which is now only present in seed form, will then be fully established.

There are many examples of the fulfillment of the Old Testament in the New. For example, when the Hebrews were complaining in the Sinai desert after their miraculous exodus from slavery in Egypt, God punished them by sending poisoned serpents that bit and killed many of the people. Realizing their sin against God, the Hebrews asked Moses to seek God for their relief. God told Moses, "Make a *saraph* [bronze serpent] and mount it on a pole, and if anyone who has been bitten looks at it, he will recover" (Num. 21:8). In the Gospel of John we read, "as Moses lifted up the serpent in the desert, so must the son of man be lifted up, that all who believe might have eternal life in Him" (John 3:14). God is the Healer of death and the Redeemer of humankind from the desert of the Old Testament to the cross outside of Jerusalem in the New.

Another example of Old Testament fulfillment by Christ involves spiritual food. We are all hungry for God in our hearts and can only be satisfied by Him. God portrays this for us in the Old Testament by feeding the Israelites with manna (heavenly food) in the desert (Ex. 16). That manna was but a prefigurement of the true heavenly food He would give to His body, the church, in the holy Eucharist. In the New Testament, the crowds question Jesus about this: "Our ancestors had manna to eat in the desert; according to Scripture, He gave them bread from the heavens to eat" (John 6:31). Jesus' answer reveals the fulfillment:

> I solemnly assure you, it was not Moses who gave you bread from the heavens; it is my Father who gives you the real heavenly bread. . . . I myself am the bread of life. No one who comes to me shall ever be hungry. . . . Your ancestors ate manna in the desert, but they died. This is the bread that comes down from heaven for a man to eat and never die. . . . the bread I will give is my flesh, for the life of the world. (vv. 32, 35, 49, 51)

Shortly after that discourse, Jesus broke bread with His disciples and gave them the gift of His Body and Blood, commanding them to partake of them in the Eucharist "as a remembrance of me" (Luke 22:19).

How beautifully and intricately the Old and New Testaments are woven together! Together they show us our rich heritage and its consummation in Christ. We need to pass on that heritage, to retell the story of the people of God and of their Savior and first love, Jesus Christ. Better yet, we need to make their Savior and Lover ours. When we know and love Him for who He is and what He has done, especially as He has been revealed in the Scriptures, we will have the evangelical dynamism—that internal burning desire to spread the good news—that we and those around us so desperately need in our narcissistic age.

I challenge you to fall in love with the Scriptures because of their richness and power and because of what they are: the words of Christ, the words of the living Word, the love letters of Love Incarnate to a love-starved world.

A NECESSARY APOLOGETIC

In spite of these wonderful truths, many people still wonder why they should study and meditate on the Bible. "After all," they reason, "didn't Christ establish the church so we would have all we needed for salvation?" That question has a two-part answer.

First, it's true that we have all we need for salvation within the church. The church is fundamentally the people of God. Christ "called a race made up of Jews and Gentiles which would be one, not according to the flesh, but in the spirit, and this race would be the new people of God."[2] We are all "a chosen race, a royal priesthood, a holy nation . . . who in times past were not a people, but now are the People of God" (1 Pet. 2:9-10).

From His earliest dealings with men and women, God has longed for a people. After fashioning Adam from the clay of the earth and breathing life into his nostrils, the Lord said, "It is not good for man to be alone" (Gen. 2:18). Man's destiny is never complete until he finds his home in family and community, the summit and ultimate model of which is the Trinity—Father, Son, and Holy Spirit living in perfect harmony, while maintaining their individual distinctions. Now, through Jesus' death, resurrection, and ascension, we are joined to God, the perfect society. Although the fulfillment of this mystery will only be complete in the kingdom to come, its prophetic sign in the temporal order is the church.

Central to the message of the gospel are its communal impli-

cations. When Jesus began His public ministry, He gathered the
twelve disciples as community. When He sent them out, He made
sure they went in twos, never alone. Just prior to His ascent into
heaven He even promised to send them the Holy Spirit, and He
commanded them to gather as a people to wait. And they did. And
when the Spirit came, the church was born (Acts 2).

There is no Christianity without the family, the church.
Jesus entrusted His mission, imparted His power, and promised
His kingdom to that family. And it was to and through that family
that His words and deeds would later be transmitted, memorial-
ized, and gathered together into what would eventually be called
the Bible. Even though many Christian writings were circulated
during the early years of the church, many more writings than appear in our Bible, after several years of discernment, the bishops
developed a list of writings (the canon) that they agreed were inspired by the Holy Spirit. These became the official sacred
writings—the Word of God—for the church.[3]

Therefore, we cannot forget the church's role in the trans-
mission, preservation, and establishment of the Bible. Breaking
open the Word of God is an integral part of the church's worship of
her Lord. The Scriptures are so important to the life of the church
that her leadership exhorts us to study them seriously and prayerfully. For example, the fathers of the Second Vatican Council in the
document *On Divine Revelation* clearly define the importance of the
Scriptures and call for greater study and preaching of the Word:

> Sacred Scripture is the speech of God as it is put down in
> writing under the breath of the Holy Spirit. . . . And the Holy
> Spirit, through whom the living voice of the Gospel rings out
> in the Church—and through her in the world—leads believers
> to the full truth, and makes the Word of Christ dwell in them
> in all its richness (Col. 3:16). Access to sacred Scripture ought
> to be open wide to the Christian faithful. . . . The sacred
> synod forcefully and specifically exhorts all the Christian
> faithful . . . to learn "the surpassing knowledge of Jesus
> Christ" (Phil. 3:8) by frequent reading of the divine
> Scriptures. . . . Let them go gladly to the sacred text
> itself . . . [but] let them remember, however, that prayer
> should accompany the reading of sacred Scripture, so that a
> dialogue takes place between God and man.[4]

Second, those who ask, "Why should we learn the Bible?" frequently raise it out of a fundamental misunderstanding of the nature of Christianity. They don't see the need for study. They argue, "Christ has saved us; what else is necessary? Our faith in Him has set us free; there's nothing else we need to do." But this understanding is mistaken. Yes, faith in Christ saves us. But He does not deliver us from sin and death so that we can sit on our hands for the rest of our existence on earth. No! Christ knows nothing of bare-minimum Christianity. He certainly didn't live that way, and He calls on us to live as He did—all out, in obedience to God, serving all people for His sake, coming to know Him in our experience and through His Word as fully as we are able. To the degree we do less, we minimize the transforming power of Christ in our lives. He invites us to come to Him and drink in the fresh, life-giving water of deep spirituality. We can look to the Scriptures as a primary source of this life. In fact, as a man, Jesus required the nourishment of the Word. When He was tempted by Satan, Jesus cited Deuteronomy 8:3 from memory: "It is written, 'Man shall not live by bread alone, but by every word that proceeds from the mouth of God.'" If He needed to know the Word to withstand evil and nourish His soul, how much more do we?

Now don't misunderstand me. I am not saying that the Bible gives us life everlasting. Jesus Himself denied this when He said to the Pharisees, the keepers of the Law, "You diligently study the scriptures because you think that by them you possess eternal life. These are the scriptures that testify about me, yet you refuse to come to me to have life" (John 5:39). The Scriptures reveal the Giver of life; they do not give life themselves. Jesus came to form a people and redeem them by His blood. The Bible simply tells about Him—the events leading to His incarnation, His earthly life, His death, His resurrection, His ascension, His intercessory ministry in heaven, His Second Coming, and His everlasting reign as King of kings and Lord of lords. The Bible records Jesus as saying, "Come to *me* all who are weary and find life burdensome, and *I* will refresh you" (Matt. 11:28). He did not say, "Read my word all who are weary . . . and it will refresh you." We need to seek the Giver of the written Word—the living Word Himself, the Word who is God. And a sure place to find Him and learn of Him is in the written Word.

Therefore, we should go to the Bible frequently, every day, and meditate on the Lord through what He says to us there. And we should always approach the Scriptures in faith, bathing our study in devotion and prayer. Some of us know the original languages of Scripture, which can give us incredible insight into the Lord's words. But this knowledge can also create linguistic technicians, who carefully define the words without allowing them to be used by God to penetrate their spirits with life-giving power. There is a time and a place for the textual analysis of the Bible, but it can never take the place of prayerful meditation for the nourishment of the soul. Have you ever been insulted by someone who examines the way you speak more closely than what you are saying? The same applies here. Jesus speaks to us through His Word. We should be listening for the wisdom in His words. Then understanding will enlighten our souls and work its wonders in our hearts and minds.

HITTING THE MARK

But let's not forget: The purpose of Scripture is to help us grow in our knowledge and love of the Lord. How can we work with them to achieve their intended end? Let's see.

First and obviously, we must know what the Word says before we can discern or obey our Lord's injunctions. And this takes time and commitment to the study process so that the Word becomes so deeply rooted in our spirits that recalling and applying it almost becomes second nature. Committing Scripture to memory is important to this process. Many of the fathers of the church committed the entire Bible to memory.

In the thirteenth century, Francis and his followers knew the Scriptures quite well. One historian writes of Francis that "he often said that man would easily move from knowledge of himself to knowledge of God if he would set himself to study the Scriptures humbly, not presumptuously".[5] Francis and the brothers knew the Scriptures so well that their minds and hearts became one with the Lord.

But an even more important example of the need for and results of learning the Word comes from Jesus Himself. He was brought up in a Jewish home and experienced what Jewish fathers bring to their sons—training in the Word. As a consequence, Jesus "grew in wisdom and stature" (Luke 2:52). At age twelve, He even astounded the religious teachers of His day with His understanding of the Scriptures (vv. 46–47). His extraordinary wisdom also helped Him later when He faced the temptations of Satan in the desert (4:1–13).

Throughout His earthly ministry, Jesus appealed to the Scriptures to prove that He was sent from God and that He was God incarnate. Out of the Scriptures, He instructed His disciples and the crowds who followed Him. He quoted from the Scriptures when he challenged the unbiblical teachings and prejudices of the Pharisees and Sadducees. Even during the darkest time of His life, He quoted Scripture: "My God, my God, why have you abandoned me?" (Matt. 27:46; Ps. 22:1).

After His resurrection from the grave, He appeared to His disciples. On the road to Emmaus He taught two of them about Himself by taking them through the Scriptures: "Beginning then with Moses and all the prophets, he interpreted for them every passage of Scripture which referred to him" (Luke 24:27). Can you imagine what a sermon that must have been? Jesus took the entire Bible and explained its central theme to the disciples.

He undoubtedly loved the Word, lived by the Word, died by the Word, and rose victoriously according to the Word. He was the Word alive. And He wants us to be alive with the Word. He wants us to love Him so much that we bathe our lives in the Scriptures, allowing Him to use them to wash our hearts and minds of sin so that we can be filled with new life.

Of course, simply memorizing and studying the Word will not accomplish this. Yes, "the sword of the Spirit" (Eph. 6:17) is the Bible, and yes, it is powerful enough even to slice through the hidden garbage in our lives as well as to beat the devil back in battle. But if we simply know the Bible in our heads without permitting it to penetrate our hearts, it will not accomplish all it can in our lives. When Satan tempted Jesus, he demonstrated an intellectual—albeit a twisted one—understanding of Scripture. He could even quote from the Bible. But his knowledge did nothing to change his life. So from his example alone, we know that memorization of the Word is not enough. If we are to experience real change—change that will restore us as Christ's image bearers (Col. 3:10)—we need to also be in a *living, personal relationship with God.* Only then can the words of Scripture come alive within us and transform us.

Once the Word begins to gel in our spirit, its power begins restoring our nature. Our thoughts conform to God's thoughts. Then our actions start conforming to our new thoughts. The apostle James wrote, "Act on this word. If all you do is listen to it, you are deceiving yourselves" (James 1:22-24). Our actions will only change if our minds and hearts are renewed. But once that inner transformation begins and is nurtured by God's Word, our motivation for action becomes our love of God and neighbor, not fear or duty.

The Bible is designed to help in our transformation from the inside out, not to be used by us to conform our behavior to external dos and don'ts that have no real impact on our souls. We must read, study, and meditate on sacred Scripture to become like its divine Author. We need to become living images, mirroring the divine life within us, magnifying the Lord, becoming living testimonies of love incarnate. This is our challenge, our vocation, our holy calling.

LOVING LIKE THE INCARNATE WORD

One of my favorite books on personal evangelism is written by Paul Little and is entitled *How to Give Away Your Faith*. In it Little says, "Life and lip are inseparable in effective evangelism."[6] Another man whom I greatly admire, Pope Paul VI, also wrote a book on the subject. In his monumental work *Evangelization in the Modern World*, he said something similar: "The good news proclaimed by the witness sooner or later has to be proclaimed by the word of life."[7] This matter of life and lip, speaking and becoming, is essential to the Christian life if we are really going to love and live as Jesus Christ did.

Do we love Him? Is He our first love? If so, we must love as He loved. Sound intimidating? It isn't if we are truly in love with Him. I am convinced that the greatest motivation for effective lifestyle evangelism is love—love for Jesus and love for those whom He loves.

If that's true, how do we love the way Jesus loved? Spiritual writers through the ages have answered this question, and they have always pointed back to the dynamic action of God in our lives as the key. Saint Paul talked about the continuing process of transformation wherein we become "complete" and "fully mature, growing up into Him who is the head" (Eph. 4:13, 15). Great writers on the interior life have talked about becoming "alter christus," other christs (of course, with a small *c*) via our submission to God's transforming work. In other words, we who are disciples of Christ are becoming like the Master. We are following His blueprint of life, which is revealed to us in His Scriptures and in a personal, dynamic, ongoing relationship with Him.

Since He's the master planner, let's look at His example to learn how He loved so that we can follow His blueprint for love.

PERSONAL

Jesus' love is profoundly personal. Throughout the Scriptures we see Him teaching, feeding, healing, forgiving, encouraging, affirming, and even correcting in a deeply passionate, personal way. He loved emotionally and tenderly. He loved with his whole self and held nothing back.

In one of the most beautiful passages in Mark's Gospel, we find a prime example of Jesus' unconditional love. There we see Him approached by a leper, who was suffering and probably weak. This social outcast reached out to Jesus and boldly said, "If you will to do so, you can cure me." How did Jesus respond? He could have turned away in fear or disgust as was the social norm in His day. But the Scriptures tell us He was "moved with pity." And in that instant, Incarnate Love stretched out His compassionate hand, touched the untouchable, and proclaimed, "I do will it. Be cured" (Mark 1:40–41).

To love as Jesus loved means loving with deep, heartfelt compassion. It means loving with a heroism that enables us to stand against our contemporary age and embrace those it has rejected. This kind of unconditional love brings about healing. I believe in physical healing and prayer for bodily healing, but there is another kind of healing that touches our interior wounds—the brokenness and woundedness that nobody is permitted to see. That kind of healing and that kind of unconditional Christlike love motivate modern-day saints like Mother Teresa to embrace the worm-eaten dying in Bombay, India, and see within their hollowed eyes the eyes of Christ. To love like the Word is to love like this.

TRUTHFUL

Jesus also loved by speaking truth—not so-called relative truth that fluctuates from person to person or culture to culture, but absolute truth, flowing from Him who is Truth. We desperately need people to speak this truth to our current generation. As my friend Chuck Colson so wonderfully summarizes in his book *Against the Night*, we live in a new dark age. The hardened heart of twentieth-century man presents us with a new barbarianism, the kind that has created

> men and women without principle, those who have elevated
> tolerance as the highest of values and in so doing have become
> blindly intolerant to those who adhere to absolute values.
> They are unbeholden to anything—except, perhaps, the god of
> self. These new barbarians, unlike the unwashed hordes that
> overcame the Roman Empire are not hairy Goths and Vandals,
> swilling fermented brew and ravishing maidens. They are
> civilized, enlightened, well-groomed men and women who are
> prominent in government, in the media, leaders in our schools
> and communities.[8]

They all too often stand and mock truth. Their questions remind us of a man named Pilate, who in the face of Truth personified cried out, "What is truth?" (John 18:38).

But as Christians, Christ followers, we serve the One who is the Way, the Truth, and the Life. Everything He did and everything He ever said and continues to say is true. To love as Jesus loved, we must speak His truth in the daily circumstances of our lives. One of the most marvelous Gospel stories which demonstrates this approach to loving is found in John 4.

As a pious Jew and rabbi, Jesus should never have been speaking with a Samaritan woman—in fact, He should not have been in the hated region of Samaria. But breaking cultural biases once again, He traveled through that country and encountered a native. When he met her, He spoke with her at great length, teaching her about living water and revealing to her His salvific role.

What a great act of love! Yet, His love involved speaking hard words of deeply personal truth.

> He said to her, "Go, call your husband, and come back here."
> "I have no husband," replied the woman.
> "You are right in saying you have no husband!" Jesus exclaimed. "The fact is, you have had five, and the man you are living with now is not your husband. What you say is true." (John 4:16–18)

How many of us would have the courage to speak a word of truth like that in the midst of an evangelistic encounter? But remember, Jesus, our great model of love, acted out of sincerity at all times. So rather than simply being offended, the Samaritan woman was led to repentance. She went forth as a wonderful evangelist, telling her fellow townspeople, "Come and see someone who told me everything I ever did! Could this not be the Messiah?" (John 4:29). She understood truth in the context of tough love, and it changed her life, just as it still changes lives today.

If we are going to love the way Jesus loved, we must be willing to speak the truth even when it hurts. I recently saw this graphically illustrated in a documentary on a Christian network. The documentary presented a woman raised in an evangelical Protestant tradition. She had also been an ardent opponent of abortion. Widowed at an early age, she had two teenage daughters and an increasingly lonely life. In the midst of her barrenness, she fell into sin, and sin resulted in pregnancy. She soon found herself considering what was at one time out of the question: abortion. Amazingly enough, she found in many "Christian" circles a sympathetic ear for her plight and an acceptance of abortion as a possible solution, but something kept gnawing at her heart. Still disturbed, she turned for compassion to the one she trusted most, her natural sister. What she heard from her sister were tough words spoken out of the kind of love Jesus had demonstrated to the Samaritan woman: "I love you and I hurt for you, but I will not let you kill my nephew or niece. You cannot transgress the law of God."

Her sister stuck by her all through her pregnancy, as did some other women in the church. They even helped give her the courage to confess her sin to her teenage daughters. Much to her delight, they understood her, embraced her, and helped her prepare for the joyful birth of a daughter. The documentary showed her small child and allowed viewers to hear this woman's testimony of love that speaks truth and brings with it divine gifts, even in the form of a tiny infant.

FORGIVING

To love as Jesus loved means to be willing to forgive at the sign of genuine repentance. Luke 7 contains a wonderful example of this.

Jesus went to one of the Pharisees' homes to eat. Among the numerous guests was a woman who was uninvited. "She brought in a vase of perfumed oil and stood behind [Jesus] at his feet, weeping so that her tears fell upon His feet. Then she wiped them with her hair, kissing them and perfuming them with the oil" (Luke 7:37–38). The other guests were appalled because of her less than unblemished reputation. And to add insult to injury to this prestigious group, she had wasted costly perfume on someone's feet—even the feet of the rabble-rouser Jesus. How could such a ghastly woman do such a ghastly thing in the midst of such respectable folk?

When we read such a story, we wonder how people could be so uncaring, so mixed up in their priorities and perspectives. But we fail to see how often and how closely our behavior and mindset resemble those of the Pharisees. Like them, we sometimes harden our own hearts and fail to practice Christlike love—even in the midst of our most "pious" activities.

But Jesus knows love when He sees it because, unlike us, He looks into the heart. He knew that the woman's actions were motivated by a deep, abiding love. Knowing the heartthrob of this woman in contrast to that of the Pharisees', He lovingly but firmly rebuked the guests for their response to her: "You see this woman? . . . She has washed my feet with her tears and wiped them with her hair. You gave me no kiss, but she has not ceased kissing my feet since I entered. You did not anoint my head with oil, but she has anointed my feet with perfume. I tell you, that is why her many sins are forgiven—because of her great love. Little is forgiven the one whose love is small" (Luke 7:44–47).

These words should burn in our hearts: "Little is forgiven the one whose love is small," or as another translation says, "it is the man who is forgiven little who shows little love" (Jerusalem Bible).

There is a direct reciprocal relationship between our own understanding of the depth of our fallenness and our capacity to love. The more we understand our sin, the more we are able to see others as they are and to love them regardless. Perhaps this understanding motivated some of the greatest heroes of our faith—a Francis of Assisi who truly saw himself as the chief among sinners, a Saint Paul who specifically referred to himself as a sinner (1 Tim. 1:15–16). Some contemporary psychologists tell us that such a self-understanding reflects a poor self-image. Although that can occur, saints Paul and Francis and countless others understood that such a realization is designed to lead us to more fully experience God's marvelous grace. The truth is: *All of us are the chief among sinners.* Only the unmerited favor of God has enabled us to enter into His presence by our faith in His Son. When we truly understand that, our self-images soar. Because we have received the salvific benefits of the depth of God's love for us, we realize how much we have been forgiven and at what a great cost. How in the light of that can we love and forgive any less?

The first disciples of Jesus wanted to know how much they should forgive. Was there a maximum number of times one should forgive an offender? The religious teachers of their day said that three times was the maximum. Knowing the graciousness and mercy of Jesus, they believed that He would up this number. So they asked Him: "Lord, when my brother wrongs me, how often must I forgive him? Seven times?'" How generous they were, raising the maximum from three to seven! Certainly Jesus would not go higher than that. But His answer stunned them: "'No,' Jesus replied, 'not seven times; I say, seventy times seven times'" (Matt. 18:21–22). Biblical scholars tell us that Jesus' answer means that we should always be ready to forgive regardless of how many times forgiveness is called for. In other words, the sky is the limit. We can never quantify forgiveness; we simply must always be ready to forgive.

However, since I am shaped by a Western worldview that places a lot of stock in numbers, I decided to quantify Jesus' teaching just to get a handle on its scope. For what it's worth, here's what I found. If we take Jesus literally, the maximum number we should forgive is seventy times seven, or 490 times. Now there are 1,440 minutes in every day. If the maximum number applies to each day, beginning at zero at the start of each day, then to reach the maximum I would have to forgive an offender once every 2.9 minutes over a twenty-four-hour period. But if I reduce the day to sixteen hours, allowing eight hours for sleeping, I would have to forgive my offenders every 1.9 minutes before I would reach the limit. That's a lot of forgiving! But if I want to love as Jesus loves, I must be quick to forgive and ready to forgive often. After all, there's not enough time in a day to harbor grudges or nurse bitterness.

EMOTIONAL

Sometimes I think we lose sight of the marvelous biblical truth of the Incarnation. Jesus was truly God and truly man. As a man, He was like us in all things, except He had no sin (Heb. 4:15). If you had lived during His tenure on earth, you could have touched His hands, washed dirt from His feet, heard Him teach, shared meals with Him, covered Him with a blanket as He slept, watched Him buy clothes or stub His big toe. The Creator and Sustainer of the universe in His deity, but one of many creatures dependent on His Father's sustaining power in His humanity—this was Jesus Christ.

As remarkable as that is, however, we rarely think of Him as an emotional being. For some reason, we see Him as a stoic—cold, unfeeling, unmoved by the pain around Him, or at least always suppressing His feelings, keeping them tightly harnessed, holding them under absolute control. But such an image does not match the Jesus of the Gospels. He was a man who not only understood, but experienced the full panorama of human emotions. Anger. Frustration. Hurt. Disappointment. Despair. Happiness. Sadness. He felt them all, and He felt them deeply. Consider, for example, the emotion He displayed over the death of Lazarus.

Lazarus and his two sisters, Mary and Martha, were Jesus' friends. Jesus found their home a place of relaxation, encouragement, and renewal. He deeply loved this family and enjoyed spending time with them. One day while traveling, Jesus received news that Lazarus was very sick. But Jesus did not change His travel plans. He knew that His friend's illness was part of God's desired plan for him. Two days later, after He was sure Lazarus was dead, Jesus left for his friend's home. This may seem like a cold response from the Lord, but He knew that Lazarus was destined to leave his tomb and rejoin his sisters.

As Jesus came close to Lazarus's home, Martha ran out to meet Him. Her greeting was anything but a welcome. She cried out to Him through her grief, "Lord, if You had been here, my brother would not have died" (John 11:21). Her loss was great, and she blamed Jesus for letting it happen. With deep compassion, Jesus reassured her that her brother would rise from the dead and that He had come to raise him.

Then Mary came out to Jesus. She fell down at Jesus' feet wailing and leveling the same charge against Him. "At the sight of her tears and those of the Jews who followed her, Jesus said in great distress, with a sigh that came straight from the heart, 'Where have you put him?'" Can't you just hear that? A sigh straight from the heart of God. Jesus' friends were crushed in their spirits, and their pain was wounding Him. How much He hurt for them and with them.

Then He heard an answer to His question. "They said, 'Lord, come and see.'" They took Him to Lazarus' grave, and when He saw it, He "wept." What tender love He must have felt for His friend, since those gathered remarked, "See how much He loved him!" (vv. 33–36).

Our Lord knows the tremendous pain of loss. He felt it—deep within His being. And He feels it now as He intercedes on our behalf before the heavenly throne of His Father and ours.

Christianity is not a bedfellow of stoicism. Emotions are divine gifts to us and can become windows to help us see our needs and motivate us to reach out to others. This presumes, however, that we are living a balanced Christian life. One of the most obvious contemporary mistakes is giving our feelings sovereignty over what we should think and how we should act. "If it feels good, do it" and "Don't worry, be happy" are popular expressions of this destructive approach to life. But putting such misuses of emotions aside, we must never forget that feelings are a vital part of being fully human, and if we should love as Jesus loved, we must feel as

He felt and channel our feelings as He did. The apostle Paul summed up this idea in an exhortation meant for all Christians: "Rejoice with those who rejoice, weep with those who weep" (Rom. 12:15).

A CALL TO LOVE

Although examples from the Gospels could be multiplied, these are enough to show that Jesus cares deeply about people, each in his or her individual joys and pains. He meets each of us personally, embracing us to heal and restore us, for our sakes and for those around us whom we can touch with His love. But why miss the full benefits of His unconditional love and unmerited favor? Our personal relationship with Jesus Christ is the door into our heavenly home. Sometimes the phrase "a personal relationship with Jesus" can sound trite and overused, but it expresses the heart of evangelical Christianity and the heart of loving as Jesus loved. Only when we accept the Lord will we receive the plenitude of His love for us and be able to love others as He wants us to. The disciple John, the beloved one of the Lord, wrote as he was growing older and wiser, "Love, then, consists in this: not that we have loved God, but that he has loved us and sent His Son to be the propitiation for our sins. Beloved, if God so loved us, we also ought to love one another" (1 John 4:10–11).

When you consider the cross and see how much God cares for us, you have to wonder, Why? Is there something about us that makes us so important, so valuable as to be worth infinite love? Secular humanism says yes, but it qualifies the answer by adding that our value has nothing to do with the supernatural. As evangelical Christians, we cringe at this qualifier, but in our attempts to refute secular humanism, we have missed its greatest danger and bypassed its core of truth. What makes this contemporary brand of humanism dangerous and unacceptable is that it is *secular*—a God above and beyond, but intimately involved in, human history has no place in its philosophical framework. But there is another brand of humanism called *Christian* humanism that has a different framework. It gives prominence to the God secular humanism rejects. Furthermore, it elevates humanity precisely because of our relationship with God, demonstrating that in this relationship we find our true dignity, identity, and value. Christian humanism also enables us to see that we were created to love. As Pope John Paul II has said, "Loving is the actualization of the highest possibility of man. Loving gives us dignity."[9] To become fully what God has destined us to be, we must love. The more we love, the more actual or real we become. And the more real we become, the more we glorify the God who is love.

Love is an action word, and loving as the Word loved means doing what the Word did. Before He ascended into heaven, the Master asked Peter three times, "Do you love me?" and Peter responded, "Yes, Lord, you know I do." Then Jesus directed Him, "Feed my sheep" (John 21:15–17). On another occasion Jesus told His followers, "Love one another as I have loved you. There is no greater love than this: to lay down one's life for one's friends. You are my friends if you do what I command you" (John 15:12–14). We are friends of Jesus—if we love as Jesus loved.

First and foremost, Christianity is Christ. And being a Christian is being like Him. Being like Him begins with a choice to enter into and sustain an intimate relationship with Him through prayer, the Word, the believing community, and the sacramental life. He must become our first love.

What is the heartthrob of *your* love life? Is it He? Is He first in your life? Is He your first love? If not, evangelical Christians of all traditions urge you to return to Him. Only He can fulfill you. Only He can elevate you to your true dignity and worth. Only He can give you the capacity to love deeply and unconditionally. Only He can give you the superabundance of His supernatural life.

CHAPTER 6

Faith and Works: The Full Family Life

Mother Teresa is a contemporary saint. As a faithful messenger of the gospel, she has become like her message—a source of salvation and hope to untold millions. Christ shines through her life as through few others you or I will ever encounter. Her very character radiates the grace, mercy, and power of God. Her words and works constantly proclaim Jesus and His gospel. Indeed, He is so preeminent in her life that she has become Jesus, not only to those to whom she ministers, but also to thousands who have never met her, only heard her speak, read about her, or watched her work from afar. From the streets of Bombay where she caresses the dying and treats worm-eaten corpses with dignity, to the streets of New York where she reaches out with a message of hope to AIDS victims, she reflects the heart of evangelical Catholic Christianity.

I'll never forget the time she came to Franciscan University to address the 1976 graduating class. The presence of Christ was so real in her that it made me want to pray continually. She challenged us all to realize the fundamental truth of the gospel: "What does it profit a man if he gains the whole world and loses his own soul?" (Matt. 16:26). And she shocked us when she said with prophetic seriousness, "The worst poverty I have seen in all of the world is the poverty in America." How could she say such a thing? Certainly America is much better off economically and spiritually than most of the other countries of the world—or is it? Mother Teresa's point was that America's religious rhetoric and financial affluence are superficial; they hide our loneliness . . . our misplaced or lost sense of significance . . . our spiritual hunger for intimacy with God. Her poignant observation became most clear to me while I was visiting our nation's capitol.

I was one of a handful of Roman Catholics in a crowd of nearly two thousand Protestants attending a leadership conference in Washington, D.C. At one of the evening banquets, I enjoyed the company of evangelical Christian leaders from throughout the country. Some of them I had met earlier when I represented the Franciscan University's student affairs office at other evangelical schools. What I found most interesting was their topic of conversation. They didn't spend a lot of time discussing management styles or business ethics or how to raise money or the church's role in the political arena or any other subject common among Christian leaders. The hot topic of conversation was a little gray-haired lady who spent most of her time overseas in obscurity. Her name? You guessed it—Mother Teresa. Apparently, she had just addressed a predominantly evangelical Protestant crowd in California, so everyone was buzzing about the content of her talk. But not just that, as I soon learned. Her impact went much deeper.

I remember one man at the table who was deeply moved by Mother Teresa's obvious holiness and Christlike nature. He asked me if I knew the key to her simplicity and love. Before I could answer, he told me he had posed the same question to her, and the answer he had received was, "Jesus and continual prayer." He had already noticed that she constantly prayed the rosary beads she held in her hand, even when she spoke. As my brother talked, I saw in his eyes a hunger to personally experience Christianity in action. He knew Jesus, but he didn't know Him in the fullness that Mother Teresa knows. In her face and life he saw what he so desperately wanted: the coming together of the Great Commission, a deep interior life, and true social action in a rich incarnational theology.

For Mother Teresa, there is no conflict between the interior life and external acts of charity. She is able to integrate an intimate relationship with Jesus with genuine piety and social action. This is the full family life—the true union of faith and works—and it is the hunger that lies at the heart of much of today's evangelical Christianity. Sadly, however, its Roman Catholic expression, except in rare cases such as Mother Teresa's, is often misunderstood by my Protestant brothers and sisters. And all too frequently, their misunderstanding can be traced to their misconception of the Catholic view of salvation.

CATHOLICISM AND SALVATION

Many Christians misunderstand the Catholic theology of salvation as one of salvation by good works. Catholics, they say, try to earn Jesus' acceptance into heaven's gate by performing deeds that would please Him. That's how such critics explain the fact that Catholics are so often engaged in feeding the hungry, housing the homeless, caring for the sick, and the like. They believe that Catholics have rejected the true gospel of salvation by faith alone and accepted the false gospel of salvation by faith plus good works.

Although some Catholics, as well as some Protestants, have adopted the "gospel" of faith + good works = salvation, this view does *not* represent Catholic theology. As we will see, there is an integral place for the deeds of faith in our salvation, but this must be understood in light of the *full* expression of the biblical concept of salvation. And this understanding flows from the biblical view of the human dilemma.

OUR DILEMMA

We sin. In numerous ways and for a variety of reasons we violate God's directives. Human beings have done this for centuries, ever since our first parents, Adam and Eve, defied God in the garden of Eden (Gen. 3). As a result of our first parents' original sin, we have received a mixed inheritance: a corrupted condition that separates us from our Creator and makes it easier for us to rebel against Him. The consequences of this fallen condition are staggering. Not only has it created a chasm between us and the Lord, but it has separated us from ourselves, from our friends, from our mates, from our spouses, from our neighbors, and from our world. Our every relationship has been affected. Now instead of exuding the natural outflow of transparency and intimacy, we hide our true selves from others and even struggle with coming to know who we really are in our selves. *Death*, which means "separation" in Scripture, has permeated our lives. As the apostle Paul observed centuries ago, "Through one person sin entered the world, and through sin, death, and thus death came to all, inasmuch as all sinned" (Rom. 5:12).

The theological terms often used in an attempt to describe the wounds caused by sin are not always helpful. The most common phrase is *fallen nature,* and, in many Protestant circles, the word *depravity.* The meaning of *fallen nature* and its extent have been debated among Christians for centuries. Some have understood it to mean that people are in complete bondage to sin; they cannot perform any good deeds, nor can they reach out to God in faith unless He first gives them the faith to exercise. Fallen humans, they say, are intrinsically evil: sin is now an integral part of their nature; it has virtually destroyed their ability to will freely, to think rationally, to feel compassionately, to behave unselfishly. In other words, man is totally and literally dead in sin; he cannot find God, hear Him, or respond to Him. Like a corpse, man is totally unresponsive to his Creator and Redeemer.

Roman Catholics, however, take issue with this picture of mankind. They believe that it overemphasizes some portions of Scripture while neglecting the clear thrust of other passages. In contrast, they appeal to the full teaching of Scripture, seeking to allow it to set fuller parameters for a Christian understanding of man's fallen nature. Within scriptural parameters, a different picture develops.

First, the Bible presents several models of human fallenness. One model is certainly that of death: Humans are dead in sin and need new life (Eph. 2:1-6; Col. 2:13). But this does not mean that we are unable to respond to God; rather, it means that sin has separated us from Him and that we need to be reunited to Him. The other biblical models confirm this. We are sick with sin and in need of healing (Mark 2:17). We are impoverished by sin and need God's riches (Luke 4:18; 2 Cor. 8:9; Eph. 2:7). We are polluted or defiled by sin and need to be cleansed (Mark 7:14-23; Eph. 5:25-27; Titus 1:15; 1 John 1:7-9). We are lost in the darkness of sin and desperately need the light of Christ (John 8:12; 12:35). We are blinded by sin and need our sight restored (Luke 4:18; 2 Cor. 4:3-6). We are enslaved to sin and need to be liberated from it (Luke 4:18; John 8:31-36; Rom. 6:16-18). All of these models depict our sad, desperate condition, but none of them even implies that we cannot respond to God.

Second, the Scriptures resoundingly declare that all human beings are marred by sin (Eccl. 7:29; Rom. 3:9-18, 23). One virgin from Nazareth, however, was preserved for the incredible task of bearing the Son of God. And in the words of Elizabeth's proclamation, the virgin Mary was and still is "blessed among women" (Luke 1:42). Catholics believe she was kept from any tarnish of sin precisely so she could bear the untarnished One, whose spotless life, substitutionary death, resurrection, and ascension would pave the way of salvation for us. Mary's preservation from sin is a mystery because she, like us, was saved by the One she bore.[1]

Third, because every aspect of man has been affected by sin, he needs to be sanctified (or purified) entirely. His mind, emotions, will, body, soul . . . all he is has been affected by sin, but sin has not destroyed him or his abilities.

Fourth, depravity could not mean that people are evil *in themselves*. Scripture is clear: *Everything* God created is still intrinsically good, and this includes all mankind (Mark 7:14–23; Rom. 8:18–23, 14:14; 1 Tim. 4:4; Titus 1:15). In addition, human beings were created as God's image bearers, and sin's entrance into the world did not destroy the divine image in them (Gen. 1:26–27; 9:6; James 3:9). We still reflect, however dimly, the character and presence of deity (Ps. 8:6). On the other hand, we have definitely been effaced by sin, much as rust effaces metal or as wind and water efface rock. But man is not essentially evil. Evil is a parasite. It exists in good things, but it cannot exist on its own. Protestant apologist Norman Geisler explains this well:

> A man born without sight is subject to an evil. The evil is the lack or privation of sight—something that belongs to the natural order. . . .
>
> To say that evil is a privation is not the same as saying that it is a mere absence or negation of good. The power of sight is found neither in a blind man nor in a rock. But it is a privation for the blind man, whereas it is a mere absence in the rock. A privation is the absence (or lack) of something that ought to be there.
>
> As well, metaphysical evil is not a mere negation or unreality. Privations are real and physical. Blindness is a real and physical lack of sight. Being maimed is a positive and real lack of a limb. Sickness is a real physical lack of good health. A rusty car, a moth-eaten garment, and a wounded body are physical examples of real corruptions in otherwise good

things. In each case, there is a real lack or corruption that leaves what remains in a state of incapacitation.[2]

Therefore, if we were devoid of good, evil could not exist in us. And if our natures were intrinsically evil, we could not exist at all—not any more than a totally moth-eaten garment or a totally rusted car could exist. In other words, we could not be *totally* depraved, if that means we are devoid of good or God-likeness.

Fifth, fallen people can and do accomplish good works. Jesus affirmed this when He said, "Which one of you would hand his son a stone when he asks for a loaf of bread, or a snake when he asks for a fish? If you then, who are wicked, know how to give good gifts to your children, how much more will your heavenly Father give good things to those who ask him" (Matt. 7:9–11). But the Scriptures also state that fallen people cannot perform any good work that could justify them (Isa. 64:6; Gal. 2:16; Eph. 2:8–9; Titus 3:3–7).

In short, the biblical view of human fallenness is that *all human beings are morally, intellectually, emotionally, spiritually, and physically corrupted because of sin.* As a consequence of the original sin of our first parents, we have inherited and surrendered ourselves to a distorted, corrupted nature. We have dug ourselves into a pit so deep that we can't climb out of it. But because we are God's creatures and image bearers, we are not *totally* depraved.

GOD'S SOLUTION TO OUR DILEMMA

So what's the solution to our dilemma? How can we get out of the pit of sin? We need someone to have mercy on us and reach down to pull us out. We need a rescuer, a savior. But this person can't be someone who shares the pit with us. This deliverer must be above the pit, on the solid ground above—he must be, in other words, without sin. He also must be able to bridge the chasm between God and man, between holiness and corruption. We need a God-man, a sinless Savior, and the only Person in human history who has ever fit that description and proved it through His words and deeds is Jesus Christ—the Son of God incarnate. When we freely place our trust in Him, God's undeserved gift of salvation from sin becomes ours. As Saint Paul said in his letter to the Christians in ancient Ephesus, "It is owing to his favor that salvation is yours through faith. This is not your own doing, it is God's gift" (Eph. 2:8).

This truth is the mainstay of evangelical Christianity, but to understand it fully, we need to see it in the context of three central ideas of the Christian religion: 1) grace, which is God's unmerited and merciful favor; 2) salvation, which deals with our deliverance from the penalty, power, and presence of sin; and 3) faith, which is the means whereby we receive God's gracious salvation. And these are clearly exhibited in Paul's theology of grace, which can be discussed in terms of justification, sanctification, and glorification. Moreover, these three correspond to the Christian virtues of faith, love, and hope. All of these terms and concepts are an integral part of any discussion of salvation.

Justification and Faith

According to Paul, the first and primary *grace* is God's free gift of Himself to humans, which is indeed "amazing grace." Through Christ, God has communicated Himself personally to each one of us, and we have the God-given potential to either accept or reject His gift.

The point at which I accept this free gift of grace is the point of my *justification*★. I am rescued from the *penalty* of sin, which is everlasting separation from God, and I am changed in the very center of my being. The biblical term most used to refer to this center is *heart*. Paul tells us, "For if you confess with your lips that Jesus is Lord, and believe in your heart that God raised him from the dead, you will be saved. Faith in the heart leads to justification, confession on the lips to salvation" (Rom. 10:9).

For modern minds, *heart* is often reduced to a technical interpretation. When we hear the word, we frequently think of the physical organ and its blood-pumping function. At times we may even think of it in relationship to our emotions. But most of us rarely think of the theological truth that *heart* also represents the

---

★Any discussion of salvation is limited by words. Even the word *justification* is used differently throughout the biblical texts. For my purposes, I will use justification to refer to a part of a fuller understanding of God's grace at work within us in the whole process of salvation.

deepest reality or core of who we are as people. Paul understood this, however, and so must we. When we talk about believing in Jesus "in our hearts" and allowing Him to be "Lord of our lives," we are really inviting Him to rule over our entire being, even to its very depths. This complete surrender begins in our hearts through *faith;* then, like the rippling effect caused by a stone tossed in a lake, it affects every facet of our being, our personality, and our behavior. This kind of surrender is essential to understanding evangelical Christianity fully. And it's the key to the proper integration of the Christian's interior life and social activity. It's in this sense that Mother Teresa "believes in her heart."

Infant Baptism—Evidence of Grace

To the Christian, the sign of this invisible reality of conversion is water baptism. Baptism is meant to be the doorway to a new way of living. It symbolically presupposes what is to come and what was left behind as it acts as a sign of the believer's initiation into the new life in Christ. The good news of the gospel is that our very nature can be transformed—saved not only from the penalty of sin, but also from the power of sin. Our corrupt nature can be purified, and our behavior can exude the holiness flowing from within us as sin's stranglehold over our nature and daily lives is broken. In baptism, the old man—our corrupt sin nature—is submerged, and the new man—our new nature in Christ—emerges clothed in Christ and His transforming power. "This means that if anyone is in Christ, he is a new creation. The old order has passed away; now all is new" (2 Cor. 5:17). Or consider yet another passage from Paul's pen: "The life I live now is not my own; Christ is living in me. I still live my human life, but it is a life of faith in the Son of God, who loved me and gave himself for me" (Gal. 2:20). This fundamental change is a result of our placing faith in Jesus Christ and receiving His Holy Spirit. The Spirit, in turn, infuses us into the holy life of Christ. As we grow in holiness, Christ becomes more real to us than we are even to ourselves because we are in the process of being transformed into His likeness.

Although we often think of baptism and salvation as an adult affair, the church recognized centuries ago that they apply to children, even to infants. In fact, we have good evidence that infant baptism was practiced in the church at least as far back as the third century.[3] This practice arose because Christian couples who began to have children expressed a desire to fulfill the call of Jesus: "'Let the children come to me and do not hinder them. It is to such as these that the kingdom of God belongs'" (Mark 10:14). By the fifth century, infant baptism was universally accepted in the church.[4] Believing parents were having their children baptized because they wanted them saved.

    This raises an obvious but important question: How can a baby be saved without acknowledging Jesus? It appears to many evangelical Christians that infant baptism renders faith obsolete as the foundation of one's relationship with the Lord. But is this true? As I see it and as the Roman Catholic Church has taught, infant baptism is just one more example of grace. Even our own exercise of faith cannot earn salvation—faith simply gives us the opportunity to receive God's gracious gift of new life and walk in it. I am not downplaying faith's critical role in God's salvation plan; rather, I am saying that it is the means by which we receive what God freely offers to all. He reaches down to us so that in childlike faith we can unclench our defiant fists, open our hands, accept His salvific present, unwrap it, and spend the rest of our lives here and in the hereafter enjoying the plenitude of its blessings. Salvation is a gift. It cannot be earned. But it can be received—by faith. Now since an infant cannot exercise faith, what role could baptism possibly play in his or her salvation? The answer involves first understanding the church as "the Family of families."

    Since its inception, a critical presupposition has underscored infant baptism, and indeed the symbolic meaning of even adult baptism. The presupposition? *The children of Christian parents are part of a faith-filled family, the "domestic church," and they are to be raised in the midst of a faith-filled local Christian community.* The church has believed that these two experiences would ensure that children would be raised as believers. It has been further presupposed that the church and the family would instruct, nurture, and lead newly baptized Christians into a *full* assent to the faith. Full assent has necessarily included a personal decision and commitment to a lifelong relationship with Jesus Christ. Unfortunately, that commitment has sometimes been lacking in contemporary Christian experience. In other words, there are sacramentalized but unevangelized Catholics. The same is true in the Protestant and

Eastern Orthodox traditions. In my own Catholic tradition, there is a tremendous effort to rediscover that full catechesis and community experience necessary for infant baptism, but much is left to be done.

Given the fact that baptism must be approached in faith and the church is the Family of families, I return to the original question: How can a baby be saved without acknowledging Jesus? Obviously, the infant cannot respond by faith, but his parents, godparents, other believing relatives, and especially the church in its local expression can respond in his behalf. The faith exercised need not be his. Does this sound radical or new? Actually, it's neither. Remember the paralytic Jesus forgave and healed? It was not his faith that prompted the Master's intervention—it was the faith of his friends.

> One day Jesus was teaching, and the power of the Lord made him heal. Sitting close by were Pharisees and teachers of the law who had come from every village of Galilee and from Judea and Jerusalem. Some men came along carrying a paralytic on a mat. They were trying to bring him in and lay him before Jesus; but they found no way of getting him through because of the crowd, so they went up on the roof. There they let him down with his mat through the tiles into the middle of the crowd before Jesus. Seeing their faith, Jesus said, "My friend, your sins are forgiven you." (Luke 5:17–20)

The faith exercised by the paralytic's friends led to the forgiveness of his sins. If this could happen to an adult who could place his own faith in Christ, how much more so for a tiny baby who cannot?

Children, even infants, can be baptized into the faith by the community of faith so that they can be nurtured in Christ until they are old enough to trust in Him personally. What a beautiful picture of unmerited divine grace in the salvation process. Salvation is truly of God alone. Infant baptism is evidence of this fact.

Of course, the proclamation of personal faith and the vows of commitment made to the Lord at baptism do not have to be a once-for-all act. In fact, much can be said in behalf of regularly proclaiming our faith and renewing our baptismal vows. For the important truth about baptism, whether received as an infant or as an adult, is that it marks the beginning of a faith walk in Christ. This fact leads us to consider sanctification and love.

Sanctification and Love

Baptism helps to equip us, by means of God's objective presence within our souls, to live lives continually transformed in love. This is the life to which the Christian is called. In traditional theological understanding, it's the process known as *sanctification*. Though we may be justified by faith in a moment, we daily experience salvation from sin's *power*—its continual pull on our lives. This day-to-day process makes us holy, not at once, but over the period of our lifetimes. The virtue of love is key to working out this daily process.

In my own church, a document entitled *Light to the Nations* comments upon the beautiful passage in the letter of 1 John 4:16 wherein the beloved disciple reminds us that God is love. The document says that "love, as the bond of perfection and fullness of the law, governs, gives meaning to, and perfects all the means of sanctification. Hence the true disciple of Christ is marked by love both of God and of his neighbor."[5]

Love for God and love for neighbor are two sides of the same coin. They must go together. In fact, as the apostle John reminds us in that same letter, "Anyone who claims to be in the light yet hates his brother is still in the darkness. Whoever loves his brother lives in the light, and there is nothing in him to make him stumble" (1 John 2:9–10). Mother Teresa is a living example of a faith walk that manifests the two sides of this coin. Her intense love for God is displayed in her intense love for His creation.

So it must be with all of us. Our journey of faith is to manifest its genuineness through the fruit of our lives. If we do not bear fruit, our justification has not been worked out yet in our lives. True justification brings a change of heart, a change in the innermost part of our being. Therefore, if we are truly transformed, our lives will reflect it. This is what the great apostle James referred to when he wrote, "Show me your faith without works, and I will show you the faith that underlies my works" (Jam. 2:18).

Evangelical Christianity has long contended that the key to true social reformation is personal regeneration. Great Protestant evangelicals such as William Wilberforce have shown us that there is no contradiction between the message of personal conversion and the message of social action rooted in gospel love. We begin with interior change and then proceed outwardly to the complexities and intricacies of our social relationships. The love of God that comes to us supernaturally, in the moment of our decision to follow Jesus Christ, awakens within us a corresponding love for the world. "God so loved the world that he sent his only son" (John 3:16). He continues to send His Son to the world through the actions of the Body of Christ—you and me—as we live out the mandate of divinely incarnated love. Similarly, we are compelled by the Holy Spirit to enter into the social arena, not to withdraw but to reach out. Jesus, in his wonderful high priestly prayer to His Father, prayed for you and me: "I do not ask you to take them out of the world, but to guard them from the evil one . . . so as you have sent me into the world, so I have sent them into the world" (John 17:15, 18).

The integral relationship between faith and works has long troubled many believers of all traditions. But the Catholic theological understanding of the biblical teaching is clear: *We receive salvation by faith, not because of our good works, and we do good works only because we have the grace to do so.* Our good works flow out of our love for God and that which God loves, His creation. Faith must express itself dynamically in a life of love. As Paul describes, it is a "faith working through love" (Gal. 5:6). Faith and works go together in God's family-life plan. Without faith, works have no everlasting value. Without works, faith has no everlasting value either. Works apart from faith are dead; faith apart from works is dead also. If faith is genuine, good works will follow, and if good works are genuinely of God, saving faith will be present. Faith and good works are inseparable.

Glorification and Hope

The continual outpouring of divine grace on us enables and empowers us to live out our lives and, ultimately, to receive the hoped-for fullness of our salvation—freedom from the *presence* of sin which includes our total and blessed *glorification*. As Catholic philosopher Peter Kreeft has said, heaven is our heart's deepest longing.[6] We were created to live in intimacy with God, but sin alienated us from Him. Throughout history, He has been pursuing us, lovingly dogging our steps, reaching out His arms of forgiveness to embrace us and pull us back to Him. For those of us who say yes to the divine proposal, He promises the full restoration of an intimate relationship with Him. But this cannot happen without the complete abolition of all that hinders such an incredible goal. And this He has promised. One day, all of creation, including we who have faithfully trusted in Him, will be set free not only from all of sin's consequences but even from its very presence (Rom. 8:18–21; Rev. 20–22). Evil and all its bad fruit will be cast away forever. All the good that remains will spend eternity in blissful worship, rest, joy, and celebration with God. This is heaven, and our experience of it will mark the completion of our salvation, the fulfillment of our deepest longing.

The Scriptures exhort us to work toward this day in hope: "Work with anxious concern to achieve your salvation" (Phil. 2:12), or as it says in the New International Version, "continue to work out your salvation in fear and trembling." We hope in God for our complete salvation, and we're confident in what He has done for us; however, we can never be sure that we will always be faithful to Him. Some of us may even turn our backs on Him in apostasy, thereby "holding him up to contempt" (Heb. 6:6). But the race belongs to those who persevere to the end, not to those who never start, nor to those who begin but never finish. Certainly God is faithful whether we are or not. But He is also love, and love is not coercive. He will not force us to love or serve Him. What C. S. Lewis said is true: "There are only two kinds of people in the end: Those who say to God, '*Thy* will be done,' and those to whom God says in the end, 'Thy will be done.'"[7] Or, as the apostle Paul wrote to the young pastor Timothy: "For if we died with Him, we shall also live with Him. If we endure, we shall also reign with Him. If we deny Him, He will also deny us" (2 Tim. 2:11–12).

For such reasons, Catholics believe that we have been saved, we are being saved, and we hope to be saved. I like the way Catholic theologian and friend Alan Schreck puts it:

> First, a Catholic can say "I have been saved." It is an objective fact that Jesus Christ already has died and been raised to save me from my sin. The salvation of the world has been accomplished by Jesus Christ. This salvation has already

begun to take effect in the life of everyone who has accepted Jesus Christ and been baptized. As St. Paul said, "If anyone is in Christ, he is a new creation" (2 Cor. 5:17). In this sense, I can say, "Yes, I have been saved."

Secondly, Catholics need to say that "I am being saved." We must realize that we are still "running the race" to our ultimate destiny of heaven. We must turn to the Lord each day for the grace to enter more deeply into his plan for our lives and to accept his gift of salvation more fully. "And we all, with unveiled face, beholding the glory of the Lord, are being changed into his likeness from one degree of glory to another" (2 Cor. 3:18). In this sense, I can say, "I am being saved."

Thirdly, Catholics say that "I hope to be saved." We must persevere in our faith in God, love for God, and obedience to his will, until the end of our lives. We have hope and confidence that God will give us that grace, and that we will respond to it and accept his gift of salvation until the day we die. In this sense, "I hope to be saved."[8]

We need to be careful of presumption. Even that great bastion of evangelical faith, Paul of Tarsus, well understood the challenge to remain faithful to the end. He reminded us that we have to "finish the race. . . . What I do is discipline my own body and master it, for fear that after having preached to others I myself should be rejected" (1 Cor. 9:27).

THE FULL FAMILY LIFE

We've covered a lot of ground in this chapter, so let me close with a brief summary of its essence and some final thoughts.

Catholic Christians do not see good works as a means to justification. The great medieval theologian Thomas Aquinas taught that we are born on the natural level, and nothing we do can merit eternal life. Only the sacrifice of Christ can merit salvation. But when we become justified at that point of inner conversion, we are raised from the natural to the supernatural level. Raised to a new height, our actions on the natural level are redeemed and transformed. They become eternally significant because they are a gauge, a litmus test of the *fact* that we have entered into the process of sanctification and transformation and of *how* we are progressing in our spiritual journey toward the fullness of our salvation.

The contrast many of us experience between faith and works may simply be caused by our inability to integrate Christian principles and morals into the secular marketplace. Whatever the cause, however, we should not separate these integral essentials of Christianity in our thinking or practice, regardless of our theological tradition. I'm always excited to see genuine efforts among Catholics and Protestants to integrate faith and works as they rediscover a biblically sound approach to social action. Perhaps this renewed discovery is why so many Protestants are so attracted to Mother Teresa. She has done what many of them are striving to do. And when you see the integration lived out in that beautiful woman of Bombay, it is nothing short of inspiring. We should see no contradiction between faith and works. As Mother Teresa reminded our graduating seniors, "We're all called to simply live a life of love." When we love, we integrate faith and good works and become one with God.

As we also say, "faith without works is dead," wrote James. His words do not imply that good works can get one to heaven. They do, however, teach that good works—that is, the life of love—is a measuring stick of whether we are on the right road. Grace, faith, and good works are complementary and necessary elements of our Christian walk. Together they produce a creative tension in the life of the individual believer and the corporate mission of the Christian church. But we must maintain them if we're to proclaim and model the *whole* gospel and thus remain "evangelical" in the fullest sense.

Not only is love the measure of the Christian, but it is the mandate of the Christian life. We are called to love God with all of our heart, mind, soul, and strength (Matt. 22:37). This is the great *shema* of Israel (Deut. 6:5). But when we actually try to live out this mandate, we quickly discover how difficult it is to surrender each of the four to the Lord. We spend our entire lives bringing ourselves into submission to Him. Some of us have the most difficulty surrendering our intellect in matters of faith. Others find it hard to trust God above their own strength to work out all situations for good. Still others guard their hearts, refusing to be vulnerable to anyone or anything—including God. Many of us can't even comprehend loving God with our whole soul. Yet we are called to love God with our whole being. And if the Scriptures make such a call to us, we can respond to it and accomplish it—not on our own, of course, but through the power available to us through the transforming ministry of the Holy Spirit.

Granting this, we must be careful to avoid confusing our obedience to the biblical commands with striving for perfectionism. Jesus called us to be perfect as our heavenly Father is perfect (Matt. 5:48), but He did not call us to embrace perfectionism. Let me explain.

Several years ago, I was personally disturbed by the scriptural command to be perfect. Like many Christians, I thought it meant that my goal was perfectionism—flawless thinking, morally pure behavior, a totally disciplined spiritual life, and so on. This interpretation was terribly depressing because I knew I could never achieve such a goal. Thank God that's not what Jesus meant. The Greek word translated "perfect" is *telios*. Because we don't have an English word that captures the full meaning of this Greek term, it is difficult to translate. Nevertheless, the New Testament scholar William Barclay provides a helpful explanation of this word.⁹ According to him, something is *telios* when it is fulfilling what it was made for. A hammer is *telios* when it is hammering a nail; a screwdriver is *telios* when it is screwing a screw. Similarly, a believer is *telios* when she is living out her vocation to be "alter christus," a little christ who is loving the Lord and allowing Him to live His life through her. This is not perfectionism. Rather, the idea is best captured by Saint Paul, who tells us, "this makes us ambassadors for Christ, God as it were appealing through us" (2 Cor. 5:20). An ambassador not only speaks the words of the king, but does his work. He actually makes him present in his kingdom. So must we make the divine King present to His earthly creation.

Some time ago, I had a legal client who had been seriously injured in a trucking accident. He was a burly, gruff, hardened man. As we got to know each other, I did what any evangelical lawyer should do: I told him about the pearl of great price, the good news about Jesus and His death on the cross for our sins. He told me he wanted to do the right thing but couldn't. He felt it was impossible to live a Christian life. I told him this was the struggle of all human beings, and I read this passage from Paul: "I cannot even understand my own actions. I do not do what I want to do but what I hate. . . . Who can free me from this body under the power of death? All praise to God, through Jesus Christ our Lord" (Rom. 7:15, 24–25).

Through the merits of Christ, we are not victims of the war for personal holiness. Instead, we are overcoming warriors. Yes, we will fight this battle our entire lives. In fact, it is the central battle of the Christian life. But one day it will end. One day, we will triumph with our King. One day, we will taste the sweetness of final victory. It doesn't matter whether this day comes at the Second Coming or when we pass through the gate of physical death into the presence of our Lord. If we endure to the end . . . if we run the race and don't give up, we will win the prize—the imperishable crown of our full salvation in the Lord of lords and King of kings, the Triune God of unconditional love. In this, evangelical Christians of all traditions can rejoice.

CHAPTER 7

Evangelical Counsels: Wisdom for Family Living

Understanding where we've been, where we are, and where we're going is critical in the Christian life. We've seen that we all begin in sin and that for those who accept and follow Christ perseveringly, their end will be total freedom from sin and all its effects. Positively speaking, this state of complete liberation is known as the beatific vision—everlasting bliss in the glorious presence of the Triune God. We've also touched on where we are as Christians—namely, that we're in the day-to-day process of becoming transformed from the inside out into Christlikeness. This process works to free us from the power sin wields daily in our lives. We've also seen that we're members of the Family of families—the family of God, the church. And as family, we're spiritually related to each other, regardless of our theological or denominational traditions or any other differences between us.

But as is true in all families, we must be concerned with our growth. Parents raise their sons and daughters to become, at least in part, contributing members to the family and society. They want their children to enrich the family's experience of work, play, education, and worship; and they want their children to assume social roles that will improve society's value for its other members. Parents know that reaching these goals requires that their children mature—that they grow intellectually, emotionally, psychologically, spiritually, and relationally. And parents know that maturity will not happen apart from sound instruction and discipline.

OUR FATHER'S DESIRE VS. OUR SEARCH FOR "PLEASURE"

In these respects, God's supernatural family is no different from a natural family. Consider some of our heavenly Father's words to us:

> And He Himself gave some to be apostles, some prophets, some evangelists, and some pastors and teachers, for the equipping of the saints for the work of ministry, for the edifying of the body of Christ, till we all come to the unity of the faith and the knowledge of the Son of God, to a perfect man, to the measure of the stature of the fullness of Christ; that we should no longer be children, tossed to and fro and carried about with every wind of doctrine, by the trickery of men, in the cunning craftiness by which they lie in wait to deceive, but, speaking the truth in love, may grow up in all things into Him who is the head—Christ—from whom the whole body, joined and knit together by what every joint supplies, according to the effective working by which every part does its share, causes growth of the body for the edifying of itself in love. (Eph. 4:11-16, NKJV)

Our Father is concerned with our understanding and our behavior. He doesn't want us to remain as little children spiritually. In fact, through the writer of Hebrews, He chastised some members of His family for their failure to grow up:

> About this we have much to say, and it is difficult to explain, for you have become sluggish in hearing. Although you should be teachers by this time, you need to have someone teach you again the basic elements of the utterances of God. You need milk, [and] not solid food. Everyone who lives on milk lacks experience of the word of righteousness, for he is a child. But solid food is for the mature, for those whose faculties are trained by practice to discern good and evil. Therefore, let us leave behind the basic teaching about Christ and advance to maturity. . . . (Heb. 5:11—6:1, RSV)

God wants us to mature in the faith so that we will use our God-given gifts to help one another grow up and will work to bring those outside of the family of faith into it. But despite our Father's desire, we see few signs in the church and society that His children are moving toward maturity in mass.

Take society, for example, especially in the United States.

> At different times in our history, different cities have
> been the focal point of a radiating American spirit. In the late
> eighteenth century, for example, Boston was the center of a
> political radicalism that ignited a shot heard round the
> world. . . . In the mid-nineteenth century, New York became
> the symbol of the idea of a melting-pot America . . . as the
> wretched refuse from all over the world disembarked at Ellis
> Island and spread over the land their strange languages and
> even stranger ways. In the early twentieth century, Chicago,
> city of big shoulders and heavy winds, came to symbolize the
> industrial energy and dynamism of America. . . .
> Today, we must look to the city of Las Vegas, Nevada,
> as a metaphor of our national character and aspiration, its
> symbol a thirty-foot-high cardboard picture of a slot machine
> and a chorus girl. For Las Vegas is a city entirely devoted to
> the idea of entertainment, and as such proclaims the spirit of a
> culture in which all public discourse increasingly takes the
> form of entertainment. Our politics, religion, news, athletics,
> education, and commerce have been transformed into
> congenial adjuncts of show business, largely without protest or
> even much popular notice. The result is that *we are a people on
> the verge of amusing ourselves to death.*[1]

Flash and image are everything; substance and character are nearly trivialized. Many of our politicians are more concerned with how they look and sound on television than with whether what they say significantly advances the public's understanding of society's problems and their possible solutions. Numerous news reporters and educators seem less worried about getting out the facts to inform and educate and more taken up with the entertainment value of their presentations. People are generally preoccupied with their leisure plans for weekends and vacations rather than with their relationships and job performance. We are, indeed, a culture obsessed with entertainment and superficiality.

Furthermore, instead of Christians modeling and working for depth of character and lifestyle in our pleasure-addicted society, we have often capitulated to society's values and expectations. For instance, numerous radio and television preachers take more stock of their ratings and the results of their financial appeals than they do of the spiritual state of their audiences. Churches play numbers-in-attendance games as if the goal of a vital spirituality were the number of heads present at a worship service or weeknight church activity. Revivals are often planned to boost attendance and financial giving rather than to penetrate hearts and minds with the claims of the gospel. We have even drawn people to the gospel by promising them that all their material wants will be satisfied if they will give themselves to God. We, along with our society, seem obsessed with offering people what they want, rather than what they need. But, as Neil Postman points out, this is a strange religious credo: "There is no great religious leader—from the Buddha to Moses to Jesus to Mohammed to Luther—who offered people what they want. Only what they need. . . . I believe I am not mistaken in saying that Christianity is a demanding and serious religion. When it is delivered as easy and amusing, it is another kind of religion altogether."[2]

DIVINE WISDOM AND DEEP SPIRITUALITY

I believe that our current notion of what it means to be an evangelical Christian is weak in the areas of personal holiness and social action, and this subtle but critical weakness can obstruct a truly evangelical lifestyle. Some evangelical Christian expressions do not seem to offer a piety that leads to a deep interior life. But it is this interior life that provides the rootedness and strength for genuine social action. Without it our "good works" may not be "God's work" but our own do-goodism.

This type of spiritual strength has been the bedrock of countless Christians throughout the centuries. Many great saints and heroes of the faith sought a personal holiness that was steeped in a deep prayer life. Out of that wellspring they were able to become God's instruments directed by His perfect will. They opened themselves to God's actions and experienced continual transformation and renewal. They were also concerned with their own personal holiness because they well understood that only by the pure witness of their holy lives could they most powerfully proclaim the gospel. We need to recapture the importance of the interior life.

My friend Glandion Carney, Dean of the Chapel at Warner Pacific College and a dynamic, sensitive man, refers to this approach to spirituality as "an inner journey with an outer focus." In his chronicle of his own spiritual journey, *Heaven within These Walls*, he says:

> Here's what I think Christian spirituality looks like.
> First, Christian spirituality does not reject or attempt to escape the material world. True spirituality treats nature, the human body, ordinary life, work, money, and play as gifts from God, and it transforms them into means for glorifying God.
> Second, Christian spirituality must be centered on Jesus Christ and knowing Him intimately. The inner journey of spirituality takes the Christian into the core of the incredible mystery of knowing Christ.
> Third, Christian spirituality belongs within the routine experience of ordinary people.
> Fourth, Christian spirituality is to be practiced in relationship with others. It is not for hermits.
> Fifth, Christian spirituality is a rhythm of life that moves inwardly and outwardly. The inner journey can progress both in times of solitude and times of frantic activity.
> Finally, Christian spirituality is an act of God's grace from beginning to end. God reaches out to us because He loves us. We can only put our trust in Christ because of God's grace. Every experience of growth which follows our conversion is the result of God's activity within us.[3]

After the interior disposition has begun to be redirected toward God, truly evangelical efforts follow. For some time now, evangelical Christians have been searching for a theology and a methodology that will enable them to bring Christianity into the marketplace. Actually, there are no fancy gimmicks. Proper social action flows out of a conviction that accompanies interior conversion.

Dealing with spiritual growth is always somewhat intangible and obscure, and gauging growth is often difficult. What we do not need is a pre-set, rationalistic, formulized methodology that will tell us if we are going to get heaven. This approach can be misleading and shallow. In a subtle way, it can gear us toward salvation as *the* goal instead of the goal being reconciliation and intimacy with God, which is achieved through a saving relationship with the Son of God. What we need is a different perspective: We should desire to pursue God, to pursue His will for our lives, and to pursue personal holiness. As our commitment to the person of Jesus Christ increases, so will our commitment to His people and His mission increase. But how can we live such a life? The rich tradition of Christianity points to the spiritual disciplines as a critical key.

DISCIPLINES FOR LIFE

Over the centuries, holy men and women, even in their vastly different personalities, have had some basic things in common. They all had a deep, abiding love for the person of Jesus Christ, a working knowledge of God's action in their lives, and a commitment to certain disciplines that kept them dynamically growing in love and acting that out through "works of mercy."

Traditional theology has used the phrase "works of mercy" to deal with concrete expressions of a life of love. The "corporal works of mercy" include feeding the hungry, giving drink to the thirsty, clothing the naked, sheltering the homeless, visiting the imprisoned, caring for the sick, and burying the dead. These forms of "social action" are precisely what Jesus speaks of in Matthew 25. However, there are also works of mercy referred to as the "spiritual works of mercy" which are equally important. Traditionally, this phrase has referred to admonishing the sinner, instructing the ignorant, advising the perplexed, comforting the unhappy, bearing wrongs patiently, forgiving all injuries, and praying and intercession. All of these works of mercy flow from a life of true, interior piety and Christian virtue.

THE EVANGELICAL COUNSELS

There are some tools that can help us measure our spiritual growth, tangible measures that can help us put flesh on our spiritual experience. They have been traditionally called the "evangelical counsels." This phrase out of our common heritage may be helpful in any discussion of evangelical action. *Evangelical* refers to their ability to promote interior growth in Christian virtue as they protect and insure the proper focus of our apostolic work—the Evangel Himself, Jesus Christ. These practices or disciplines are called *counsels* because they are sources of wisdom, guidance, and inspiration which are used by the Holy Spirit to help us mature in the Christian life.

With the polarizations that have unfortunately accompanied

the splits in the Christian church, the rich tradition of the evangelical counsels has often been lost. I believe it is time to rediscover the evangelical counsels as the normative vehicle for both interior change and external action.

What are the counsels?

- Poverty
- Chastity
- Obedience

The evangelical counsels in today's Catholic understanding have all too often been relegated to the Catholic religious and reserved to monks and nuns. Yet all Christians are called to live out these counsels within their state in life. In fact, all Christians can live them out and grow in the interior life as a result. Embracing these counsels would do a world of good for contemporary evangelical Christianity.

Saint Francis De Sales, in *The Introduction to the Devout Life*, stresses that our state in life reflects the degree to which we practice the counsels: "Every state of life must practice some particular virtue. All men should possess all the virtues, yet all are not bound to exercise them in equal measure. Each person must practice in a special manner the virtues needed by the kind of life he is called to."[4] In other words, it would be inappropriate for a housewife to live the call of chastity in the same way as a cloistered Carmelite nun. Similarly, all of us are called to obedience, but a child is called to a different form of obedience than is a person responsible to a spiritual director.

These evangelical counsels are tools to be voluntarily embraced, and they give shape to the command to love; as such they are distinct from the Ten Commandments, which are binding for salvation.[5] Poverty, chastity, and obedience will help us imitate Christ because they reflect the way Jesus lived His life. Let's consider each counsel, especially in light of their biblical foundation and contemporary relevance.

Poverty

The spiritual discipline of poverty involves both what we possess and what possesses us. It is not against our having what we need to live, but it is against our being had by our attitude toward what we have. In and of themselves, possessions are not evil. But we can allow possessions, whether they are ours or someone else's, to possess us—and that is evil. Jesus encountered a rich young man who had just this problem. When Jesus reminded him of the commandments concerning adultery, stealing, false testimony, defrauding, and honoring one's parents, he respectfully responded, " 'Teacher . . . all these I have kept since I was a boy.' Jesus looked at him and loved him. 'One thing you lack,' he said. 'Go, sell everything you have and give to the poor, and you will have treasure in heaven. Then come, follow me.' At this the man's face fell. He went away sad, because he had great wealth. Jesus looked around and said to his disciples, 'How hard it is for the rich to enter the kingdom of God!' " (Mark 10:20–23, NIV). The Lord knew that though this man was rich in material goods, he was poor in spiritual gain. His love for his wealth had impoverished his soul. The only way he could regain his life was for him to lose what he loved more than Christ. But he refused and walked away. His master was money, not the Messiah, and he would not change masters.

Jesus well understood the grip possessions can have on each of us. It is a great and holy enterprise to use what we have to benefit others and further the gospel, but all too often we use what we have to further selfish ends while congratulating ourselves for our otherwise pious talk and walk. Possessing without being possessed is hard, but Christ calls us to a life of nothing less. "Blessed are the poor in spirit, for theirs is the kingdom of heaven," Jesus said (Matt. 5:3, NIV). Our material goods are worthless if they are not used for Him. Heaven comes to those who give, not to those who keep. Jesus proved this by becoming poor for our sakes:

> Who, being in very nature God,
>   did not consider equality with
>   God something to be grasped,
>   but made himself nothing,
>   taking the very nature of a
>   servant,
>   being made in human likeness.
> And being found in appearance as
>   a man,
>   he humbled himself
>   and became obedient to death—
>   even death on a cross!
>   (Phil. 2:6–8, NIV)

And how did the heavenly Father respond to His Son's voluntary poverty?

> Therefore God exalted him to the
>   highest place
>   and gave him the name that is above every
>   name,
> that at the name of Jesus every knee should
>   bow,
>   in heaven and on earth and under the earth,
> and every tongue confess that Jesus Christ is
>   Lord,
>   to the glory of God the Father.   (vv. 9–11,
>   NIV)

Today, however, many Christians have gotten off balance and fallen into two opposite but equally dangerous errors. Some have idealized material poverty and rendered what is actually a curse a blessing. It was not the original intention of the Creator for His creation to be deprived of the means for life and a livelihood. The deprivation has come as a result of human rebellion, and it has often been forced on others through social and racial bigotry, withholding educational opportunities and sufficient job training, and even outright greed. However, as with many other things in the spiritual life, the very deprivation when embraced voluntarily and *in love* can become a vehicle for sanctification. In other words, when one embraces poverty as a holy mistress, much like Francis of Assisi did, it can become a means to holiness and Christlike living.

The other extreme error that I believe is even more predominant in Christian circles today is an attempt to baptize materialism. There is a school of thinkers who have posited a theory often referred to as the "prosperity gospel," which has damaged a genuine view of poverty. According to these leaders, God wants us to have heaven on earth now. If we will simply put enough faith in Him, He will give us our every desire—a successful, thriving business, a Mercedes or Rolls Royce, a bulging bank account . . . name it, claim it, and it's yours. But this realized eschatology leaves no room for the cross; it crowds it out with self-indulgence and self-adulation. It downplays sacrifice and suffering, exalts instant gratification, and baptizes consumerism. Its emphasis is not God's ultimate glory, but our here-and-now one hundredfold return on our "faith." Love of Christ and His work on the cross becomes a blurred and forgotten reality. We must always remember Jesus' mandate: "If anyone wishes to come after me, he must deny himself and take up his cross daily and follow me" (Luke 9:23). We dare not allow ourselves to be trapped by this world's riches, no matter how we sugarcoat our self-centeredness with pious jargon. One can live in simplicity making $7,000 a year or making $700,000 a year (although a good argument could be made that the latter is much more difficult). Regardless of our earnings, all Christians are called to a life of simplicity, a life of almsgiving and sharing with those in need. This is not an optional call. It's the heart of a truly evangelical Christianity.

Spiritual poverty has two features: lack of possessions and insecurity about future possessions.[6] The first is a more tangible expression of poverty. Our hearts must be open to heavenly values and perspectives, but they cannot be if they are filled with desires for transitory, material possessions. Our goods must not become gods. Everything we have has been given to us by God so we can use it for His ends, not ours. Consequently, we should hold our goods loosely, standing ready to open our hands and use our valuables for the value of others. (This, by the way, not only applies to material possessions but to our time, our love, or any other thing that is difficult to release.) God will greatly repay that kind of generosity in heaven (Matt. 5:12).

The second feature of poverty is not as easy to see. It is more of an attitude that we should develop and nurture. We need to meditate on how we are nothing in relation to Him who is everything. God sustains our moment-by-moment existence, our every breath. As such, He makes our every action, our every experience possible. Since He is so intimately and fundamentally involved in our lives, we need to be convicted that He will take care of our needs. We should be able to abandon our will to the Father instead of depending on our own powers and capabilities. When we depend on what we can do rather than on what He can, we remove Him from His rightful place on His throne, and we place ourselves on it instead. Everything then gets out of focus. Havoc reigns. But when God reigns on the throne of our lives, true peace and poverty will permeate our hearts and home.

Trusting God allows freedom, freedom to give away what

was freely given because there is no room for fear or anxiety about our daily needs. What was freely given can be given again. And we have Jesus' assurance that God will meet our basic needs each day:

> Therefore I tell you, do not worry about your life what you will eat [or drink], or about your body, what you will wear. Is not life more than food and the body more than clothing? Look at the birds in the sky; they do not sow or reap, they gather nothing into barns, yet your heavenly Father feeds them. Are not you more important than they? . . . Why are you anxious about clothes? Learn from the way the wild flowers grow. They do not work or spin. . . . If God so clothes the grass of the field, which grows today and is thrown into the oven tomorrow, will he not much more provide for you, O you of little faith? So do not worry and say, 'What are we to eat?' or 'What are we to drink?' or 'What are we to wear?' . . . But seek first the kingdom [of God] and his righteousness, and all these things will be given you besides. (Matt. 6:25–26, 28, 30–31, 33)

But how do we seek first His kingdom and righteousness through the discipline of poverty? According to our particular call in life. Everyone cannot practice poverty in the same manner, just as everyone cannot pray the same amount, sacrifice to the same degree, or love the same way.

For some, specifically the religious (priests, sisters, and brothers) in my own Catholic tradition, poverty is embraced in the form of a vow. For the religious, personal possessions are relinquished and replaced with single-minded devotion to God and His church. Their commitment stands as one of the greatest prophetic signs of the life to come. These men and women challenge us all to see through heaven's eyes, to be free from this world's possessions, and to be totally consumed by love for the Pearl of great price. But this degree of practicing poverty, though a beautiful and mysterious witness to the riches yet to come, is an extraordinary call—it is not for everyone, not even for most of us.

The ordinary, or normative, way to embrace poverty is not as a vow, but as a discipline. Possessing and possessions are neither good nor evil. As the apostle Paul observed, the love of money—not money itself—is the root of all evil (1 Tim. 6:10). Our perspective of and attitude toward what we own or wish to own are the central and most difficult issues. They can lead us into sin or into service, into hell or heaven. Possessions are merely means for good or evil. What is done with them is up to us.

This points us to the most fundamental issue of the spiritual discipline of poverty: our attitude toward what we have and don't have but want. In his powerful and illuminating book, *The Spirit of the Disciplines,* Protestant philosopher and theologian Dallas Willard makes some critical distinctions that will help us see the importance of attitude:

> To possess riches is to have a right to say how they will or will not be used. To use riches, on the other hand, is to cause them to be consumed or to be transferred to others in exchange for something we desire. The difference between possession and use immediately becomes clear when we think about how we sometimes use and control the use of riches we do not own, as when we influence the decisions of those who do own them. It's possible to use or consume goods we do not own, and it is possible to own what we do not and perhaps cannot use.
>
> To trust in riches, on the other hand, is to count upon them to obtain or secure what we treasure most. It is to think that they will bring us happiness and well-being. When we also possess the riches we trust in, we may suppose that we are secure, like the rich fool of the Gospel account (Luke 12:19), or even suppose that we are better than those who are poor. If we trust in riches we will also love them and come to serve them. In our actions we will place them above the truly ultimate values of human life, even above God and his service.
>
> In the light of these distinctions it becomes clear that we can possess without using or trusting. Possession only gives us a substantial say over how goods may be used. And we can use without possessing or trusting. And we are painfully aware how we can trust (and serve) wealth without either possessing or using it. Those poor people whose faith is in riches they neither own nor can use are among the most unhappy people on earth.[7]

Lay people are called to manage this world's goods with heavenly values and for heavenly purposes. If we are burdened by a misunderstanding of poverty, we will feel guilty. We need to see poverty in its proper light, as a discipline of the mind and will and as an attitude of the heart, designed to promote godliness in the midst of godlessness.

When it comes to poverty, what we have, don't have, keep, or give away means little. Our attitude, however, means everything.

The person who has grown to the place where he or she can truly say with Paul, "One thing I do . . . press toward the goal for the prize of the upward call of God in Christ Jesus" (Phil. 3:13, NKJV), who can truly "seek first his kingdom and his righteousness" (Matt. 6:33, NIV), is a person who has entered in to poverty. The practice of poverty "makes possessions safe and fruitful for the glory of God."[8] And our proper use of them stores up for us an incomparable treasure "in heaven, where moth and rust do not destroy, and where thieves do not break in and steal" (Matt. 6:20, NIV).

Chastity

Chastity, even voluntary celibacy, have their basis in Scripture. Matthew 19:12 tells us, "Some are incapable of marriage because they were born so; some, because they were made so by others; some because they have renounced marriage for the sake of the kingdom of heaven. Whoever can accept this ought to accept it." Many did accept it, including Saint Paul. He saw voluntary celibacy as a tremendous opportunity to be more available to the Lord and His people.

"The unmarried man can be busy with the Lord's affairs, maintain single-minded devotion to Him, and be concerned with pleasing the Lord alone. But the married man is busy with this world's demands and occupied with pleasing his wife. The virgin—indeed any unmarried woman—can devote herself to the things of the Lord and pursue holiness in body and spirit. The married woman, on the other hand, is easily absorbed by the cares of this world and pleasing her husband" (1 Cor. 7:32–34). These differences do not make one life necessarily better than another; they merely point out why it is easier to pursue God as a single person than it is as a married one.

Voluntary celibacy is only one way to live out the counsel of chastity. It may be hard to believe, but chastity is a gospel mandate for all Christians, even Christians who are married. In fact, a revival of a proper understanding of marital chastity might do us all a world of good in our efforts to correct the terrible blight of infidelity that has swept even the Christian church.

We are living in a day of tremendous moral collapse. Notions of right and wrong have been either abandoned, redefined so they are hardly recognizable, or declared relative to individuals, situations, cultures, or governments. Our world is filled with shades of moral grays; blacks and whites are gone. This situation has created, among other things, sharp increases in family disintegration, marital infidelity, and sexual immorality. Children are growing up with two or more *sets* of parents. Spouses are trying on and throwing away spouses as fast as they change fashions. And people, even young teens, are sleeping with anyone who even appears to be moderately interested in them.

We desperately need to rediscover the spiritual discipline of sexual chastity. Its practice among all Christians could help the church and the world return to an undefiled concept of love, to rebuild family life, and to restore long-lasting and satisfying marriages. But this will not begin until we first reclaim a clear understanding of chastity.

Chastity is demonstrated through fidelity, and much like obedience, it is a discipline of the body and includes two main concepts: the sacredness of reproductive creativity and sexuality as a way to show our love for God. The key to understanding the importance of chastity is to grasp the divine design of sexuality as creative, sacred, and purposeful. We can even say that it is a "prerequisite for man's communion with the Divine."[9]

We are by nature sexual beings. In fact, our sexuality is an aspect of our divine image (Gen. 1:37). Without our sexuality, we could not fulfill our divine commission to "be fertile and multiply" (v. 28). Therefore, our sexual desires are natural and good, but we need to be careful to not fulfill them in impure ways. In fact, we need to learn to control them—hence our need to practice chastity.

A chaste single person is one who tempers sexual satisfaction by not having the experience outside of marriage. Chaste married couples are those who are sexually faithful to one another, who respect and reverence each other as sacred temples created by God and recreated to be the dwelling place of the Holy Spirit. Chastity in marriage can also be demonstrated through temporary and mutually agreed upon sexual abstinence (1 Cor. 7:5). About this, Dallas Willard makes some insightful comments:

> Contrary to much modern thought, it is absolutely vital to the health of any marriage that sexual gratification not be placed at the center. Voluntary abstention helps us appreciate and love our mates as whole persons, of which their sexuality is but one part. And it confirms us in the practice of being very close to people without sexual entanglements. Chastity thus has an important part to play within marriage, but the main effect we seek through it is the proper disposal of sexual acts, feelings, thoughts, and attitudes within our life as a whole, inside of marriage and out. Sexuality cannot be allowed to permeate our lives if we are to live as children of God and brothers and sisters of Jesus Christ.[10]

Indeed, like all the other disciplines, chastity must first reside in the heart before it can work itself out in conduct. Just as "out of the heart of men, proceed evil thoughts" (Mark 7:21, NKJV), so genuine chastity flows from a heart set on God and demonstrates its presence through personal discipline and respect for others. True chastity thus enables us to love others purely.

Obedience

This brings us to the third evangelical counsel—*obedience*, the greatest antidote to our self-centered age. Our first parents disobeyed when they refused to obey the living God. Their profound act of disobedience has been repeated by practically every human being since then. It is our most basic generational problem. It runs deep. It is known theologically as "original sin."

Fortunately for mankind, the "second Eve," a beautiful title given by the early Christians to Mary, the mother of Jesus, undid the "no" of the first Eve. She said yes to God: "I am the handmaid of the Lord. May it be done to me according to your Word" (Luke 1:38). She and her Son stand together as the most beautiful examples of the kind of servanthood to which we are all called. Jesus tells us, "whoever desires to be great among you, let him be your servant . . . —just as the Son of Man did not come to be served, but to serve, and to give His life a ransom for many" (Matt. 20:26–28, NKJV).

Our practice of obedience must begin with the Source of all authority—the Lord of the universe. Even God's Son so submitted His will to the Father that He could say, "the Son can do nothing of Himself, but what He sees the Father do; for whatever He does, the Son also does in like manner" (John 5:19, NKJV). This level of obedience cannot be achieved apart from a life devoted to prayer. Jesus knew this. Even a cursory reading of the four Gospels demonstrates that He bathed His life in prayer. He prayed at His baptism, during His first preaching tour, when He healed, when He chose twelve men to be His closest disciples, before and after feeding the five thousand, during the feeding of the four thousand, before Peter's revelatory confession of Jesus' identity, before Jesus' transfiguration, after the seventy disciples returned from ministry, prior to presenting what we know as the Lord's prayer, while standing before Lazarus's tomb, when children gathered around Him, while presiding over the Last Supper, hanging on the cross, after rising from the dead and teaching the two disciples on the road to Emmaus, and just prior to His ascension into heaven.[11] The Son of God immersed Himself in prayer. As a result, He made it possible for Himself in His humanness to obey the Father and perfectly fulfill His will.

Ironically enough, Jesus' utter obedience to the Father made Him not less independent, but more independent than His contemporaries. By freely submitting to God and His will, Jesus was free to live a truly counter-cultural life. Don't misunderstand me. He was not disobedient to authority. Remember, He was the one who refused to be turned into a political Messiah who would overthrow the Roman rule over Palestine; He was the one who said, "Render therefore to Caesar the things that are Caesar's, and to God the things that are God's" (Matt. 22:21, NKJV). Nevertheless, He constantly challenged the religious and social norms of His day. He spoke to hated Samaritans. He touched and healed dreaded lepers. He drove merchants, who were buying and selling wares, out of the house of God. He spent much of his time ministering to prostitutes, tax collectors, drunkards . . . all types of social outcasts.

His behavior was so contrary to the cultural expectations for a good Jew that He gained a sordid reputation. He was called "a glutton and a drunkard, a friend of tax collectors and sinners"

(Matt. 11:19). But such charges did not pose any threats to Him—in fact, they magnified the reality of His total obedience to His Father. He knew His Father would take care of Him. He was even willing, though it almost crushed His spirit, to die according to His Father's will (Luke 22:41-44). He realized, however, that regardless of the circumstance or challenges, God would reward His submission.

The Lord promises the same for us. He will reward our obedience now by using it to give us such fruit of the Spirit as a holy character, perseverance, increased trust, humility, and patience. He will also reward us in heaven with the unimaginable intimacy and unconditional love of the eternal beatific vision. In that incredible state of heavenly unity, superabundant goodness will flood and completely transform every facet of our being. Every trial, every hurt, every pain, every tear, every misunderstanding, every violation will be wiped away—*forever*. That's the ultimate reward for our obedience. What else do we really need?

As we submit to God's authority, we will also find that it includes submission to human authority. We are commanded to obey civil government, employers, parents, and church leaders.[12] As long as such human authorities do not violate the dictates of God, we must obey them.

But as we all have experienced, because of our fallen nature we are more inclined to follow our own will rather than God's. Our flesh rebels against the movement of the Spirit within us. "I shall not serve" reverberates through our fallenness. But thanks be to God, Jesus Christ, as the new Adam, has overcome our fallenness. Because of the cross, we can experience victory over the flesh as we become obedient through the power of the Spirit to the demands of the gospel. Obedience keeps us close to the Master and steeped in His commands. So shall we be saved! Saint Francis de Sales captures the significance of obedience as he states, "Blessed are the obedient for God will never let them go astray."

But obedience does not just yield personal or inner fruit. As many of the great social action missionaries of our time, including Mother Teresa, have discovered, fruitful social change follows only from true devotion to God. Mother Teresa of Calcutta, for example, begins each day with mass and then Eucharistic adoration. She acknowledges that she could not do the work that she does without

His strength. She humbly realizes that our own abilities and most intense motivation cannot accomplish any lasting social change; that is God's gift alone. Yes, the gift is received through obedient hands, but it is still a gift. God lets us share the fruit of our obedient efforts—not because He has to, but because He wants to. How good is our Lord.

THE KEY TO THE COUNSELS

God has given us an incredible gift in the evangelical counsels. All of us who are in His Family of families, regardless of our various traditions, can embrace these counsels out of our individual and corporate love for the Lord. And as we do, we will find ourselves increasingly in opposition to our culture. This will not be the opposition of a political revolutionary, but the opposition that flows from an inner disposition and outer lifestyle focused on and conformed to Him who is love.

Loving is the key to true works of mercy, practicing the counsels, and long-lasting social change. One cannot be an evangelical Christian—Catholic or Protestant or Orthodox—without embracing this understanding. I find that most evangelical churches today make a genuine effort to grab hold of this perspective of the Great Commission—to "do" as well as to "say." As an evangelical Catholic, my understanding of the call to love is consistent with my view of man, who was created in the image of God. That image was tarnished and flawed by sin, but it has been restored by the cross. That image reflects God and is present in every human being, even in every unbeliever. And when one embraces Jesus Christ personally by faith, one's image is graciously and divinely restored.

I believe that if we rediscover what the evangelical counsels are really all about, we will find not only that they promote the full and rich development of an interior life based on a vibrant, persevering relationship with God, but they compel us to an evangelical social action flowing out of our convictions about poverty, chastity, and obedience. Perhaps this is why the little nun from Calcutta challenges all of us. She makes practicing the evangelical counsels look so simple, doesn't she? Well, perhaps it really is.

PART III

Our Evangelical Heritage

CHAPTER 8

Our Family Tree

The fire softly crackles in a room of subtle evening shadows and subdued light. Curled up next to the fireplace is the family cat, head tucked between her front paws and tail gently resting against her body and wrapped around more than half of it, appearing almost as a snow-white border around a photograph. The love seat, three-cushion couch, and old wood rocking chair show many years of use, but somehow the way they have aged tell more of the love they have shared rather than the years they have survived. In the rocker, draped with a multi-colored afghan, sits an elderly, majestic woman enjoying the fire's warmth and sounds, while holding in her arms a usually overactive seven-year-old boy. Though his arms and legs are resting, his lips are still chattering away, asking questions to satisfy his curiosity about his family heritage.

"Grandma, what was Grandpa like? . . ."

"Tell me about Daddy when he was my age. Did he get in trouble sometimes too? . . ."

"Mommy says she always walked to school, even when it snowed. Is that really true? . . ."

For what seems hours they laugh and talk—the young grandson discovering the treasures of his family tree and within that his identity, and the grandmother reliving afresh the sometimes dusty but life-shaping memories of her and her family's past. She understands the value of her heritage and the need to pass it on. He is just beginning to learn. But she willingly, even joyfully, shares the family's heritage so her grandson will sink his roots deep into its rich soil and there find nourishment for the hopefully healthy branches he will add to the family tree.

As spiritual children of our heavenly Father, we too have a rich family heritage. It reaches all the way back to our first earthly parents, Adam and Eve, but it becomes the most clearly defined through the second Adam, Jesus Christ, and the history of the family He began, the apostolic church. Our family tree encompasses the countless millions who have embraced Jesus as Savior and Lord. It also includes a divinely inspired book of our heritage which takes us through the first century A.D. From there we can turn to the writings and liturgical legacies of our family members to learn even more. We can even sit and talk with other Christians within and without our particular traditions to glean more insight into our family's incredible past. We have so many sources and so much to learn from one another. If we have eyes to see clearly and ears to hear patiently, we can find our identity in the past. And that knowledge—that collected and common insight—will shape our lives, beckoning us to look ahead to add even healthier, stronger branches to an already firmly planted tree.

So come join me for a brisk walk down the memory lane of our family's past. Granted, we'll catch only glimpses of our heritage, but even through those we'll begin to see the inspiring fruit of our common evangelical roots.

THE EVANGELICAL PREACHERS

We'll begin with the evangelical preachers, and probably the greatest among them was the apostle Paul. He stands as a prime example of a transformed life, a life that became a powerful tool for the kingdom.

He began his mission after his conversion from Judaism, and it took him throughout much of the Roman Empire. He traveled to Cilicia, Antioch, Cyprus, and Asia Minor, at which point the churches of Galatia were founded. After the Council of Jerusalem in A.D. 50, he began evangelizing Philippi, Thessalonica, Berea, and Corinth. The churches he founded were among the most stable on the mission field.[1]

Paul then moved across the Aegean Sea and spent a great deal of time in Ephesus. Because of his time and efforts, Asia became a Mediterranean pillar of Christianity. His final recorded evangelical enterprise, and perhaps his most powerful witness, was his trip to Rome and the ministry that evolved there. In Rome he was jailed for the sake of the gospel, but even as a prisoner he became a messenger of liberation to unbelievers and a source of encouragement for Christians in Rome (Acts 28).

Paul was the premier evangelical Christian. He preached and struggled to live out the gospel message until his death. He preached with power and conviction, convinced of the importance and the implications of his mission. Christ's death and resurrection permeated his teaching and preaching; they were the strength and hope from which Paul moved. As a result of his commitment to our Lord, he has left us a written treasure of power, a storehouse of truth, and an encouraging portrait of perseverance.

Evangelical Christians since Paul have relied on his insight, his faithfulness, and his written word—the word that amazingly touches all conceivable situations of life. This is a wonderful testimony to the timelessness of the gospel message. The worldview of the first century was obviously quite different from our twentieth century perspective, but even though the accidents of culture change, the substance of being human never alters. Paul's message was aimed at the heart of what it means to be human, at what it means to desire truth, at what it means to love. These basics are timeless and that is why Paul's words will never become outdated or obsolete.

Many of the well-known evangelists were and are power preachers, relying heavily on the words of sacred Scripture. John Chrysostom, one of the Eastern Fathers of the Church, was most famous for his ministry of forceful, prophetic preaching. But we have sometimes forgotten that his ministry was partially motivated by his concern for the sinful state of the world. Listen to how he put it: "My work is like that of a man who is trying to clean a piece of ground into which a muddy stream is constantly flowing."[2] That's not despair—that's reality.

Later, in the thirteenth century, we see Dominic establishing the first group of church-sanctioned itinerant preachers. One of the charisms of this group of men was their ability to preach with so much zeal that when their order was formally established, they were called the "order of preachers." Dominic, one of the great preachers and defenders of the faith, converted many souls to the Savior.

Looking ahead to the post-Reformation, we discover such

men as John Wesley, Charles Finney, and D. L. Moody, all men
who relied solely on the power of the proclamation of the Word to
evangelize. Wesley preached the fundamentals of Christianity,
mainly the doctrines of justification (what God does for us) and the
new birth (what God does in us).[3] The Wesley brothers' ministry
was itinerant. Fired by their own experience of saving grace, they
traveled extensively, preaching the message of the gospel with un-
quenchable zeal. In fact, identified with these two preachers is the
classic phrase, "I look upon the world as my parish."[4]

In the early 1830s, another evangelical leader, Charles Finney, promoted the practice of revivals and toured many major cities
in the United States, including New York, Philadelphia, and Boston. Due to his efforts, revivalism became a major force in evangelism. In fact, D. L. Moody transformed the technique of revivalism, changing it from one-night camp meetings and single church
affairs to power-packed, nightly events which spanned several
weeks and grew from collaborative efforts of many denominations.

Revivals were and still are an experience of extended, inten-
sive proclamation of the Word. The participants are drawn by powerful moments of praise and worship, so key for openness to the
voice of God. If the meeting begins in the power of the Holy Spirit,
the effects of the preaching will be intensified. Moody fortunately
knew how to organize these revivals and follow the inspirations of
the Holy Spirit. Thank God he did. Thousands were brought to the
Lord through the power of such approaches to revivalism.

Clarence Walworth, a nineteenth-century Catholic priest,
was converted to Christianity in a revivalist meeting and became
one of the most forceful parish mission preachers of his time. He
adopted a revivalist style of preaching that was described this way:
"First he would speak in a quiet, gentle manner, then he screamed
out so that the walls of the Cathedral reechoed it back again; it
reverberated and resounded. It was magnificent and terrible and
the people cried, groaned, beat their breasts."[5] Another penned
these observations about Walworth: "During his sermons he not
only pointed to the mission cross, but he even clung to it, till it
swayed back and forth with the weight of his body, whilst the people, conscience-stricken and pale with emotion, watched and listened with almost breathless silence."[6] That is anointed preaching,
the kind that brings about conversion.

In our own century, we can see many examples of wonderful missionary preachers, but perhaps none more obvious than our own twentieth-century Paul, Billy Graham. More than any other evangelical Christian, Reverend Graham is responsible for restructuring mass evangelism. Mass media and convenient means of travel have enabled Dr. Graham to reach almost every country in the world. He and those like him have engaged in a truly global mission of evangelization.

Another major mass evangelization organization is FIRE, a Catholic alliance of Faith, Intercession, Repentance, and Evangelism based at the Franciscan University of Steubenville. Working from Luke 12:49—"I have come to cast fire on the earth and would that it were already set ablaze"—members of FIRE proclaim the gospel of salvation: the fire of judgment, the fire of the Holy Spirit, and the fire of God's love. Testimonies of conversions, restoration of relationships, physical and emotional healings, and spiritual rebirths are the fruit of this evangelistic ministry, a sign that the hearts of many who hear the gospel message are willing to receive it personally.

Charismatic renewal conferences, much like revival meetings, have drawn thousands to a deeper experience of God and radically committed Christian lifestyles. For instance, the 1977 interdenominational charismatic conference in Kansas City was a good example of an evangelical event of magnitude. More than fifty thousand Christians attended, and the Word was preached in power and truth. Amidst the praise, prayer, and teaching, Christians mightily experienced the excitement of our common faith, the excitement of being Christian.

THE SOCIAL ACTIVISTS

While Word-centered preachers and evangelists such as those we just scanned are desperately needed, we also need social activists, for evangelism entails social action as well as preaching. Take Jesus, for example. His ministry encompassed much more than preaching and teaching. He attended to the needs of the poor and hungry, the emotionally and physically sick, the children, the lonely—the profoundly helpless who needed the touch of love. He saw the interrelatedness of the gospel and social action so clearly that when He spoke of the Last Judgment, He revealed that social involvement was a prerequisite for entering the Kingdom: "'Come, you who are blessed by my Father. Inherit the kingdom prepared for you from the foundation of the world. For I was hungry and you gave me food, I was thirsty and you gave me drink, a stranger and you welcomed me, naked and you clothed me, ill and you cared for me, in prison and you visited me.'" (Matt. 25:34–36).

Charity permeates the record of Jesus' life. In His teachings (particularly the parables) and His actions, He demonstrated the significance of reaching out in genuine love and concern for others. In the story of the good Samaritan, for instance, Jesus illustrated the importance of compassion. He told of a Jewish man who was badly beaten then left on the side of the road to die, visible to all who passed. Two men, a priest and a Levite, passed by without helping this half-dead man. The third individual, a Samaritan, saw him and was moved with pity. He approached him and dressed his wounds, "pouring oil in and wine. He then hoisted him on his own breast and brought him to an inn, where he cared for him. The next day, he took out two silver pieces and gave them to the innkeeper with the request: 'Look after him, and if there is any further expense I will repay you on my way back.'"

Jesus then asked His hearer, "'Which of these three [the priest, Levite, or Samaritan] . . . was neighbor to the robbers' victim?' He answered, 'The one who treated him with mercy.' Jesus said to him, 'Go and do likewise'" (Luke 10:30–37). Go and be compassionate.

Jesus was the greatest social activist of all time, and many after Him followed in His tradition, including the apostles, who were often involved in the ministry of healing and deliverance. Moreover, the apostolate of all of the great saints of history has always entailed compassion for the poor and suffering. I immediately think of Francis of Assisi and his ongoing ministry to and love for the lepers. Originally, Francis was so repulsed by their physical appearance that he was unable to even look at their oozing sores. But when the love of Jesus overcame him, Francis no longer saw the sores of a leper—he saw the wounds of Christ. He saw pain that needed relief; he saw people in need; he saw the alienation of being marked, of being different, of being cast down. He saw all things through the eyes of Love, through the eyes of Christ.

Leprosy finds its modern counterpart in the tragedy of AIDS. How compassionate are we to the victims of this disease? Do we try to find ways to help them, or do we reinforce the alienation that is heaped upon them, or worse, do we judge them? Do we have a desire to serve God by serving his children? Francis and the brothers did not run when service was difficult. Embracing the difficulty for the sake of Christ, they chose to love.

Developing social conscience and acting on it are necessary to a truly Christian life, but they are only authentic when they flow out of the gospel values of love and service. Social action should never be a substitute for evangelism; rather, it's a handmaid. Charity in the form of social awareness should flow from a love affair with Jesus and a desire to help others enter into a personal relationship with Him by bringing them into relationship with His presence in each of us.

Probably the most well-known example of a twentieth-century Christian committed to social action is Mother Teresa and the Sisters of Charity. These sisters have a specific apostolate to the forgotten, the homeless, the dying. They spend the entire day walking around the streets of Calcutta (or any other city with a branch of the order), picking up people on the brink of death. They help them all, even if all they can do is provide an opportunity for them to die with dignity and in peace. To die in peace is a key concept here. Not only do the sisters clean these people and provide humane conditions in which to die, but they also introduce them to the Lord. After all, no one can truly die in peace without coming to terms with the Savior.

Mother Teresa walks with spiritual eyes; when she looks, she sees only Christ and the things of Christ. She therefore radiates Christ in all she says and does, and her fruit shows it.

Since the beginning of her ministry, she has never once met anyone who refused to accept the love of the Lord while in her presence. What an incredible testimony to the impact of the Christian life on others!

THE LITERARY EVANGELISTS

A whole other branch of the Christian family tree is remote from the physical pain of the poor and the desperate. Pain of a different type exists in this branch, though, and it needs to be healed just the same. I'm talking about the world of letters, the world of the intellectual. Faith is often very difficult for those who insist on reasonable, objective proof of the existence, nature, and work of God. Consequently, they need to be approached with the claims of faith in a way that will appeal to the intellect, not just the heart.

Through the ages, our Christian family has been blessed with many profoundly faith-filled intellectuals. The early Church Fathers were some of the finest scholars and apologists the church has ever had. During the Middle Ages, the Benedictine monks, Augustine, and other scholastics and scholars continued to protect and preserve the faith. Some of the most profound theology as well as some of the great spiritual classics emerged during this historical period. Probably the greatest medieval mind and arguably one of the great minds ever was the Dominican scholar, Thomas Aquinas. Many scholars consider his *Summa Theologica* to be his finest contribution. It is a theological masterpiece in which Aquinas treats almost every imaginable issue of our human experience. Not only does he show how incredibly reasonable it is to believe in God, but he also explores such themes as love, hate, sin, virtue, justice, mercy, emotions, nature, grace, angels, heaven, and hell. The reasonableness of his positions make him appealing to the scholar. He addresses the possible difficulties with his position and systematically refutes them. Moreover, he validates his arguments with numerous sources, including the Bible and the writings of Aristotle and Augustine. Thomas Aquinas is the premier doctor of the church, and to this day, scholarly members of the Christian family study his works to break open his timeless insight and wisdom.

Another wonderful doctor of the church in the 1300s was Catherine of Siena, another Dominican. Catherine, along with Teresa of Avila, was one of only two woman doctors of the church. She was a defender of the faith in a critical time for the church and was instrumental in the Pope's return to Rome from Avignon. Most of Catherine's thoughts are recorded in two major sources—her correspondence and her dialogues with God. Catherine had a truly contemplative life of prayer, which means that she met God in prayer in so personal a way that she was often overcome with His presence. Much of her prayer time was spent in ecstasy, gazing on the face of the Lord. Through her intimacy with the Lord, which she nurtured in long hours of prayer, daily Eucharist, and service to the church, Catherine became a living mouthpiece for the Lord. He spoke clearly through her and to her. A wonderful source of meditation and food for thought is her *Dialogue,* a book of conversations between her and God. Through this communication with Him, many in our generation have come to a thoughtful and profound understanding of God's presence and love.

One hundred or so years after Catherine and immediately before the Reformation stands one of the great scholars of all time, Ignatius of Loyola. Ignatius founded the Society of Jesus (the Jesuits), which is still recognized as the great order of Catholic priests of scholars, thinkers, and writers. Many Christians have found the *Spiritual Exercises* of Ignatius tremendously helpful for growth in holiness.

In the twentieth century, one of the finest Christian thinkers and imaginative writers is C. S. Lewis. His books include *Mere Christianity, The Screwtape Letters, The Great Divorce, The Abolition of Man, The Four Loves,* and *The Problem of Pain.* Lewis has a unique touch for drawing the reader into a fantasy world that is all too real. The reader emerges from that world somewhat uncomfortably challenged in her Christian walk. *The Screwtape Letters,* for instance, is a fictional collection of correspondence between Screwtape, an agent for the devil, and his nephew, Wormwood. The letters outline the plan of destruction for the individual human soul to whom Wormwood is assigned. Lewis chillingly awakens us to the possibility that, just as we all have a personal guardian angel, we may all have a personal angel of darkness whose entire function is to lead us to destruction. Lewis reveals gospel truth subtly, pointing to the temptations that we face and also to the ways in which we cleverly rationalize our sin until we finally become desensitized to it altogether. Provocative and full of cryptic messages, his writing commands the reader's attention.

Those more drawn to the genre of literature can find their fill of the gospel in many writers who have nourished the Christian family tree. Many have found consolation and challenge in the writings of Dante, John Milton, and John Donne; the poetry of John of the Cross and Teresa of Avila; and in our own century the work of Graham Greene, T. S. Eliot, and G. K. Chesterton. Chesterton and Eliot are particularly intriguing because of their personal styles and their insight into the twentieth century.

Chesterton was a fearless thinker, an outspoken orator, and a wonderful apologist with a specific concern for human rights. He used literature as a medium for expressing his values and beliefs. He has many works, including *Heretics, What's Wrong with the World,* and *Autobiography,* but the most intriguing synthesis of his philosophy and faith, as well as the best example of the originality and brilliance of his thought, is found in his masterpiece entitled *Orthodoxy.*

Chesterton defines orthodoxy as the "only satisfactory answer to the riddle of the universe."[7] Like many Christians, Chesterton struggled with his faith for years but eventually came to the truth. When the truth was revealed to him, he responded to it. He followed the call of the Holy Spirit, and the Spirit made him orthodox. His book *Orthodoxy* recounts his story of coming to terms with a faith that is not rationalistic, that does not allow for neat and tidy explanations, a faith that calls for an ultimate surrender of what is most attractive and safe for the intellectual—reason. For only when reason is placed under the authority of Him who is intrinsically rational will it find genuine satisfaction and sound answers.

T. S. Eliot, another modern writer, uses poetry, drama, and prose to express his faith experience and to challenge his readers. He has a great volume of work, much of which parallels his own progression of faith. For example, it wasn't until his later years when he fully embraced his beliefs, that he began writing powerful, moving, and pointed poetry about the spiritual condition of humankind in the twentieth century. His best known and respected piece of work, *The Wasteland,* is a portrait of the spiritual aridity of modern man, who is caught up in the mechanized, dehumanized, sexually deviant, unrepentant, self-seeking, insensitive modern world. He definitely paints a grim portrait of modern civilization, but only to help us see that our priorities are confused, that we have no center or system of beliefs to fall back on, that everything is focused on "me." To get us back on center, he forces us to face the consequences of our attitudes, beliefs, and lifestyles. He forces us to think about our own spiritual condition. Is it dry? Is it lifeless? Is it like a desert? Is it, as the title suggests, a wasteland? An existence without life, without purpose, without meaning? If so, we need to return to the Purpose of all life, Jesus Christ.

Through the power of great writing and sound scholarship, these Christians, and many others like them, have provided a medium for evangelization that has impacted untold numbers who may never have come to the cross otherwise.

ADDING HEALTHY BRANCHES

Have you enjoyed our walk? A bit out of breath? I warned you it would be brisk. But I trust you found it memorable and enlightening.

I find it wonderful and encouraging to look at our evangelical heritage from such different approaches over many generations. It helps us see that God has created each and every human being uniquely with different needs, different gifts and talents, and with different approaches to a faith experience. The rich and varied heritage of our Christian family tree acknowledges our individual uniquenesses as it preserves and proclaims our unity in Christ.

Given our human uniquenesses and divinely bestowed and various gifts, it's vital that we who know the truth reach out to others who need the truth. We need to appeal to the people who need an evangelical fervor behind the Word of God, to the people who need to be ministered to by action, and to the intellectuals who need to exercise the gift of reason even more actively in their search for and faith in Christ.

God knows our needs, and He has faithfully provided men and women imbued with the Spirit of the gospel who have gone out in the world and worked for the Kingdom, taken chances, risked, fought, been persecuted, trusted in God, acted on their convictions, and loved. Looking at their lives is rather convicting because they are just ordinary human beings like you and me who chose to respond to God's supernatural grace and call. What if some of these Christians had ignored the call that God placed on their hearts? Christianity would have a different face today.

God wants to use all of us in a mighty way. Don't ignore His call. Sit at His feet. Learn about our common heritage. Sink your roots deep into its rich soil. Find inspiration. Be encouraged. Accept the challenge. And move out in the power of God's Spirit, seeking to start more healthy branches on our common family tree.

CHAPTER **9**

The Children of the
Great Divorce

We saw in the previous chapter some of the most beautiful aspects of our Christian family tree, and we considered the inspiring challenge that gives us to respond obediently and faithfully to God's call for our individual lives and thereby contribute to the growth and beauty of our heritage. But all is not well. A debilitating, destructive disease has invaded our tree. Although it can't ultimately uproot our tree since its trunk and life-giving source is Christ, it can surely mar our beauty, stunt our growth, and putrefy our wood. In fact, this disease has already left a terrible blight on our history and threatens to further scar our future. Perhaps the best way to see its impact is to view it in terms of a different metaphor—that of the family.

All families, regardless of their apparent or real health, are dysfunctional. Granted, the type, number, and degree of the dysfunctions vary from family to family, but they are always present. Some of the most serious dysfunctions arise out of the depth of injury inflicted on children in a family affected by divorce, drug or alcohol abuse, trauma, or domestic violence. What we're discovering is something we should not find surprising: "the sins of the fathers are visited upon the children." What does seem surprising, however, is the depth of pain these dysfunctions create and its debilitating effect on its victims for generations.

The family of God, the church, is no different. We, too, suffer from the sins of our fathers. Indeed, I would suggest that we begin to understand the current inability of the members of the whole Christian family to recognize each other—let alone work together—as fellow believers is perhaps the greatest, most far-reaching example of this phenomenon. This problem began in the eleventh century when some disputes over political, ecclesiastical, theological, and even liturgical issues finally led to a split between Western and Eastern Christians. Known as the Great Schism of 1054, it created the first break in the unity of the church. From that moment, the Roman Catholic Church and the Greek Orthodox Church went different ways. Although much reconciliation and healing still need to take place between Catholics and Orthodox, official steps were begun on December 7, 1965, when Pope Paul VI and Athenagoras revoked the mutual excommunication decrees that had been blocking reunification efforts between the two churches for almost a thousand years.

The scars left by the Great Schism, however, did not lead to the depth of hurt, anger, and divisiveness that we now see throughout the church. That legacy falls on the shoulders of the Reformation. It began with a call within Catholicism to correct abuses in the church, but it ended with Catholics leaving the church and beginning new movements outside the church's umbrella. The protest leaders and their followers came to be known as Protestants. Once outside of the church, however, they had little impetus and no overarching authority to hold them together. They soon splintered into more groups, creating the numerous denominations within Protestantism we see today.

I have no intention to assess blame against Protestants or Catholics for this terrible split. Enough mistakes were made on both sides. Neither do I ignore the positive impact and necessary correctives the Reformation caused in and outside the Roman Catholic Church (which all church leaders, including my own, have acknowledged). But the fact of the matter is that the Reformation movement and the Church's response to it led to a traumatic family split—a radical divorce—and hundreds of years later we are still suffering from its impact. We are children of this great divorce, descendants of a single family tree divided by mistrust, failure, and abuse. We can see its devastation everywhere, even in what is left unsaid or ignored.

Just recently I became distressed as I watched Pat Robertson, whom I deeply admire, report on his tour of Eastern Europe. I shared his excitement at the ripe opportunity presented by the fallen wall that once divided East and West Berlin. I rejoiced at the warm welcome he was shown. And I delighted at the pictures of

Eastern European Christians packing the small Protestant churches he visited. What was said did not disturb me. But I was distressed by what was missing—any mention of the countless thousands of family members in the Orthodox and Catholic churches who lived, worshipped, and ministered in Eastern Europe. What part did they have to play in the wall's collapse? None was the impression viewers received. The prayers of believers in the West apparently cast the deciding blow.

I must disagree. It is presumptuous to believe that our prayers in the West alone brought down the Berlin Wall. Saint Jerome powerfully proclaimed hundreds of years ago, the "blood of the martyrs is the seed of the church." And enough martyrdom, sacrifice, fasting, and prayer have arisen from the whole family of God to pierce the heavens and rouse our common Father to action. These cries have come from Germany, Russia, Poland, Lithuania, and throughout the Eastern Bloc. But apparently the assumption among Western believers is that Orthodox and Catholic Christians are not full Christians, or at least their involvement in Eastern European political affairs is negligible. That is sad. Perhaps the reality is that they have earned the name Christian more than we in the West have. Remember, from Poland's bloodied, fertile ground, enriched by martyrs of the faith, has come Pope John Paul II, who now proclaims the gospel in power to all peoples worldwide. Who are we Western Christians to believe that our prayers . . . our faith . . . our anything tilted the scales of power?

Furthermore, there is a longstanding tradition in our Christian family of "white martyrdom." It refers to those who sacrificially offer their lives for Christ but are never privileged to shed their blood. Some white martyrs seem to suffer the most, and there have been millions of them in Russia, Poland, Hungary, Lithuania, Estonia, and throughout the rest of the Eastern Bloc. Pastors, priests, monks, nuns, bishops, evangelists, teachers, preachers, and millions of lay faithful have given their all so some might be saved. Must I ask it again? Who do we think we are?

Without his intending it, Robertson's report may have also led his audience to the assumption that most people in the Eastern Bloc need to be saved. No doubt many do, but I sincerely believe many Christians from the East will soon reevangelize the secularized West. Paul Weyrich, president of the Free Congress Foundation, went to Hungary, Estonia, and the Soviet Union. What he reported should make all of us in the West sit up and listen.

> One thing that I found fascinating was the situation regarding the Orthodox Church. Some 3,000 churches have been returned to use in the past two years. I attended St. Michael the Archangel Russian Orthodox Church in the outskirts of Moscow on a Sunday where hundreds of believers packed into a building which, up until February of 1989, was used to store tractors.
>
> The main part of the church was under restoration, so the iconographers and plasterers were there trying to restore the church, which meant the services had to be held in a foyer with a temporary altar. People were literally stuffed into this church, and hundreds more were outside.
>
> John Exnicios and I witnessed twenty baptisms, and many of these were young men who, at 18 to 20 years old, were obviously not coerced by their parents, but were stepping forward as believing Christians. The priests officiating couldn't have been more than 22 or 23 years old.
>
> In Zagorsk, the home of the largest operating monasteries in the Soviet Union, I was able to talk to the director of the academic system for the Moscow Patriarchate. He said that they just opened new seminaries this year in Minsk and Kiev and that they are also training priests in parochial schools. But they can't train enough of them so anyone who expresses interest in becoming a priest is being ordained without theological or liturgical training. Because they didn't have 3,000 clergy to operate the churches that have been turned over to them, they have many untrained people running parishes. It is a very difficult situation.[1]

Similar reports regarding Orthodox Christians abound and are paralleled by reports of the heroic faith of Catholic Christians in the Eastern Bloc countries.

Each of these churches is part of the family. Consequently, when "one member suffers we all suffer; when one member rejoices, we all rejoice" (Rom. 12:15). Right? That's the biblical ideal, but it's not the usual response of Christians to one another. More often than not, our shared rejoicing and suffering don't even involve fellow believers, unless they're our immediate relatives.

Most of us don't even recognize our fellow Christians as Christians. To us, only those in or close to our theological or ecclesiastical persuasions are true believers; all others are on the outside looking in.

So it is with a divorce. Even generations later the effects of the trauma still manifest themselves, not so much in issues as in prejudice and ignorance. We may not remember or even know what brought about the divorce, but we sure know whose side we're on and *who was "right."*

Since 1973 I have been involved in what is often called the Catholic Charismatic Renewal or the Catholic Pentecostal Movement. (I guess that makes me a pentecostal, evangelical, Catholic Christian!) I have also been directly involved in the Communitarian Wing of that renewal. The communities, or fellowships, born of this movement literally span the globe. These groups have struggled with many differences of opinion. Indeed, deep and painful rifts have led to separations. Through all this I have observed a phenomenon which is typically present in our Christian family history—one which we all too often refuse to admit.

THE PATTERN IN THE SPLIT

What seems to happen before divisions occur is a serious, unresolved relationship struggle, which often takes place between key leaders. The pain of the struggle is so great that it is never properly resolved—hence reconciliation and healing remain elusive. Soon the issues, which often weren't insurmountable at first, become the ammunition everyone fires at each other. People then begin to develop theological and philosophical platforms, which they mount first for protection and then for war. All too soon, the relationship struggle—which led to the conflict—falls to the wayside, and the issues—which were generally smoke screens—come to the front. Loyal followers of each of the warring leaders embrace the cause, so the war escalates. Lying under a crusade often cloaked in "righteousness" or "right doctrine" is a deep, untreated wound, which becomes infected and poisons many well-intentioned warriors.

I propose that the major splits the Christian church has suffered follow just such a pattern. I am not downplaying the genuine and important issues related to any or all of the splits. But in relationship to maintaining our unity and love as members of the Family of families, these issues pale in significance. We must maintain a focus on our family relationship. After all, it is the heart-throb of Jesus for us all.

In my own short experience of building community, I have seen some of the wounds of divorce fester, but I have also seen many more heal. Tragically, however, the experience of the broader Christian church is quite different. Catholics and Protestants oppose one another in Mexico, Northern Ireland, Latin America, and many other places throughout the world—and the devil laughs. After all, he too knows that "a kingdom divided against itself cannot stand," and he wants the church to collapse in relational rubble. We have cooperated with him well. The deep injuries of divorce have been faithfully passed on from generation to generation. Our challenge is to stop the chain of pain by healing the relational wounds festering below the surface.

As we stand at the end of one century and the threshhold of another, I propose that the opportunity for such a healing has perhaps never been greater. The whole Christian church—Protestant, Catholic, and Orthodox—is in need of reevangelization, renewal, and reformation. The world literally awaits the gospel message. Can we rise to the challenge? Can we cooperate with one another, standing together as a unified beacon of light penetrating the dark with the good news about Christ, our common Savior and Lord? Can we begin to reexamine our long-held prejudices and rediscover our common family heritage? Can we break the insidious cycle of move, countermove, pain, and mistrust? A dying world is waiting for our answer. What will we tell it?

TRIUMPHALISM: AN UNACCEPTABLE ANSWER

As is often true for the children of a domestic divorce, the choosing of sides in the division of the church too frequently entails an imputation of righteousness for "us" and unrighteousness for "them." We are all too good at self-justification. "Look at what you did. I didn't deserve that. Besides, think about all I've done for you, and you still mistreat me and refuse to thank me." Perspectives and attitudes like these plague a family suffering divorce, including our church family. Many Protestants see the Catholic Church as enamored with itself, seeing itself as the "only church" and having little room for adjustment. Many Catholics have felt the same way about Protestant churches. Consequently, Catholics and Protestants often see themselves as the sole possessors of truth. They look upon each other condescendingly, refuse to move toward each other in dialogue but try to evangelize one another, assuming that the "other side" has embraced a false gospel and needs to be set straight. This is triumphalism, and it knows no denominational or ecclesiastical boundaries. Anytime a Christian church sees itself as the only one containing all the truth and looks condescendingly on other members of the Christian family as false or severely errant brethren, it skirts dangerously close to triumphalism, if not adopting it. When such divisive attitudes and approaches express themselves in evangelistic and missionary endeavors, they are particularly harmful and ugly. Consider Nicaragua, for example.

Nicaragua

Sometime ago, my wife Laurine phoned me at my office with wonderful news. Our friend and former next-door neighbor heard from her husband that the long reign of Sandinista Communism had come to an end in Nicaragua. Her husband, Humberto Belli, is the head of our sociology department at Franciscan University and a former Sandinista himself. He experienced a marvelous conversion, returned to the Catholic Church, and has become a tremendous voice for both political freedom and the gospel of Jesus Christ. Just last month he returned to his homeland to serve the country as its Vice Minister of Education. This miracle occurred, according to Humberto, as a direct result of God's mercy and Christians' prayers.

Author of *Breaking Faith: The Betrayal of the Sandinista Revolution*, Humberto has long maintained that the atheistic Marxism of the Sandinistas betrayed the early revolution. This particular day he called his wife Rosario from Nicaragua and told her that crowds were dancing in the streets with joy. Together Humberto and Rosario praised the Lord for another example of God's power and deliverance in response to His people's prayers. That anticipated election would open one more ripe opportunity for the gospel to take an even deeper root in this nation so long plagued with oppression. Also, it was seen as one more event in an accelerating sequence of world events, which only a few years ago would have seemed more fantasy than fact.

At a local prayer meeting sponsored by the Servants of Christ the King, the Catholic lay community I serve, Humberto shared his experiences as an election observer for a human rights group in Nicaragua. He told us that the Marxists were extremely confident before the election. They had distributed one million toys to children; organized rock and salsa band concerts; distributed free T-shirts and banners; virtually controlled media advertising; and lowered the voting age to sixteen on the assumption that they were popular with teenagers. What could go wrong? Almost all of the press, staying in the same hotel as Humberto, were confident—some delighted—in the coming "Sandinista victory," wearing the T-shirts and celebrating before the results came in.

But two events led Humberto to anticipate an unexpected upset. First, on a country road he picked up a teenager who had walked two days through the hills to vote in a central voting place, fearful that the lines and the pressure at his hometown would preclude him from "voting for freedom." Second, the bus driver assigned to transport the observers chose to risk two to four months' salary to go home and vote.

When the election results started being tallied, Humberto began to smile. Others in the main ballroom of the hotel showed shock, some anger, and some disappointment. Humberto said, *"Viva Christo Rey"*—Long live Christ the King. God had responded. The people had voted. The Sandinistan reign was over.

Humberto maintains that the prayers of the faithful brought about this "miracle," especially since almost six hundred thousand Nicaraguan exiles were not allowed to vote. Catholics and other Christians had flooded Nicaraguan churches for a three-day prayer vigil prior to election. The City of God community, a Catholic charismatic covenant community in Nicaragua, had fasted and prayed for months. In fact, evangelical Catholics within the country had held on and preserved the gospel in Nicaragua as they had done along with Orthodox Christians in Eastern Europe.

When I first met Humberto about six years ago, he was speaking to a group of leaders from predominantly Catholic communities throughout the world which had developed out of the Catholic Charismatic Renewal, an evangelical movement. The evening after he spoke, we received news that his coffin was being carried through Managua, signifying that he was an enemy of the state. Thank God it was empty!

Living next door to him for four years in Steubenville, Ohio, showed me that his evangelical Catholic Christian faith affected his whole life—the way he loved his wife, raised his children, and treated his neighbors. He's a hero. And there are countless thousands more like him in Nicaragua. They never left the country during the long reign of Sandinistan Marxism.

On the morning after the election victory, Cardinal Obando celebrated a Liturgy of Thanksgiving. Humberto said he cried through it, realizing that we serve a "God of Miracles."

Another heroic evangelical Catholic in Nicaragua is Charlie Montica. He leads the lay Catholic community called the City of God, which has planted similar communities throughout the countryside of Nicaragua. They have worked with the Cursillo movement and Charismatic Renewal. They have interceded, prayed, fasted, and literally risked their lives for the gospel for over a decade. The prayers of this community and others like it, under the brave leadership of Cardinal Obando and many other Christian leaders, have hastened the end of state-sponsored atheism in Nicaragua. Certainly the prayers of Western Christians have helped, but they were not the sole cause of such incredible changes in Nicaragua. The church was alive and well in that country before Western believers even knew through the media that it was a communist stronghold. How presumptuous for anyone to think that simply because the Nicaraguan church was primarily Catholic that it could not have had any impact on the reinstatement of freedom there.

We will have little, if any, influence on Nicaragua or Eastern Europe or any other mission field if we go in with a false paternalism. We need to enter other countries ready to serve the saints and heroes of the faith who already live and serve there, who have emerged through their particular trials by fire, no matter what part of the family they belong to—Protestant, Orthodox, or Catholic. Triumphalism will only impede our common goal of proclaiming the basic *kerygma*—the goods news of a God who so loved the world that He gave His only Son to free us all.

In fact, wouldn't it be ironic if Eastern European or African or South American Christians ended up reevangelizing the West? Many believers in other countries are beginning to view the West as a mission field. Perhaps they're right.

A missionary strategy we would be wise to adopt would begin with recognizing what is already happening in Nicaragua or Poland and supporting it—in Nicaragua to support the Humberto Bellis and the thousands of other evangelical Catholics who have held on through intense oppression and who already serve in the churches and the communities, in the Cursillo movement and Charismatic Renewal—in Russia to support the faithful believers in the Orthodox churches of the East who have endured persecution after persecution.

Consider also Lithuania.

Lithuania

Catholics such as Father Sigitas Tamkevicius and Sister Nijoie Sadunaite have persevered in the faith through the Soviet occupation of Lithuania. On May 6, 1963, Father Tamkevicius was arrested and banished to a labor camp. Among the charges brought against him were delivering anti-Soviet sermons, catechizing children, providing assistance to political prisoners and their families, organizing a Christmas party for parish youth, and organizing an All Souls Day procession to a cemetery. During his labor camp term, Tamkevicius was twice offered release if he would sign a confession of guilt. He refused both times. Eventually, however, his sentence was reduced, and he was transferred to exile in Siberias Tomskaya Oblast in May of 1988, where he remained until his release in 1990. He now serves as the spiritual director of the larger of two Lithuanian seminaries training leaders for the church of the twenty-first century.

Sister Nijoie (or Sister Terese, as she is known in her community, the Sister Servants of Mary) secretly professed religious life in Poland because all Catholic religious orders were banned by Soviet law. In her memoirs *How I Became a Target of the KGB*, she recounts her arrest by the KGB in 1974. She served three years at hard labor in Mordovia and three years of internal exile, but none of it took the angelic smile off her face or the gleam of God's love from her radiant eyes. She now frequently speaks internationally of the power of prayer and God's faithfulness.

Recently, I had the privilege of spending the afternoon with

Father Tamkevicius and Sister Sadunaite. They sat in front of me and, through an interpreter, shared their love for Christ and their need for prayer. It was a deeply moving evangelical moment for me.

There are so many more heroes like them. Yet too often Christians gear their most prominent evangelistic efforts toward other Christians. To presume that these other children of the great divorce aren't Christians and to impose an Americanized Protestant evangelical Christianity, with its attendant culture, on them is terribly judgmental and narrow-minded. We should be, instead, going to serve them with a basin, towel, and washcloth, recognizing what the Spirit of God is already doing in all Christian churches in Latin America and Eastern Europe and throughout the world.

THE ISSUES THAT REALLY MATTER

In a very short time, we have witnessed the fall of a primary symbol of totalitarianism—the wall in Berlin. From that wall a shout and cry for freedom are leading to a radical restructuring of the whole Eastern Europe. The yoke of atheistic Communism seems to be falling from the necks of oppressed people elsewhere as well. For all of this we should rejoice. Yet we must not deceive ourselves into assuming that our Western values will be a sufficient replacement for Communism. In *Against the Night,* Chuck Colson provides a prophetic picture of the West's decline. He suggests that the basic moorings of the freedom enjoyed for so long by the West and envied by others have been uprooted. There is a crisis in the West! And it is impacting every level and facet of our culture.

That crisis, like the political shifts in Nicaragua and Eastern Europe, can be turned around, but not by the rival efforts of Christian splinter groups. We must face the crisis together, confronting it on the basis of a common evangelical agenda—an agenda that acknowledges the existence of evangelical Christians in all Christian communions and recognizes our common apostolic heritage. Advocates of such an agenda must be characterized by mutual respect and a compelling desire to see Jesus Christ loved and honored.

What message will believers in Jesus Christ bring to the millions of ears straining to hear the call to freedom? Will we focus our proclamation on the only true path to freedom, Jesus Christ? Or will we offer in place of the dialectical materialism behind much of today's human misery the negative values of a radical Western consumerism? Or will we communicate an arrogant triumphalism that will make the world look for love and salvation elsewhere? The answers to these questions rest squarely with the response of the whole Christian people—Protestant, Catholic, and Orthodox. As we prepare to move into the next millennium, will we do it together, recognizing that what we have in common far exceeds what separates us? Or will we allow our internal divisions to hold us back from fulfilling our heritage?

These are the real challenges of the hour and the fundamental questions of this book. But facing and answering them are not easy; overcoming the devastation of divorce never is. We will make mistakes. I and those I have worked with have made many errors in our ecumenical efforts, some of which I will share in the next chapter. Nevertheless, we can't bring about change if we don't make any moves. Learning comes by doing. We can learn how to work together if we try doing it, but if we don't try we'll never learn, and if we don't learn, the world may never know as it could who Jesus is and why He came to die. Jesus said as much centuries ago:

> "My prayer is not for them alone. I pray also for those who will believe in me through their message, that all of them may be one, Father, just as you are in me and I am in you. May they also be in us so that the world may believe that you have sent me. I have given them the glory that you gave me, that they may be one as we are one: I in them and you in me. May they be brought to complete unity to let the world know that you sent me and have loved them even as you have loved me." (John 17:20–23, NIV)

Can we overcome the prejudice and bitterness and misunderstandings that divide us? Yes, we can. With God, all things are possible, and we know that unity is God's will for His family. The question is not, Can we? The real question is, Will we? That must be answered by each of us. What is your answer?

PART IV

Restoring Our Evangelical Family

CHAPTER 10

Humpty Dumpty Solutions

"All the king's horses and all the king's men couldn't put Humpty together again."

—*Mother Goose*

Since the 1960s, efforts at ecumenism have flowered and waned, surfaced and floundered, been hailed as revival and condemned as the work of Satan. We Christians who have sought to understand and restore the relationship of the whole family have sometimes mistaken false ecumenism for the true ecumenism God wills for us. False ecumenism is often well-intended but is misguided in its efforts to build unity on the "least common denominator." It seeks an artificial unity, denying the differences among denominations in favor of a fleeting and deceptive togetherness built only on what we hold in common. Of course, I have argued that we do have much in common. But when we build on that and deny or ignore our differences, we build on quicksand and even risk becoming dishonest with one another.

Differences between us do exist, but they are differences, not insurmountable barriers. We must always carefully present our positions clearly without watering down what we believe. As a Catholic Christian, I embrace the warning of the Second Vatican Council document on ecumenism: "Nothing is so foreign to the spirit of ecumenism as a false irenicism which harms the purity of Catholic doctrine and obscures its genuine and certain meaning."[1]

I know for some of my readers that the word *ecumenical* conjures up fear, and much of that has come of least-common-denominator attempts at ecumenism. But as a lawyer, I have a great love for words. We cannot discard them when they are misused, and we will make a serious mistake if we abandon this one in particular. We can redeem it if we do it through our witness of life. An analysis of some experiences of my own membership in an ecumenical work called the Sword of the Spirit may help in examining the differences between false and true ecumenism.

THE SWORD OF THE SPIRIT

In November 1982, I stood in the third go-round of one evangelical effort at community building in an assembly of leaders of an international alliance of communities which would come to be known as the Sword of the Spirit. Along with all those gathered, I was overwhelmed by their shared vision of a unified international Christian community, giving flesh to Jesus' prayer of unity for His church. The excitement in the air was electric. We had all gathered for what we believed was to be an historic event. Most of us had been touched by the Charismatic Renewal, an evangelical movement within mainline Christian churches and beyond. Most of those who have been touched by the grace of this renewal have testified to encountering Jesus Christ and the power of the Holy Spirit in a new and fresh way. Could we have been chosen to establish an international Christian community? Oh, I knew we were but a drop in the bucket in a small part of the Lord's wonderful worldwide work, but I was proud to be a part of this drop. I knew I would always cherish this experience, but I did not know how much pain the ensuing years would bring. Fortunately, they also brought some wisdom.

The evening was celebrated in two parts. The first part, which years later I came to recognize as the more important, involved the Word of God Community itself, an ecumenical Christian community in Washtenaw County, Michigan. It was (and still is) comprised of mainstream Protestant believers—Reformed, Lutheran, and Free Church—along with Roman Catholics. Each of those four groupings has developed, with approval from their church bodies, a fellowship related to its ecclesial body in a clearly defined structure. The community itself embraces all four. The first part of the ceremony involved the four fellowships of the Word of God Community coming together to sign a "compact," agreeing to work with one another in mutual evangelistic enterprises and to share as much of a common life as possible. They desired to stand prophetically for the Christian unity for which they all longed. The second part of the ceremony involved Word of God representatives and all of us leaders of other covenant communities. We had come together to form what we thought could become an international ecumenical Christian community with a common mission and Christian culture.

For years we have tried to make that dream a reality. We have had some success but also many failures. Still, the dream endures. I cherish my association with the Sword of the Spirit, but the years have brought repeated readjustments. They have also brought purification, spiritual warfare, attack, repentance, and humility. My Sword-of-the-Spirit experience has paralleled what the Christian life is supposed to be all about—growth and purification leading to holiness. And part of that process has been the realization that we, like so many others, tried to put Humpty Dumpty back together again. I am proud of our successes, and I am learning to cherish even our failures, for through them we have grown even more.

We have dealt with issues that won't go away when Christians from various traditions seek to work together. They involve the major schools of theological debate: ecclesiology (the nature of the church); soteriology (the nature of salvation); anthropology (the nature of man); and missiology (the nature of the church's mission). They also involve various understandings of eschatology (the study of the last things, including the Second Coming); the effect of the Incarnation; worldview; the nature of grace; and so much more. These are not easy subjects, but we have faced them with varying degrees of success and failure. In our zeal for unity, we used to say that the worst we would say of one another is, "That's an understandable mistake that a good Christian could make." Well, I still think that expression of tolerance is better than contemporary Christian examples of intolerance, but it has often missed the mark.

In our common desire to proclaim the good news, we had come together from various groups over the last decade. Each of our groups desired to build community. We hungered for what we saw as the New Testament model of church life: believers coming together in committed dynamic relationships with the missionary purpose to bring the world to Christ. We wanted more than a prayer meeting. We wanted a radically committed Christian life. We wanted to be disciples. And through the grace of the Holy Spirit, we had come to believe that our unity together as Christians was a top priority. We came from different Christian churches and traditions. But burning in our hearts as a fruit of this encounter with the Holy Spirit was a hunger for the restoration of the whole family—a hunger, we believed, was also in the heart of God. I believe that's true, but I have seen how all too often our efforts at unity fall prey to human strategizing and a minimalist approach to our individual church memberships, doctrinal convictions, and cultural expressions. What is most important is to recognize that churches, traditions, and denominations are not problems but vehicles for building a mature Christian unity. It is disingenuous to pretend that there aren't any differences between us. That kind of Humpty Dumpty solution will produce, at best, a fragile egg, subject to falling off the wall as soon as the wind picks up even slightly.

THE CHARISMATIC RENEWAL MOVEMENT

The Sword of the Spirit is not the only group that has fallen prey to some Humpty Dumpty strategizing. It seems to be endemic to much of the Charismatic Renewal from which the Sword of the Spirit was birthed. How well I remember the early Charismatic Renewal conferences, standing in an assembly of thousands singing "They Will Know We Are Christians By Our Love." How genuine and sincere we were. We still must be, but during those days we often talked as if there weren't any differences between us. This denial led us to develop a dangerous theology of the Holy Spirit. We were setting our spiritual renewal over our places in the Body of Christ. For example, I heard Catholics who had encountered a new conversion experience, which they often referred to as the "baptism in the Spirit," saying they had much more in common with Protestant Christians than they did with members of their own parishes. They meant well. They certainly did have much in common because they followed the same Spirit and the same Lord. But they ad differences as well, differences that cannot be ignored without trivializing our convictions. One of these important differences involves various understanding of the sacraments. To name one, we don't partake of a common loaf and a common cup. Even our understandings of the place and role of the Eucharist, or the Lord's Supper, are different and that difference in doctrine necessitates a difference in practice.

As a Catholic Christian, I believe the Eucharist is the sacrament of unity. And because the church is divided, I embrace my church's position that I cannot participate in the Eucharist with Christians of other traditions. We are not one. We must long to be one, and it should grieve our hearts that we cannot go to a common table. Our hunger for unity should lead us to impassioned prayer and aggressive relationship building. But we cannot pretend there aren't differences in our understandings of the Eucharist, or the Lord's Supper. There are differences, and they are real and important.

COMMUNITY BUILDING IN STEUBENVILLE

As I detailed in Chapter 4, my experience on the campus of Franciscan University of Steubenville has been nothing short of miraculous. God has done a tremendous work there, and all of us on that campus are deeply grateful for that. But it would be dishonest to claim that mistakes were never made or that our best intentions were always fulfilled. We enjoyed many successes, but they have been mixed vigorously with numerous struggles and failures, including the areas of ecumenical efforts of community building.

In 1969 Father David Tickerhoof, a Franciscan and close associate of Father Michael Scanlan, came back from Ann Arbor, Michigan, where he had visited the Word of God Community and had experienced the baptism in the Holy Spirit. He returned with a new desire to bring people together in a genuine Christian community experience.

In 1975 I joined the momentum he had begun when I transferred to the then College of Steubenville. My love for the Lord had compelled me to a deep love for His people. I wanted Jesus and I wanted His people. A group of us, most of us fresh from the college campus, gathered under the leadership of Father Michael Scanlan, Father David Tickerhoof, Tom Kneier, and others. We had experienced a marvelous prayer meeting in the college chapel. As the prayer meeting grew, it also took on an outreach of evangelism. We called ourselves, then, the Community of God's Love. Members of that community came together and made a unqualified commitment to follow the Lord together and to do His work in the Ohio Valley. We all wanted to build and live in a Christian community centered on mission. Since we didn't really know where to begin, we sought help. A sister community, the Word of God, had preceded us in this effort in Ann Arbor, Michigan. Under the leadership of Ralph Martin and Steve Clark, this early community, made up of mostly graduates of the University of Michigan, had begun to live the vision of Christian community of which the Community of God's Love only dreamed. In the early days of the Charismatic Renewal, the Word of God's literature became our bread and butter. We also regularly listened to their tapes on "Christian Personal Relationships," "The Fruit of the Spirit," "Living in Christian Community," and many others. Because of such contacts with the Word of God community, we were able to build an early foundation for our newly formed community. Hungering for much more, however, we approached the Word of God for assistance in community building, and they graciously responded. For several years they worked with us, raising up leadership, teaching us how to come together in small home groups, enabling us to apply the sacred Scriptures to our daily lives in practical, gutsy ways. Our affection and bond with the Word of God community grew.

Over time, we also found ourselves working with several other groups. Our first effort at community building internationally involved other inspiring groups of Christians such as the People of Praise in South Bend, Indiana. Under the leadership of Kevin Ranaghan, Paul Decelles, and later, Bill Beatty, they had formed a work similar to ours with a marvelous outreach. Through various stages we struggled to bring numerous such works together. In its first incarnation, our effort was called The Association of Communities. Unfortunately, although many of the groups were ecumenical, we underestimated how deep the wounds of division in the Christian churches really were and how difficult ecumenical efforts are. We also underestimated the reality of what Scripture calls "the flesh" in personal relationships. Maybe in our naivete we felt leaders involved in a prophetic work were somehow exempt from the flesh's ugly impact. We readily learned that they were not and neither were we. But that didn't stop us. We kept trying.

The next incarnation of our effort was smaller, but it, too, failed and left more hurt and wounded people in its wake. We witnessed a break in personal relationships among leaders, a difference in vision, and an inability to move ahead together. Many of us intuitively knew there was unresolved conflict, but like the secrets of divided and dysfunctional families, it wasn't talked about. The People of Praise, other communities, and associations of communities continued their missionary efforts but did so separately. We grieved over this, but not enough. The hurt lasted for years.

Our community at Steubenville continued on with the Word of God and other groups in what came to be known as The Federation of Communities. But eventually it too met with an unhappy demise. There was continual tension between the efforts to develop a common culture and central government; the existence of our distinct cultures, which were rooted in our different church traditions; and attempts to exercise primary ecclesial oversight in our individual and corporate lives. These attempts to strategize and put Humpty Dumpty together again didn't produce the kind of unity for which we all longed. So further divisions came about, and with them more pain and even more divisions.

Our next effort came to be known as the Sword of the Spirit. We wouldn't give up our dream of a truly ecumenical global missionary effort. Nothing was wrong with our dream, but I now believe we tried to achieve it with mixed motives. Primarily, we were seeking to follow God's heart for unity among His people, but I think our strategizing was running ahead of the Spirit. We also didn't understand at the time how deep our naivete and ignorance really were.

EFFORT IS NOT ENOUGH

Naivete and ignorance often impede efforts to achieve true unity, and they frequently contribute to false ecumenism. This was highlighted for me in an unforgettable experience I had at a conference on prophecy in Mobile, Alabama. The conferees were predominantly evangelical Protestant believers, and some of the speakers were from a certain wing of the Charismatic Renewal movement within Protestantism. As one of a handful of Catholics present, I immensely enjoyed the conference.

On the Saturday evening of the conference, a man whom I deeply admire took the podium to speak about the dangers of extra-biblical revelation. In the course of his highly charged presentation, he began speaking about cults. In one sentence he lumped together Jehovah's Witnesses, Mormons, Christian Scientists, and Roman Catholics. He went on to refer to Roman Catholicism as a cult filled with false extra-biblical revelation. Needless to say, I was distressed. To lump an ancient Christian church with religious groups that are clearly not Christian was, at best, extremely insensitive, and at worst, defamatory.

For the next hour I sat in my chair and listened, seeking the Lord as to how I should respond. Out of the corner of my eye, I saw a brother in the Sword of the Spirit, Ken Wilson. Ken pastors a Free Church fellowship in Ann Arbor, Michigan. He is a man I also deeply admire. Ken came across the room, embraced me, and said, "Keith, I'm sorry that happened. In fact, I want to speak to that man. I'm offended by what he said. It can't go without being addressed. I'd like your permission to speak to him and to the leader of the conference." I gave Ken my permission, and he acted.

The next morning an apology was made from the podium. I am sure it was uncomfortable, but it underscored for me the courage of the sponsoring organization, the importance of my relationship with Ken Wilson, and the basic goodness of the efforts we made in the Sword-of-the-Spirit work.

I am deeply indebted to the evangelical and pentecostal Protestant traditions. It was through evangelical Protestants preaching the gospel in Jerusalem, Israel, that my Jewish friend gave his life to Yeshua, the Messiah, and then led me back to the faith of my childhood. It was through the courage of pentecostals like Charles Parham in Topeka, Kansas, the prevailing prayer warriors of Azusa Street, and people like David Wilkerson that the experience referred to as the baptism of the Holy Spirit touched the lives of Catholic students at Duquesne University in the 1960s and finally reached me. Yet over the years my distress and frustration have continued whenever I encounter believers who have no room for me in the construct of their faith and worldview. It happens all too often.

In my work on "Purpose For Living," a national Catholic radio ministry I hosted for two years, I received a large volume of mail from Christians of other traditions. Frequently I would hear, "When are you going to come out from among her?" Too often I received anti-Catholic literature. Too often I found a lack of historic understanding that the Catholic Church is indeed a Christian church and, at least in my opinion, the Mother church. Tragically, much misunderstanding and fear are promoted by both Catholics and Protestants. We could do a far better job carrying out our common mission if we could at least accept one another, if not embrace one another, as true believers in the faith. But ignorance keeps getting in the way.

Many misunderstandings are founded on misconceptions about piety and practice. I often find in my ecumenical work, for instance, that many Christians outside of the Catholic church believe that Catholics worship Mary. This does not have to be a major bone of contention. Even a cursory exploration of solid Catholic Marian theology points to the inaccuracy of this position. The Catholic Church has long held that Mary should be honored for her special place in the life of Jesus and in all of our lives. Yet she is not to be worshiped or adored, only honored. Now, unfortunately, some piety practiced by Catholics is hard for many of those in other traditions to understand, and in all honesty, there have been abuses within Catholicism, but misinformation about this, and many other Catholic practices, has unnecessarily damaged relationships between Catholic and Protestant churches.

The strategy of our common enemy has always been to divide the kingdom. Jesus Himself reminds us that a kingdom divided against itself will not stand. Too many of the divisions among Christians are self-imposed. They spring from ignorance, long-held prejudice, and a lack of charity. And although many communities that have grown out of different renewal movements are seeking to live out a grass roots ecumenical commitment, they are doing so naively and on a faulty base of a least-common-denominator approach pushed more by human strategizing than prayer and piety. Humpty Dumpty solutions will not endure. Strategy alone will not bring the church back together. Only God can accomplish that. Ecumenical efforts based on ignorance and human strategy alone serve only to build a subtle layer of false ecumenism that does nothing to heal the wounds of the great divorce. The defensiveness and anger between us have not yet been worked out. We have so much to do for God's people and so little time in which to do it, but, sadly, we expend as much—if not more—time and energy on fighting a war among ourselves than we do spending it fighting the real enemy and our common foe, Satan. More than ever, Christian churches are tearing down instead of building one another up as we are instructed to do: "He Himself [Jesus] gave some to be apostles, some prophets, some evangelists, and some pastors and teachers . . . for the edifying of the body of Christ, till we all come to the unity of the faith and knowledge of the Son of God . . ." (Eph. 4:11–13, NKJV). This is particularly true on television and radio programs, where the slander seems to be a way of life (or should I say, death?).

As Christians, we are responsible to the Lord for what we say about our brothers and sisters. He will hold us accountable. Fear of this, however, should not be our primary motivator for striving for unity. Rather, our foundational reason should be a spiritual love for other Christians as children of God. When you tear someone down, you are really saying that you do not see Christ in them and that you don't love them. More division within the Body is caused by Christians seeking faults in their brothers and sisters instead of encouraging one another on to holiness.

My very good friend, Tom Kneier leads the Servants of Christ the King, the Christian community to which I belong in Steubenville, Ohio. We've walked together in the Lord for a long time. In our early years, we had many disagreements and frequently found ourselves almost grudgingly cooperating in ministry. One day it dawned on both of us that we were experiencing one another as adversaries in our disagreements when we needed to become advocates for one another. This fundamentally changed the way we worked and walked together. After all, we discovered the Holy Spirit is an *advocate*. He convicts us to lead us to repentance and change, and protects us against Satan, whom Scripture describes as our adversary. It is the devil who condemns us to lead us to despair, not the Lord.

Maybe the children of the divorce really need to begin by becoming one another's advocates in prayer, in life, in ministry. We need to reject the temptation to be adversaries and the lie that we are no longer family. We *are* family. We have the same Head, the same Savior, the same Elder Brother, and the same Bridegroom— He who is at the heart of our evangelical fervor, Jesus Christ.

GOD'S WILL FOR HIS CHURCH FAMILY

For too long we have failed to see one another as members of the Family of families. The mistake has been made on all sides. In the documents of the Second Vatican Council and subsequent documents, Roman Catholic leaders have acknowledged our participation in the rifts, and John Paul II has sought to move boulders out of the middle of the road so Christians could once again experience the full unity for which we were intended. Similarly, recent historic meetings between Billy Graham, other evangelical church leaders, and John Paul II signal a growing recognition of the missionary challenge of our times. However, I must admit that my heart grieves at how much work is yet to be done and how little impact such leaders' actions seems to have had at the grass roots level. We—you and I—can come together and paint a new scenario.

Picture with me, if you will, a time when we would once again speak of the church in Chicago and include (just as it did in the apostolic days when one referred to the church at Thessalonica) all those with a common bond in Christ Jesus. For some of you, even imagining such a scene immediately musters up fears of a false church. Though I understand some of the historical factors leading to your fear and the theological suspicions behind it, I believe it is the most dangerous impediment to a true, common evangelical agenda for the twenty-first century. It is simply one more straw man keeping us apart, keeping us divorced and dangerously divided. Certainly a false church could emerge in the future, but it doesn't appear to be confined to one ecclesiastical body. After all, there's enough apostasy to go around.

Our common enemy, Satan, is subtle and dangerous. He wants us divorced. He knows that as long as we're separated, our effectiveness as witnesses for Christ suffers. Should we let him have his way? Must we continue to fall prey to Satan's efforts to keep us divided? Or will we learn from the last five hundred years of Christianity that splintering leads to further splintering, and splintering leads to lost spirituality, lost evangelism, and lost souls? It is time to acknowledge that our divisions, wrought often by genuine and important theological issues, have largely hindered us and our mission. In fact, they have done more to serve Satan than they have to serve Christ. The Lord's prayer for unity must be answered: "May they be brought to complete unity to let the world know that you sent me" (John 17:23, NIV). Achieving unity will not be easy—it will be painful. Satan will fight us every step of the way. But we must not let that deter us.

I can tell you that I sometimes grow weary of the struggle. It seems I am constantly having to win the trust of evangelical Protestant brethren. First of all, many must be convinced that I am truly saved or born again. When I pass that test, I have only entered the door for polite discussion. Sometimes I'm greeted by a condescending arrogance accompanied by scrutiny or, worse, a "come outism" that has little respect or tolerance for varying opinions or doctrinal convictions. I am a Roman Catholic, not by accident or mistake but by heartfelt conviction.

I will never forget my first visit to the National Religious Broadcasters Convention in Washington, D.C. I had only recently undertaken a radio program for Franciscan University called "Purpose For Living." I had a room in the large hotel that housed the convention. Though I wasn't sure what I was to do there, I thoroughly enjoyed my first day attending seminars and hearing wonderful evangelical leaders proclaim the gospel. I went to sleep that evening with a joy in my heart, a joy that for me always accompanies true ecumenical work.

The next morning I woke and found several brochures that had been slipped under my door during the night. Now, this hotel housed thousands of people. I am sure I was one of perhaps a handful of Catholics present at this convention. I still don't know how I was "discovered," but there under my door were virulent, false, and angry anti-Catholic tracts. My heart broke. In my morning prayer I asked the Lord, "How long, oh God, how long will it continue? How long will the enemy wreak havoc within the household of the faith?" Then and there I reaffirmed a decision I had made years ago: as long as it depends on me, the enemy will be stopped at every juncture with truth; he will no longer be allowed to undermine the power of the proclamation of the gospel and the unity of Christians, at least in my presence.

Perhaps many of you have had similar experiences. And maybe in your case, Catholics or Orthodox were the instigators of hurt and misunderstanding. Inasmuch as I share in any fault for any such treatment, I repent. But where do we head from here?

Ecumenical efforts are messy, frustrating, risky, and wonderful. For me to be Catholic is to be ecumenical. In fact, to be Christian is to be ecumenical. Since that's true, what next? How do we begin to heal the wounds created by the great divorce?

First, we must acknowledge that it was never the Lord's intention for His people to be divided. The divorce was our fault, not His.

Second, we must understand that God is the One who will bring the church back together again. We can only cooperate with Him. And when we do cooperate, imagine the evangelistic efforts, the works of mercy, the worship we could have as a single body.

Third, we must realize that the greatest impediments to true Christian evangelism are usually Christians.

Fourth, we need to move ahead in prayer and divine power to restore the Family. This will involve a commitment to *true* ecumenism, a subject so vital that the rest of this book is dedicated to explaining and illustrating it.

CHAPTER 11

Genuine Ecumenism: The Road Back Home

Even though the Sword of the Spirit did not achieve its dream in 1982, and, in fact, still struggles to move forward, the grass roots unity, rediscovery of our common heritage, and dogged commitment to solid ecumenical endeavors still endures. So do our deep friendships and our communities. But our structures, our primary relationship to our churches, and our clear understanding of our traditions have deepened and changed. For many of us, our growth in the Spirit has led us back into the heart of our various traditions and church communions with a desire to reevangelize them. Rather than ecumenism diluting our fundamental faith convictions, it has helped us appreciate and identify with them even more. As a result, we have found much that we had failed to see and value in our earlier years. For example, my hope for at least the last two years has been that the Sword of the Spirit would evolve into an alliance of Christians fully rooted within their respective church traditions and communions while together moving out in action-oriented ecumenical efforts. Although this was not my original goal for the community, it represents a perspective gradually shaped by my own thinking about ecumenism and my own experience in ecumenical movements.

My analysis relates to my personal involvement in the Sword of the Spirit. Some of my brothers in the work whom I deeply cherish would probably disagree with my assessment. I love them and respect them, but our very disagreement is one of the reasons why I think the Sword of the Spirit effort is important and prophetic. It is producing dialogue, growth, common missionary efforts, and genuine Christian relationships among separated brethren. It is discovering genuine ecumenism.

170

An ecumenism that recognized the whole family as family will promote its growth, respect family differences, and seek to heal the wounds of the divorce by bringing family members together for common efforts. While it falls short of the hoped-for reunion at the family table, it can certainly kick the devil in the teeth and challenge his territory.

Pastor Richard John Neuhaus, an outstanding Lutheran scholar and leader, recently addressed our theology students at Franciscan University with a call to an unrelenting pursuit of genuine ecumenism and a warning against the false Humpty Dumpty solutions discussed in Chapter 10. He told us to avoid a

> kind of pseudo-ecumenism that was not premised upon the Spirit-given imperative in the divine gift of unity that is prior to our efforts to actualize that unity, but premised rather upon a kind of superfical 'let's all be nice to one another and pretend that our deepest differences make no difference.' That is pseudo-ecumenism. It has a terribly well-intended but terribly superficial understanding of Christian unity.
>
> Reconfessionalized ecumenism is the ecumenism in which we each go deeper into the various traditions of theology, piety, liturgy, Christian experience, and encounter one another precisely with our differences unfurled—if you wish. Because the only way you can, in your Christian life and your community and its communal life, enrich other persons and other communities is to be bringing your differences. If we say from the beginning that we are all alike, if we don't have much to give to each other, if you're just like I am, I already 'got by definition everything you got,' then I don't need you that much. It is in your difference and I in mine, and our communities and theirs that we engage in genuine ecumenism.[1]

I recently had two experiences that gave me great hope that genuine ecumenism is cracking the wall of hostility between Christians. The first one involved a telephone conversation I had with a major evangelical Protestant leader whom I deeply respect. His relationship with Catholics has already cost him popularity among some of his constituents, so I will not mention his name here. He said, "Keith, the leaders of your church are shaming us all in the evangelical Protestant world with their courage in the fight for life.

They have become our conscience. Thank God for great church-men like Cardinal O'Connor." I accepted this back-door compli-ment because I knew it knocked a chip in the wall. That's how it began in Berlin, and before long they were tearing down whole seg-ments of the wall that had divided them.

The second incident happened during a meeting I recently attended of the American Congress of Christian Citizens, an ecu-menical group that Pat Robertson founded to oppose the rising ride of anti-Christian bigotry in the media. In our meeting room were major evangelical leaders I've admired for years—Dr. Charles Stan-ley, Dr. Jerry Falwell, Dr. D. James Kennedy, Pat Robertson, and many others. I found not only a tremendous openness to my pres-ence, but also a growing respect for my church and a thawing in what had been hard ice in the past. Perhaps the comments by Dr. Falwell were most illustrative. With a sincerity born of battle fa-tigue, he told the whole group not even to consider trying to affect public policy with only a narrow evangelical Protestant church coa-lition. He said that from its inception any such effort must include Catholics and consultation with great churchmen such as Cardinal Law and Cardinal O'Connor. Clearly not backing off one bit from his self-described "narrowness of doctrine," Dr. Falwell showed a refreshing openness.

Bringing the good news to the darkness of our time will be difficult, but none of us has to do it alone. The West can be won to Christ, but it will not be reevangelized by one church. The task is too great and the enemy too strong. The reevangelization of the West will require an ecumenical missiology that builds on the foun-dational methodological approach so well enunciated by Paul him-self:

> To the Jews I became like a Jew to win over the Jews; to those
> under the law I became like one under the law—though I
> myself am not under the law—to win over those under the
> law. To those outside the law I became like one outside the
> law—though I am not outside God's law but within the law
> of Christ—to win over those outside the law. To the weak, I
> became weak to win over the weak. I have become all things
> to all, to save at least some. (1 Cor. 9:20–22)

How can we work together to carry out the evangelistic task? By building on true ecumenism.

PRINCIPLES OF TRUE ECUMENISM

The word *ecumenical* means "general or universal—of the Christian church as a whole; or furthering religious unity especially among the Christians."[2] Authentic ecumenism seeks unity in the Body of Christ, striving for all Christians to become part of the restored universal church. It strives for unity in the scope of the whole truth. Persons involved in ecumenical dialogue should seek and be open to the full revelation of truth. But contrary to popular belief, ecumenism is not another label for compromise. Rather, true ecumenism is rooted in:

- Acknowledgement of the whole family and our membership in it;
- An ability to grieve over our family's separation and long for its full unity;
- A recognition of the challenge we face in the contemporary mission field;
- A willingness to embrace our own traditions with confidence and humility;
- The humility to learn from one another and allow one another to operate freely in our respective parts of the family;
- The desire to work together for the sake of the gospel.

Firm adherence to these ideas will allow Catholic believers to rejoice at the sight of a thriving Romanian Baptist church and permit Protestant believers to rejoice at the swelling crowds present in a Polish cathedral. Why? Because they are meeting our common Father, being saved through the merits of our common Savior, and being led by the same Spirit. But we need to be flexible about culture and respectful of disagreements within the family.

Far too often the ingredient most lacking in our missionary efforts is humility. Paul reminds the Philippians, "Your attitude should be the same as that of Christ Jesus: Who . . . made himself nothing . . . [and] humbled himself" (Phil. 2:5–8, NIV). We need to empty ourselves of pride. Recently pastor John Wimber pierced my heart with a statement. He told a capacity crowd of leaders, "The Lord is looking for a generation of faceless leaders." I believe He is. The Lord is seeking men and women who care more about

Jesus Christ being exalted than they do about their own names or versions of family living.

Tom and Marie Pucci are good friends of mine and benefactors of Franciscan University. They have successfully raised a wonderful family and are enjoying their "children's children" (Ps. 128:6). They have a lot of wisdom about in-law relationships and explained to me that their wisdom was born of their first feeling like *out*-laws. When their sons and daughters married, the Puccis had to develop a whole holiday pattern which acknowledged that to marry a spouse is to marry a family, allowing time and space for that family's traditions. They became flexible enough about long-held family traditions to hold the family—the whole family—together. Their wisdom recurred to me when I read an intriguing report in *Christianity Today* (Feb. 5, 1990) on English evangelicalism. The headline read, "Roman Catholics No Longer Outlaws." Well, at least it is a step in the right direction—maybe not that far away from being rediscovered as *in*-laws, as part of the Family of families by our Protestant brethren.

In many regions of the world, Christians are fighting one another, particularly in those areas that are ripe for cooperative evangelism. These Christians might benefit from the Puccis' recognition that to move their whole family into the future they would have to exercise some flexibility. Global evangelistic efforts will only be successful if our warring against one another is replaced with a willingness to negotiate both our space and our togetherness. The time has come for Christian people to respond to the growing momentum of and urgency for an authentic ecumenical effort.

I hope that we will move toward a missiology that seeks to find where the family is and strengthen it. Where Catholic, Orthodox, or Protestant churches are alive and thriving, we can strengthen them with the message of evangelical faith in Jesus Christ as personal Savior and Lord without prejudice toward or intolerance of their respective traditions.

Let me repeat once again: I am not calling for a least-common-denominator ecumenism. I've experienced that and it doesn't work. I believe in what the Catholic Church teaches (though I must admit it isn't perfectly lived). I welcome inquiries from Christians of other churches about my convictions. But non-Catholic Christian churches are not my primary mission field. As long as many people have never heard the gospel and many in my own church have allowed it to fall on rocky ground, my work is there.

So, where do we begin? At the beginning. One person, one relationship at a time. If each of us examined how the great divorce has affected our opinions of one another and resolved to rediscover one another's gifts, we would make much progress. If we could admit that we are family, separated brethren, we could begin rediscovering our common history and mission.

In the case of the Sword of the Spirit, the least-common-denominator approach of our early days has evolved into a mutuality of respect toward our differences. Even as I write this chapter, the leaders of the Sword of the Spirit are meeting in a formal assembly to discuss adjustments in structure, leadership, mission, and, most importantly, relationships. I don't know what the result will be. I do believe, however, that the years of effort are bearing new fruit. Yes, we've made mistakes, but risks are a part of all advancement in Christian work. I am proud to have stood and to continue to stand with brothers like Steve Clark, Ralph Martin, Bruce Yocum, Paco Gavrillides, Randy Cirner, and so many others in this work.

I can't lay out a blueprint or a manual for common evangelical efforts. Even if I could, it would be presumptuous because I don't have the jurisdiction to speak to all the churches, nor do I have the ability or understanding to design a global missionary strategy. I can only suggest some things I've experienced that might help. Of the principles I try to adhere to in ecumenical activity, I list the following as a general and central guide:

1. *Ecumenical efforts are part of God's plan for this generation.* They can and must stand as a prophetic call and resource for Christian unity. But ecumenical groups must respect individual church memberships and conviction above the ecumenical purpose. Ecumenical communities cannot replace church; they should be supplementary. If membership in an ecumenical group becomes primary, that group takes on the indicia of church and ultimately promotes indifference toward church affiliation. In so doing, it makes major mistakes pastorally, spiritually, juridically, and historically. Enough of these mistakes have been made already.

2. *Long-term evangelization must be seen as a process.* It is

never finished. Consequently, though there is room for cooperation between Protestants and Catholics in personal evangelism, long-term evangelization should be pursued according to individual church conviction and tradition. It must of necessity be directed to church life and have as its primary goal the full embrace of the Christian life in a church communion. Ecumenical communities should not be the object of evangelization, but rather a vehicle to promote deeper church life in their respective church bodies.

3. *Efforts at building ecumenical groups and communities should not avoid but rather openly acknowledge distinctives in church tradition and practice.* Primary pastoral care for members of ecumenical groups should come from members of their own church. There must also be genuine respect and submission to appropriate church authorities.

4. *Though ecumenical groups and communities can develop elements of a common Christian culture, the individual's church culture must be primary.* Children who are Catholic and members of Catholic families participating in ecumenical activities should know their Catholic identity, tradition, and culture, and should be able to live them out. Children of a family in a Reformed tradition should be able to do likewise, and so on across the confessional spectrum.

5. *When church groups and communities participate as a whole in ecumenical activities, their primary commitment and allegiance must be to their church in substance, not just form.* Although we embrace a common creed on the faith's essentials (see Chapter 1), we have differing beliefs about other important beliefs and practices. A genuine ecumenical effort will allow, even encourage, its participants to embrace fully the doctrinal, ecclesiastical, and liturgical convictions of their distinctive traditions. Indeed, it's these differences that can help us all come to a fuller understanding of the whole counsel of God. We misuse our differences, however, when we raise them as divisive barriers rather than sharing them with one another in honest, humble dialogue. We have much to learn from each other, but we won't learn anything if we cover up our differences or ignore them or refuse to listen to each other.

If we adhere to these principles, I believe we will find that the whole church is like a very large, multi-faceted jewel. We may not see the beauty of it all at once, but if we're honest, flexible, and humble, we will see her more as God does: the precious Bride of the

Lamb who was slain, resurrected, and exalted for the sake of the world. With this in mind, let's take a closer look at the many facets of genuine ecumenism.

INFORMED ECUMENISM

Much of the counseling and support philosophy that accompanies recovery for those affected by dysfunctional families applies to the children of the great divorce as well. These groups are refreshingly honest, as we must be. In time, they come to understand that the greatest antidote to fear is faith; to confusion, understanding; and to suspicion, trust. As Christians—Orthodox, Catholic, or Protestant—we must make it our business to learn about our whole family history and heritage. There is a distinct difference between informed disagreement and uninformed quarreling.

It is startling how little Christians know about one another's beliefs, culture, and practice. How much of our antagonism and distrust is built on misinformation that we pass along generationally. Careful study of all Christian traditions is important. How can we agree or disagree with anyone whose beliefs we don't know? Each person has arrived at his relationship with God for a reason, and only through sensitive discussion can we understand his or her reasoning. Then, and only then, may we be able to offer a portion of the truth to them that may still elude their grasp.

My friend Alan Schreck of our theology department at Franciscan University provides solid, clear teaching about Catholic Christianity. The Lord has raised up other men and women in other Christian traditions who are doing the same thing from other Christian perspectives. In his marvelous book, *Catholic and Christian: An Explanation of Commonly Misunderstood Catholic Beliefs and Practices*, Alan explains Catholic doctrine in a fresh and readable way. I highly recommend this book to my Christian friends of other traditions, not as a polemic but as a bridge toward understanding Catholicism.

In addition to studying carefully other traditions, all ecumenical dialogue calls for a keen understanding of one's personal faith. If you have trouble understanding your beliefs, you will obviously have difficulty explaining them to others. We need to become educated and firm in our positions, but also prayerfully open to the truth. The truth will always prevail if the channels are open. We can't have a dialogue if we already think we know all the truth before we begin discussion. Dialogue is the interchange of ideas, not two sides talking at each other.

One-to-one exchange among friends and neighbors is critical to unity. Ecumenism builds and grows on the ground level, among the people. Not just theologians, clergy, and scholars, but all Christians are responsible for seeking unity within the Body.

> The concern for restoring unity involves the whole church, faithful and clergy alike. It extends to everyone, according to the talent of each, whether it be exercised in daily Christian living or in theological and historical studies. This concern itself already reveals to some extent the bond of brotherhood existing among all Christians. It leads toward full and perfect unity, in accordance with what God and His kindness wills.[3]

Much contemporary missiology is built on the concept of *contextualization,* which simply recognizes the reality of culture and seeks to insert the gospel into it without diluting the gospel message or violating cultural distinctives. While it's true some efforts in adaptation have gone awry, the concept of contextualization is as ancient as Paul's missionary strategy (1 Cor. 9:19–23) and the conclusion reached by the first Council of Jerusalem (Acts 15). I propose we adopt it as we learn more about one another.

I am a Catholic Christian, and as such I have embraced a culture, a context for living out my faith. This church culture has much in common with other Christian cultures, but it also has its own signs, symbols, language, heritage, and tradition. I find it rich and fulfilling. You may be a Reformed Christian or an Anabaptist. No matter. Whatever your church culture, it has elements in it that are common with others, and other elements that are distinctively its own.

If you consider yourself "nondenominational," I believe you apply a term to yourself that is a misnomer. Belonging to Christ has immediate corporate connections. You can't have the head without the body, and you can't live a bodiless, disjointed Christianity. You live within a church cultural framework, knowingly or not.

It's time we learned one another's church cultures and discovered the richness of our whole family. We have much to learn from one another and a whole lot of lost ground to reclaim.

LOVING AND TRUSTING ECUMENISM

All ecumenical efforts must be rooted in sincere love that seeks only the best for another. We want to strive for unity, not simply for the sake of togetherness, but because unity in the truth is the call of every Christian: ". . . endeavoring to keep the unity of the Spirit in the bond of peace" (Eph. 4:3, NKJV). Our bond as children of God should move us to find the shared tenets of our faith and love each other in them. For instance, as Christians we embrace a common belief that the Father sent Jesus Christ who died for us as the Savior of the world. Christians also agree that the Word of God was inspired by Him; that Jesus will one day return; that the Holy Spirit makes possible godly living; that the virtues of faith, hope, and love are foundational to the Christian life. We can love one another as fellow believers in these shared truths.

Humble charity must be the impetus behind all ecumenical activity. Our goal is not to get everyone to be like me or you, but to move everyone into the fullness of truth, the deepest possible relationship with the Lord. Arrogance and pride in a particular tradition don't belong in a loving exchange among Christians. Ecumenism cannot be approached with the attitude of "I have the truth and you don't, so listen to me." That attitude has already failed miserably for hundreds of years.

Yet I as a Catholic Christian do believe that I am following the Lord's plan for me and for His church. I am more deeply and freely Catholic today than I was five years ago. I am also more ecumenical. These realities are not contradictory but complementary. I cannot be fully Catholic without being committed to ecumenism. I think the same relationship exists between any evangelical tradition and genuine ecumenism. One Protestant friend who shares this belief is Harald Bredesen.

Harald Bredesen, whom I believe is one of the greatest apostles of the Spirit and unity today, is deeply and proudly pentecostal. He acts out of his Lutheran convictions with a wonderful grasp of grace, but he couples this with a free-wheeling, refreshing approach to following the Holy Spirit. In each of these areas, we express ourselves quite differently, and yet despite our cultural and theological differences, we work together because we both see the urgency of the times and know that only the gospel of Jesus Christ can save.

In 1989 Franciscan University conferred an honorary doctorate upon Harald for his apostolic endeavors toward true unity. He attended the Baccalaureate Liturgy at which our local bishop presided. For me it was an experience of "the best of the old and the best of the new," as Jesus says in Matthew 13:52. The liturgy was filled with spontaneous worship expressed at appropriate moments; the spiritual gifts came alive but with a solemnity and deep reverence appropriate to just such a liturgy. Because it was a special event, we also used sacramentals, such as incense, and we blended traditional church hymns with newer musical expressions of praise and worship that have grown up on our campus. In the middle of it all, Harald turned to me and said, "Brother, this is the kind of worship that is fitting and proper for a holy God. We led you Catholics into a deeper experience of the Holy Spirit; now you need to lead us into a deeper encounter with worship." This is a genuinely ecumenical attitude.

EVANGELISTIC ECUMENISM

Before any substantial global unity in the family can occur, it needs to be a burden on the hearts of the people. We have seen this issue grow, particularly in the Catholic church since the Second Vatican Council. The issue of unity cannot be properly addressed, however, until we all begin living our faith first. When we fail to witness the truth with our lives, we rob our brothers and sisters of tangible access to it. The fathers of the Second Vatican Council told Catholics, "their primary duty is to make a careful and honest appraisal of whatever needs to be renewed and done in the Catholic household itself, in order that its life may bear witness more clearly and faithfully to the teachings and institutions which have been handed down from Christ through the apostles."[4] There can be no ecumenism without interior conversion. We need to see the Spirit as our guide and let Him take control of our lives. True spiritual ecumenism is allowing the Holy Spirit to animate our thoughts and actions, but that will not happen apart from a personal salvific encounter with Jesus Christ.

All Christians, Catholic or Protestant or Orthodox, need to rediscover individually the basic *kerygma*, the good news. We need to insure—not simply presume—that those who occupy our churches have met Jesus Christ personally. For some of us that will mean reaffirming our baptism as children; for others of us it will involve a first-time encounter; for all of us, however, it must involve a deep, abiding encounter, not simply with doctrine (though I believe doctrine is critically important) but with a person, Jesus Christ. The source of the Christian faith is not doctrine, sacraments, church government, or missionary efforts. The source of the Christian faith is the Person of Jesus Christ. As a Catholic I deeply believe that these many elements are important, but we all have, to some degree, fallen prey to the greatest sin of presumption the world has ever seen: We presume people have met the Lord Jesus Christ personally because they've been "through the system." That is simply and dangerously a false presumption. We can have sacramentalized but unevangelized Catholics. We can also have unevangelized Baptists, no matter how many times they have responded to altar calls. We must seek to evangelize and reevangelize those in our assemblies. If we refuse or fail, we will abort our mission to the whole world.

Moreover, we dare not assume or teach that once we have met Christ personally, that is enough. It isn't. Coming to know Christ personally has a beginning but no end. Our initial act of faith begins an enduring relationship. We must meet Him over and over and over again, deepening our ties to Him, seeking to serve Him more faithfully and fully.

When I was a boy, I looked forward to Easter morning. Though we were very poor, my father made sure we experienced the lavishness of love when we celebrated Christmas and Easter. On Easter morning we always woke up to a packed Easter basket and a chocolate bunny. We certainly knew that Easter was not about bunnies, but I sure looked forward to eating that delicious rabbit. Every Easter morning I scurried down the stairs eager to find out just how big my bunny would be. Of course, size wasn't the only issue. I also wanted to know if the bunny was solid or hollow. You really can't tell by looking at an Easter bunny whether it's solid or hollow, but I sure could tell when I bit into it.

Christians are like candy bunnies. They may appear similar on the outside, but on the inside they are either hollow or solid. I have met many hollow Christians, and their presence spans all ecclesiastical boundaries. I'm not saying that they don't look like Christians; I'm not even presuming that I can usually tell whether they are empty inside or not. I am saying, however, that the solid core—a vibrant personal relationship with Jesus Christ—has too often been lacking in Christians. They may have at one time given themselves to the Savior, but they have not continued to pursue a relationship with Him.

We must rediscover and proclaim the full gospel in all of our church traditions and within our own jurisdictions. And that full gospel includes an ongoing, personal, ever-deepening relationship with the Lord of our salvation. This message is the essence of revival.

Earlier I shared with you about my experience at Franciscan University, a Catholic school in the midst of a classical revival, but there are many other examples of revival throughout the churches in these days. Nevertheless, the job is far from over. I'm speaking not about a revival as simply a planned event (though it may include some planning), but about revival as a move of God and precipitated by His people's falling to their knees in repentance. It is a move of God furthered by the holiness and conversion demonstrated by His church. How much we need a lifestyle of revival, individually and corporately. We need to recognize that these times demand holy living and sacrifice, a truly radical Christianity.

Radical is one more word that needs redemption; we have lost sight of its etymology. It simply means a return to the root. We must return to the root of evangelism, the cross of Jesus Christ. There is no room for false ecumenism here. Without the cross of Jesus Christ, there is no salvation, there is no hope, there is no historic Christianity.

Two years ago I received a phone call from a man in Moundsville, West Virginia. He listened to our radio program "Purpose for Living" regularly and wanted to discuss it. He was a member of the Hare Krishna temple outside of Moundsville. I said to him, "I find it interesting that you, a Hindu, are listening to a

Catholic layman share the gospel." He told me that several members of his religious community were listening. Well, my evangelical blood began running faster. Here was an occasion to share the gospel. And so I did. I began a telephone relationship with this man that still continues. Although he has not yet indicated that he has accepted Jesus, our conversations have been stimulating and challenging. At one point he said, "I believe in Jesus. After all, isn't the teaching of Jesus really important, what He said and did? Why all this talk about His death?" Well, therein lies the real issue. I said to him, "Duane, without the cross of Jesus Christ, there is no Christianity. Unlike every other religion that sees man attempting to climb the mountain of salvation on his own, in Christianity God came among us in the Person of Jesus Christ and climbed that mountain for us. The mountain was Calvary. There He died for you and me. Unlike the teaching of your religion which indicates that you are bound by the *karma* of sin, Christianity proclaims that you have been set free if you will embrace the sacrifice for sin, the life of the incarnate Son of God on the cross of Calvary. There God's justice and mercy met. The cross is the bridge to heaven, the way out for you."

I pray fervently that this man finds freedom in Jesus Christ, for a Christianity without the cross will not save. Indeed, no religion without the cross will bring life instead of death. The cross is the only bridge to God, reconciliation, and life everlasting.

Furthermore, through Christ's resurrection, we can be raised to a new life and be born anew into a family in which Jesus Christ is the first-born Son. That family, of course, is the church. That church will one day reign with Him in a new heaven and a new earth. This is the good news entrusted to us, and we are called to bring it to the nations. This is the evangelical agenda we hold in common. But will we rise to the occasion and link arms for the charge?

I believe there are practical ways we can express this kind of true, grassroots ecumenism. One way is through common evangelical efforts. It is important that I explain what I mean here. As a Catholic I understand evangelization to be a process involving both the proclamation of the faith and the eventual implantation of believers into the church. It is not my intention, at this point, to explain more fully the Catholic concept of conversion as a continual process that necessarily takes place within the church. Suffice it to say that the kind of evangelical cooperative effort I am speaking of involves the first phase of this understanding, namely, the proclamation of the gospel message.

In his recent apostolic exhortation to the lay faithful, John Paul II said something rather astounding:

> Whole countries and nations where religion and the Christian life were formerly flourishing and capable of fostering a viable and working community of faith are not put to a hard test and in some cases are even undergoing a radical transformation as a result of a constant spreading of an indifference to religion, of secularism and atheism. This particularly concerns countries and nations of the so-called First World, in which economical well-being and consumerism, even if coexistent with a tragic situation of poverty and misery, inspires and sustains a life lived "as if God did not exist." This indifference to religion and the practice of religion devoid of true meaning in the face of life's very serious problems is not less worrying and upsetting when compared with declared atheism. Sometimes the Christian faith as well, while maintaining some of the externals of its tradition and rituals, tends to be separated from those moments of human existence which have the most significance, such as birth, suffering and death.[5]

The task facing believers as we approach the threshold of the twenty-first century is not only bringing those who do not yet know Christ to faith in Him, but reevangelizing the Christian church itself.

We have learned much about how to do this from Dr. Bill Bright, Dr. D. James Kennedy, and Dr. Billy Graham, but the work must continue until every Christian sees himself or herself as a missionary. I have all too often experienced the shock of others toward my own personal efforts at evangelism. They don't expect a Roman Catholic Christian to share the faith. Thankfully, those days of surprise are coming to an end. The task of personal evangelism is being carried out by more and more Catholics. And so it should be. According to the Scriptures, it is the task of all Christians.

The nineties and indeed the next millennium present us with evangelical opportunities unlike any we have seen in our lifetime. These opportunities call for ecumenical action—not like the ecumenism of the sixties, seventies, or eighties, which was often characterized by only dialogue (which can be helpful); nor will it be a false ecumenism that pretends nothing separates us. But it will grow out of a conviction that our common bond in Christ mandates evangelical cooperation.

MORAL ECUMENISM

Our world is slowly deteriorating into a new pagan society. It needs people to fight the onslaught of darkness. In *The Wasteland*, T. S. Eliot described the spiritual aridity and desolation of the 1920s' society of wasted souls. Eliot's frighteningly bleak but realistic portrait of sexual license, manipulation, idolatry, escape, occultism, numbed consciences, broken marriages, and fragmented lives was also a rather prophetic vision. If the world was a "wasteland" in 1923 when he wrote his book, what is it now? Some seventy years later we have fulfilled Eliot's worst-case scenario in our mechanized, man-centered society. Later, after converting to the Christian faith, Eliot asserted that "the choice for the future was between the Christian culture and the acceptance of a pagan one."[6] What have we chosen?

The darkness is hungry. Not satiated by the secular world, it has begun to consume even the church. Chuck Colson cites an example of an Episcopalian bishop who not only condones but "celebrate[s] and welcome[s] the presence of our gay and lesbian fellow human beings." This bishop calls on the church to express its "willingness and eager desire to bless and affirm the love that binds two persons of the same gender into a life-giving relationship of mutual commitment."[7] These are the words of an Episcopalian bishop—a leader of the church leading the faithful down dangerous paths.

The Christian church has long affirmed Saint Paul's admonition: "Do not be deceived: neither fornicators nor idolaters nor adulterers nor boy prostitutes nor practicing homosexuals . . . will inherit God's kingdom" (1 Cor. 6:9–10). If we believe the Word of God is the same yesterday, today, and forever, we believe that active homosexual practice is sin. It is not to be tolerated, much less celebrated. Long-standing church teachings on temptation and sexual orientation give hope to those who struggle with sexual confusion.

But condoning objectively sinful lifestyles doesn't help at all, nor does it bring good news of liberation from deviant and compulsive behavior. Of course, not only active homosexual practice but also all kinds of sexual promiscuity, drug and alcohol abuse, abortion, birth control, and euthanasia are presented as amoral issues today. This bishop certainly has society's support.

We cannot continue accepting or tolerating amoral or immoral positions on issues that radically affect the moral face of our world and the lives of so many. Jesus was never morally neutral. In fact, He directed several warnings to the middle-of-the-road, fence-sitting, lukewarm believers of the first century. The Lord's stern warning to the church in Laodicea should be echoed today: "I know your works; I know that you are neither cold nor hot. I wish you were either cold or hot. So, because you are lukewarm, neither hot nor cold, I will spit you out of my mouth" (Rev. 3:15–16).

All of this is not meant to project a hopeless worldview. Nor is it meant to be wrongly critical. Rather, it's important that we understand the reality of what is happening to our world and within our church. Foundations are crumbling and desperately need to be rebuilt. The sense of urgency is gripping. Thanks be to God, we can do all things through Christ who is our strength (Phil. 4:13), but we need to pull together in Christ if we are gong to enter the battle full force. At the moment, the forces of evil seem to have the upper hand, but we have the advantage of appealing to the human heart, the heart that by grace is created for light and truth. "Today the Christian people—and all people—are searching with a lamp for persons who radiate something of the light, something of nearness to the source."[8]

Christians unite! Let us become an eternal flame obliterating the power of darkness in our world. We can rebuild the Body by working hand in hand. Some of us are doing it. Many more must. The world is waiting—and it's growing darker every day we wait.

SACRIFICIAL ECUMENISM

In World War II, the Allies were comprised of very different troops. The French did not pretend to be English; nor did the English pretend to be American. But they stood together in the trenches fighting the same impending darkness. They recognized that the world of their time was being swept up in a movement, an ideology, which was attempting to unleash its fury and its lies throughout the world. We confront that kind of hungry darkness in these days. We stand in the midst of what Chuck Colson has called a "new dark age." But Christians have been through dark ages before. Indeed, God gave us the light of Christ so we would reflect and magnify His brilliance and thereby dispel the darkness. We need not fear the dark. We need to confront it with the light of the gospel. But it is an urgent time, and the challenge requires true ecumenical activity. Our lights alone may not withstand it, but our lights together will push back the night.

Perhaps the area of ecumenical action that holds the most promise is our common fight for life. How society treats unborn children, the elderly, and the infirmed is a barometer of its heart. The heart of America has waxed cold. Sometime ago, my good friend Father Michael Scanlan accompanied our local bishop, Albert Ottenweller, to Youngstown, Ohio, to provide pastoral oversight to a group of pro-life demonstrators. The demonstration led to the arrest of many, including Father Mike and Bishop Albert. They all later came to be known as "the Youngstown 47."

I assumed that Father Mike and Bishop Albert would be released immediately. After all, the authorities could not think of holding two prominent churchmen in jail, could they? One day turned into two and then three. I couldn't sit still any longer. When Nick Healy, the vice president of university relations, returned from vacation to take on the administrative tasks at the University, I was then free to do what I felt compelled to do as a friend and lawyer. I had to help get Father Mike, the Bishop, and the students out of jail. It was an experience I will never forget.

At every step of the effort I had to fight the obvious spiritual forces at work. By God's grace, the efforts of some excellent Youngstown attorneys such as David Betras and Tom Charles, and the intercessory prayers of God's people, the Youngstown 47 were finally released. But their release was not as incredible or inspiring as their imprisonment.

The Youngstown 47 were housed in an armory. They were a group of believers from different Christian churches, but they were united as one in the valiant effort to protect the unborn, and they deeply respected each other. Not to be defeated by their situation, they turned their time in jail into a retreat. They arose early each morning for personal, private prayer. They then prayed for hours together in intercession and praise. For the Catholics a Eucharistic liturgy was celebrated every day. For the Christians of other traditions other services were held. Informal classes on different aspects of Christian living were set up. One of our theology professors at Franciscan University, Dr. Mark Miravalle, even taught an optional class on aspects of Catholic life and practice and the teachings of John Paul II. Interestingly, many evangelical Protestants chose to attend that class. The group also gathered for meager meals, which they turned into agape celebrations. The bond these believers developed and strengthened during their jail stay has not weakened. Just recently the Youngstown 47 held a joyful, worshipful reunion.

For me these Christians underscored what I have heard so many times from persecuted Christians, including my Nicaraguan friend Humberto Belli: When the battle heats up, Christians discover their true priorities and their spiritual unity; they find their common roots and stand together as the Allies did in World War II.

Since my Youngstown experience, I believe more strongly than ever that the pro-life movement is a model for action-oriented, sacrificial ecumenism on all fronts. It is the primary issue of our day, the litmus test of our moral and spiritual convictions. How we respond to this test will determine much in the next millennium. We simply cannot compromise on this one. Our view of life reveals our worldview. Remember, the Son of God occupied the womb of a holy woman, and the Father kept Him safe from infanticide (Matt. 1–2). The unbroken teaching of all the Christian churches for almost two thousand years is clear. Contemporary attempts to justify the killing of children in the womb simply must not receive any credence from any evangelical Christian. The attack on unborn children is an attack on family, on life, and on the nature of God and the truth of the gospel. Life is precious from conception to natural death and beyond. To embrace anything less is heresy. If we cannot join forces on this issue, on what can we?

RETURNING HOME

It is still the burden of God's heart and the commission of the whole Christian people to go into all the world and proclaim the good news. In order to respond today, we must now, in our own way, through our relationship with one another, fulfill the great prophecy of Isaiah and "beat our swords into plowshares and our spears into pruning hooks" (Isa. 2:4). "The harvest indeed is plentiful and the laborers are very few" (Luke 10:2). We have a common mission, and we are part of the same family. We are allies in a cause far more important than any mankind has ever fought for. But we must join forces on a genuinely ecumenical basis—one that is informed, loving and trusting, evangelistic, moral, and sacrificial.

What would such an ecumenical effort look like? In the next chapter, we'll examine several groups and individuals which display many, if not all, of the characteristics of genuine ecumenism. They are traveling the road back home, and by following their lead, we can return home as well.

CHAPTER 12

Family Examples of Ecumenism at Work

One of the wonderful privileges of my position as dean of evangelism at Franciscan University of Steubenville is my opportunity to work with so many different believers. I can find myself one month with the Apostolate for Family Consecration, a conservative Catholic group located in Kenosha, Wisconsin, committed to the restoration of Christian family life. I am inspired by their love for the Lord, their love for the church, and their deep piety. The next month I may find myself engaged in a wonderful dialogue with Chuck Colson, a prophet for our times. I still remember with joy my opportunity to address Prison Fellowship's morning devotions. There I stood, a lay Catholic, in the midst of a group of Protestant brethren engaged in a beautiful evangelical work of mercy and true Christian social action. I shared our common gospel and read an excerpt from Bernard of Clairvaux, a member of our common family heritage.

Not too long thereafter I found myself in the midst of a meeting of the American Congress of Christian Citizens, an assembly of like-minded Christians who are coming together to confront what we all believe is an anti-Christian bigotry in the media. I sat in the ballroom of the Mayflower Hotel with Jerry Falwell, James Kennedy, Pat Robertson, Charles Stanley, and representatives of major evangelical groups. Overjoyed with their warmth and their great respect for Catholic churchmen like pro-life warriors Cardinal O'Connor and Cardinal Law, I sensed a new openness and a thaw in what had seemed like a glacier.

I am free to move in all these circles because of the increasing realization that we are being led by the same Holy Spirit, we serve the same Savior, and ultimately we will occupy the same

Kingdom together. This is no dreamy, wild-eyed ecumenism. I know full well that our bedrock differences in doctrine and practice are serious and must be discussed and worked through. That process is under way. But the missionary challenge of the twenty-first century compels us to come to the foot of the cross together. In plain terms, we need each other but we need each other saved before we can offer salvation to others. Let me explain.

Almost every major Christian leader is proclaiming a challenge not only to evangelize the nations but to reevangelize the churches. Shortly after I read Pope John Paul II's marvelous book *An Apostolic Exhortation to the Lay Faithful,* I read a wonderful article by Dr. Bill Bright of Campus Crusade for Christ.[1] Both writers used a word that I have heard repeatedly since then. The word is *reevangelize.* They pointed out the serious missionary challenge we face within all Christian churches. No church body is immune from the secularization of our age. We have seen the effects of a dilution and, in some instances, a tremendous pollution of Christian proclamation and practice. Unfortunately, we are often too quick to see it in other people's churches and less able to acknowledge it in our own. It's reminiscent of the log-and-splinter problem discussed by Jesus (Matt. 7:3-4).

Earlier I shared the experience of my time in Bible college. It was there that I rediscovered my convictions as a Catholic Christian and had them rekindled by the evangelical influence around me. It was also there, during a fervent prayer time, that I read the call of Isaiah. The prophet heard the Spirit of God say, "'Whom shall I send? Who will go for Me?'" And he responded, "'Here I am Lord, send me'" (Isa. 6:8). I knew then that I was called to share the gospel as a Catholic and that my predominant mission field would be the Catholic Church in the area of reevangelization.

It is important in these times that we develop an ecumenical approach that enables Catholics to reevangelize Catholics, reformed Christians to reevangelize reformed Christians, and so on. We then must recognize the need to develop an agenda for cooperative Christian action for those who do not yet know Jesus Christ. God's plan is and will always be salvation. He has given us one another to work through our salvation with each other, to build upon one another, and to build each other up so we can reach out to others. But what have we done instead? We have torn each other down. We need to help one another and to help all of those who don't even know the Lord. But we can't bring others to the Lord when we can't even live in the Lord together, when we slander each other from our pulpits, when we fail to work together, when we indulge in subtle undertones of bigotry and prejudice. If we are to be true Christians and faithful to our mission, we need to come together.

This is a tall order given the huge gaps to be bridged, but ecumenical efforts are our only way to fill the order. So we need models of groups and individuals who have shared the burden of rebuilding and renewing the Body of Christ. Fortunately, we have many, and more are coming. Some I will mention here. But these models are not perfect. On the other hand, they have all tried, made mistakes, reevaluated, and modified their plans of action to meet the needs of Christ's Body. Therefore, we have good reason to admire, imitate, and be inspired by their example. After all, even in their mistakes and through many persecutions, these are the courageous few who have made an inner decision that ecumenism is not an option but a gospel mandate.

THE PERSONAL DIMENSION

Two movements within the Catholic Church have dramatically affected thousands of people. The focus of both movements is personal evangelism. They have enabled thousands of people to come into a deeper relationship with Jesus Christ. In some instances they have helped people find Him for the first time; in many more they have awakened a dormant walk; at times they have even positively impacted other parts of the family for Christ. The movements are the Cursillo movement and the Catholic Charismatic Renewal movement.

CURSILLO

Cursillo originated in Spain in 1949. Gerry Hughes, executive director of the National Cursillo Center, defines Cursillo as "a movement of the church with its own method that makes it possible to live what is fundamental for being a Christian in order to create small groups of Christians who would evangelize their environment with the gospel and help structure Christianity."[2] The idea of small groups comes from the Spanish word *cursillo,* which means little or short course. The actual full title of the movement, *Los Cursillos de Christianded,* means "the little course in living Christianity."

Cursillo is best known for its special ministry weekends, a community experience in which the participants live and work together—listening to talks, discussing them, and making practical applications. In a Catholic Cursillo they also celebrate the Eucharistic liturgy. In all Cursillos they hold group prayer together, which is an essential part of the experience. But one of the most interesting and sustaining things about Cursillo is the follow-up program: in small weekly reunions, participants share experiences and insights from their prayer lives, studies, and outreaches.

The long-range goal of the movement is that Christ become the preeminent influence in society. The primary objective is two-fold: (1) to develop in its members a consciousness of their power and mission to become leaders in the work of Christian renewal, and (2) to sustain them as they provide a Christian witness to the world. Gerry Hughes states:

> We challenge men and women to really do what they are supposed to do as Christians and help them to discover that. . . . We tell people, "If you want to live your Christianity in the world, find a group of friends, meet with them regularly, share your Christianity with them, your living union with the Lord, how you are reforming your mentality to be more in line with the gospel, and what you are doing to build the kingdom in your family, your neighborhood, your place of work, or wherever."

Cursillo has certainly affected many families, neighborhoods, work places, and indeed churches. It has even affected my family. My wife Laurine can attribute her own personal conversion to Jesus Christ to the Cursillo movement. When she went on a Cursillo weekend in the diocese of Peoria, Illinois, she was not a believer but more of an agnostic. She was definitely not a Catholic. In fact, she had been raised in a home that was, at least, cold toward Catholics, if not directly anti-Catholic. The experience of that weekend confirmed a process within her that began through the witness of a friend named Marge Helgoth. Marge had a deep and personal relationship with Jesus Christ. She was also Catholic. Her witness affected Laurine as did the witness of a customer in Marge's beauty business. Fortunately, a wonderful priest in the Peoria diocese responded to Laurine in her point of need. On that Cursillo weekend, Laurine came face to face with Jesus Christ. It was an evangelical moment that led to a vibrant relationship that has endured. Shortly thereafter, Laurine sought admission to the Catholic Church. Within six months from that we met, and the rest is a wonderful history.

Laurine's father, Mac, was also changed through a Cursillo weekend. Years after Laurine's initial confession of faith, Mac, too, encountered the saving power of Jesus Christ in a new way. He attended a Cursillo weekend sponsored by The Upper Room, a Methodist outreach. There he got in touch with the One who has been his constant companion ever since.

Cursillo has opened the door for great renewal in our time due to its direct and indirect influence on all the subsequent renewal movements.

THE CATHOLIC CHARISMATIC RENEWAL

The Catholic expression of the Charismatic Renewal began at Duquesne University in 1967 during a retreat weekend for students and faculty. As the weekend progressed, many knew they were being confronted with what it would mean to surrender fully to the Lord. Patty Mansfield, then a student, says, "Jesus was asking us to let Him reign, not simply to acknowledge Him as an important person, but to allow Him into the very center of our lives."[2] That statement may seem quite ordinary today, but in 1967 it was fresh and radical. Think of it! "Jesus was asking us to let Him reign . . . to allow Him into the very center of our lives." Think about what that meant at the beginning, before it was common to say that "Jesus is Lord." The Holy Spirit was working mightily. While these Christian men and women had loved the Lord, prayed, and desired to serve Him, they realized in retrospect that loving Him and being fully surrendered to Him were two different things. And they realized that prayer under our willpower and with the best of intentions was still vastly different from prayer in the conscious, experienced power of the Holy Spirit.

The Charismatic Renewal has spread like fire and had a global impact on Catholics. The experience referred to in the Charismatic Renewal movement as baptism in the Spirit is a deeper conversion and encounter with God—it is an evangelical moment. Catholics are in a sense "Johnny come latelies" to this experience. In fact, the experience was brought through the generosity and affection of Protestant brethren. Great men and women of God who suffered persecution as the result of their walk in the Spirit were not afraid to bring the treasure they had unearthed to these Catholic students at Duquesne. We are so thankful for individuals such as David DuPlessis and Harald Bredesen who understood that the work of the Holy Spirit is for the whole Christian family, not just Protestants.

Both of these movements focus on a particular dimension of evangelical Christianity—encountering Jesus Christ personally. Their effect has been like a pebble thrown into the middle of a still pond. Ripples have gone out and affected the whole Christian family for the Savior.

COMMUNITY LIFE

Another vital part of a truly evangelical Christian life is the rediscovery that to belong to Christ is to belong to His people.

The impact of the Cursillo movement and the Charismatic Renewal only deepened the hunger of many Catholics and Christians of other traditions to respond to the call of community. Many groups seeking closer relationships with the Lord and His people have joined together. One expression of such community life is what has been called covenant communities. The name derives from the fact that the members of these groups have made an agreement with the Lord and one another to be committed to a way of living—a way of living which so often provides a tremendous model of the evangelical counsels and a truly evangelical lifestyle. Among these groups are People of Praise, the International Brotherhood of Communities, Christ the King Association, Catholic Fraternity, the communities associated with FIRE (a Catholic alliance of Faith, Intercession, Repentance, and Evangelism), and the Mother of

God community. These communities traverse the globe. Efforts at connecting them have produced mixed results. However, their existence and impact is a breath of fresh air and an inspiration for all believers who call themselves evangelical Christians. The covenant community I have been most closely associated with is, as I mentioned earlier, the Sword of the Spirit.

The Sword of the Spirit is only one of the many international associations of communities that have emerged in the last twenty years. Like many of its sister networks, it has tried to keep the flames of ecumenism alive by explicitly supporting ecumenical communities like the Word of God in Ann Arbor, Michigan. It has also promoted church-based communities like the one to which I belong in Steubenville, Ohio, the Servants of Christ the King. Servants of Christ the King is a fully Catholic community. It has also been given fellowship parish status by our local bishop, Albert Ottenweller.

Throughout its history, Sword of the Spirit has repeatedly readjusted its expressions and understanding of ecumenism to comply with the teaching authorities of the churches to which its members belong. Like individuals, communities go through a process of maturation. That process has brought a clearer and deeper revelation to members of Sword of the Spirit as to what it really means to be fully Catholic or fully Lutheran or fully Presbyterian. What has emerged is a realization that membership in the individual church body is exceedingly important. These readjustments in understanding, leadership structures, and relationships among communities, though often difficult, have not deterred the leaders of the Sword of the Spirit from standing for ecumenism. They continue to seek to demonstrate willing submission to appropriate church authorities, joining it with a prophetic conviction about Christian unity. That's one tough but rewarding task!

The Sword of the Spirit has been fruitful through its outreaches. One such outreach is the Center for Pastoral Renewal. The goal of the Center is explicitly evangelical and ecumenical. It strives to strengthen the whole Body of Christ by first strengthening its leadership. The Center sponsors conferences called Allies for Faith and Renewal (AFR), featuring speakers from all Christian denominations uniting in our common commitment to the good news. The Center's main activities are nationwide seminars and a periodical entitled *Pastoral Renewal*.

Leaders of AFR have become aware of the danger of the de-Christianization of Western society and have realized that the church must be a witness to holiness and truth. Members believe that Christians must unite to reassert the fundamental elements of the Christian faith we hold in common and join together in loyalty to the authority of God's Word. As a group of Catholics, Protestants, and Orthodox, AFR members recognize one another as brothers and sisters, separated by differences but united in a desire to obey the one Lord. They supplement their ecumenical thrust with an effort at evangelism on university campuses called University Christian Outreach. Their goal is for all to work together in practical ways to strengthen one another, defend Christian teaching, and bring the world to Christ. Now isn't that a model we can follow? Isn't that what Christ wants us to do, to recognize and see Him in one another, to build one another up as brothers and sisters in His family as we touch others for Him?

Although this goal is a high priority of AFR and Sword of the Spirit, its leaders are not naive. Accepting one another is only a necessary first step to positive ecumenism and to our *ultimate* goal—complete unity. We need to pray with each other for the coming about of the full communion in faith and charity of all Christians. This union can only be the fruit of grace, a sign of the forgiveness of God for His sinful people.

FAMILY LIFE

Another dimension of true evangelical Christianity is the full recognition that a relationship with Jesus Christ is not simply personal. It must also affect family living—how we relate to our parents, spouses, children, cousins, and so on. After all, the natural family is the first cell of the church. It has long been hailed throughout Christian history as the *domestic church*. Without an evangelical renewal of Christian family life, there will be no evangelical renewal of Christian churches.

In our day, we have been truly blessed with family movements that have directly affected thousands. Three Catholic movements have moved beyond their own church family to impact the broader Christian church. They are Couples for Christ, Marriage in the Holy Spirit, and Worldwide Marriage Encounter. And one

Protestant group, Focus on the Family, has reached across all church and confessional lines, providing sound spiritual and psychological counsel to families everywhere. Let's briefly look at each group.

COUPLES FOR CHRIST

Couples for Christ (CFC) began in 1981 when members of a Christian community in the Philippines (Joy of the Lord) realized the need for family outreach and began bringing couples into private homes on a weekly basis to share the power of God in their lives. CFC's primary goal is the renewal and strengthening of the natural family as the basic unit of society. CFC members provide support, guidance, and Spirit-directed strength to many families trying to live gospel values in the contemporary world. They help one another grow into maturity as men and women of God, showing them how to fulfill their primary vocation of raising families under the lordship of Jesus Christ and for the service of His Kingdom. CFC moves toward this goal step by step, beginning first with each individual's personal encounter with Christ. After each partner renews his or her commitment to God and becomes open to a fuller working of His Holy Spirit, he or she can then recommit to each other in a vital way. When the parents are strong in the Lord, their example touches the entire family; then once united, the family can become an example and a source of evangelism to the church at large.

Before becoming a member of CFC, a person must attend a series of introductory teachings, sharings, and fellowships called Christian Life Program. Twelve weekly sessions focus mainly on the basics of Christian life; on the call of each Christian, with particular emphasis on family; and finally on total commitment to Christ. These sessions pave the way for an initial encounter with Christ and offer a basis for continuing spiritual growth. If couples wish to dig deeper, they are placed in a small group of five to seven couples who meet weekly for support, encouragement, and prayer. In this ongoing connection to friends and leaders, CFC provides an effective means for the transformation of families into the pure image of God.

MARRIAGE IN THE HOLY SPIRIT

Marriage in the Holy Spirit (MHS) was founded by the People of Hope, a Christian community in northeastern New Jersey, in response to the growing need for couples to submit their marriages to the lordship of Jesus Christ. Out of this community's prayer and reflection came a pattern for a weekend retreat of teachings, prayer, and sharing.

The goals of the weekend are twofold: to enable each couple to learn about God's plan for their marriage, and to deepen each couple's awareness of the Holy Spirit's work in their marriage. The teachings are coupled with times of prayer, relaxation, sharing, witnessing, and personal time. Before the end of the weekend, each person spends individual time in prayer and writes a recommitment to his or her marriage vows. This statement includes details on what recommitment will look and sound like—that is, what is going to be done about it and how communication will be improved. Then each person exchanges commitments with his or her spouse so these can become statements of direction for them after they return home.

This weekend program has changed numerous marriages by planting seeds of strong family life, consistent prayer, and reliance on the Holy Spirit. Spokespersons for MHS say that their ultimate purpose is to give hope to people, to reassure them that marriage can work and that marriage according to God's design is not a mistake. Power is still available for marriages, and it flows from the true source of love, the Holy Spirit. MHS is a testimony to this fact.

WORLDWIDE MARRIAGE ENCOUNTER

Worldwide Marriage Encounter (WME) ministers to married couples, priests in the Catholic Church, and Christians of most major traditions within Protestant Christianity. WME leaders realize that all God's people share a common thread in their relationship with and in the Lord. Their vision is of a new world—a world made new by the power of love, which is a vision that comes from Jesus Himself and has been handed down by His church for generations.

Married couples and priests have a call beyond baptism to the special gifts and graces appropriate to their respective sacraments. The lives of married couples uniquely reveal the mystery of the Trinity wherein, as Augustine once said, you find a Lover (the Father), a Loved One (the Son), and a Spirit of Love (the Holy Spirit). Their lives also stand as illuminating examples of Christ's special love for His church (Eph. 5:22–23). And the priest's loving service to his people tangibly reveals the depth and power of Christ's own love for them. So on a practical level, WME encourages the renewal of the sacraments of marriage and priesthood to renew the church for the sake of the whole world. They do this in a weekend encounter that challenges participants to live a new way of life in full, intimate relationship—a radical lifestyle of reevaluation and intimacy through dialogue. They teach that pursuing values such as responsible relationship, intimate communication, and sacramental living will produce dynamic growth in and for Christ. During the weekend, couples share marriage values, weaknesses, and strengths. WME encourages couples to see marital encounters as a way of life, for as their mission statement says, "It is through awakening in couples an awareness of the gift that they are as the Sacrament of Matrimony, that we will assist in strengthening and renewing the Church and aid in its work of changing the world."

FOCUS ON THE FAMILY

Of course, any treatment of evangelical renewal and family life would be incomplete without mentioning the marvelous work of Dr. James Dobson and Focus on the Family. We were privileged to honor Dr. Dobson and Focus on the Family at Franciscan University of Steubenville. We bestowed upon him an honorary doctorate as a statement of our support for him and his work. God has certainly used him as a healing balm to countless numbers of families. Through numerous means, including radio, a magazine, and books, he faithfully brings an evangelical fervor along with good practical help to the fractured homes of Christian families from virtually all church traditions.

These four much-needed and successful movements look to the crucial problems of broken marriages and dysfunctional families. They minister to those who have made vows in Christ and who seek to strengthen those vows, to grow together in holiness, to work through their salvation with one another in the context of family life.

GROUPS FOR SOCIAL JUSTICE

Social justice is a necessary part of a truly evangelical renewal, and there are signs that at least some Christians are taking this seriously. One of the greatest signs is the work of Prison Fellowship Ministries (PFM).

PFM was founded in 1976 by former presidential aide Charles Colson after he served prison time for his involvement in the Watergate scandal. While in prison, Chuck experienced firsthand the loneliness, bitterness, fear, and pain of men and women who live without hope for the future. Fortunately, however, through the care and ministry of others, he became a committed Christian during his confinement. After his release, Chuck was unable to ignore the pain he witnessed in the hearts of many prisoners. Now convicted by God, he began a small discipleship program for inmates with just two staff members and three volunteers. God blessed his outreach. Today PFM is a worldwide ministry with branches in thirty-four countries. In the United States alone, twenty-two thousand PFM volunteers minister to inmates in 550 prisons. The ministry also extends to former inmates and to families that have been touched by prison experience.

PFM is a fellowship of men and women who, motivated by their love for the Lord Jesus Christ and in obedience to His commands, have joined together to exhort and assist His church in the prisons and in the community in its ministry to prisoners and ex-prisoners and their families. PFM also seeks to promote biblical standards of justice in the criminal justice system. The ministry includes in-prison seminars, discipleship seminars, Bible studies, marriage seminars, one-to-one visitation, inmate correspondence (pen pals), community service projects, family assistance, aftercare for released inmates, and Project Angel Tree—a program that supplies Christmas gifts for the children of indigent inmates. Gifts are given in the name of Jesus on behalf of the parent.

Justice Fellowship, a subdivision of PFM, promotes reforms that hold offenders responsible for their crimes, restores victims, and protects the public. It advocates biblically based concepts such as restitution and community service punishments for appropriate offenders, victim assistance and compensation programs, and reconciliation opportunities for victims and offenders. It also promotes the fair and effective use of prisons for offenders who must be imprisoned.

PFM is exploding with outreach opportunities, and because their focus is reaching out with Christ's love, church tradition and identification scarcely becomes an issue. The PFM staff and volunteers simply want to touch unbelievers and fellow Christians with the love of Christ. So when their work takes them to predominantly Catholic countries and Catholic environments, they strive to work with Catholic Christians. When they minister in predominantly Baptist environments, they try to work with and through Baptist Christians. A Prison Fellowship chapter has even been started on the campus of Franciscan University.

Undoubtedly, PFM is a model for ecumenical activity that is forward-thinking, prophetic, and definitely worth following. It demonstrates the mutuality of respect for different church communions that is the message of this book.

Other works of mercy are being done among the poor and hungry. Love Incorporated, Ferdinand Mahfood's Food for the Poor, Mother Teresa's Missionaries of Charity, and numerous other groups are manifesting Jesus among the materially destitute.

Many other social justice groups are doing marvelous and difficult works focused on the next generation. Operation Rescue is one of many ecumenical pro-life groups attempting to protect the unborn against the most heinous form of selfishness and prejudice—abortion. In respect to evangelism, teenagers throughout the world are reached for Christ through National Evangelization teams, begun and supported by my Catholic tradition. Our own efforts at Franciscan University through our Youth Evangelization Alliance have also touched the lives of many.

One youth work that has particularly impressed me is Youth with a Mission. Leland Paris, one of its key leaders, is a man on fire with a desire to see the nations come to Christ through the next generation. And that fire has enough burning embers to light Christians of all traditions. Although Leland is a Protestant, he carries on the work of Youth with a Mission in Catholic areas, using the talents of Catholic youth. He and Youth with a Mission understand that the Spirit of God knows no boundaries in the work of revival.

GLOBAL EVANGELISM

LAUSANNE

Another powerful example of Christians coming together emerged in Lausanne, Switzerland, in 1974. This city hosted the first international congress on world evangelization which was possibly the widest-ranging meeting of Christians ever. Twenty-seven hundred evangelical leaders from all denominations gathered at this congress to consider the task of winning the world for Christ. They worked to draft a document that any church could adopt to help launch evangelistic efforts. After much discussion and debate, delegates to the congress drafted the Lausanne Covenant, which affirmed their commitment to pray, study, plan, and work together to fulfill the mission of spreading the good news commanded by Christ in the Great Commission.

Significant cooperative evangelistic efforts began, but eventually many leaders made an urgent plea for a second congress. In July 1989, Lausanne II was held in Manila. Numerous participants and observers believe that this congress was the most strategic gathering of Christians committed to world evangelism in the twentieth century.

The point behind the Lausanne Covenant is that the task of evangelism is unfinished and that all Christians must come together on their common beliefs to spread the gospel. The Covenant speaks to many issues, all of them rooted in a central mission: "We [the participants] are deeply stirred by what God is doing in our day, moved to penitence by our failures and challenged by the unfinished task of evangelization. We believe the gospel is God's good news for the whole world, and we are determined by his grace to obey Christ's commission to proclaim it to all mankind and to make disciples of every nation."

One of the leaders of the Congress simply and clearly expresses the spirit of Lausanne: "It is only when we meet face to face, and struggle to hear and understand each other, that our type-cast image of each other (developed in separation) are modified, and we grow in mutual respect and shared conviction. This is the 'spirit of Lausanne'—a spirit of openness, integrity, and love."

Lausanne has reached out to Christians of every church communion. Their efforts to bring Catholics, Protestants, and Orthodox together have not been easy. They are being carefully scrutinized by different church authorities, but this should not be feared. If there is need for readjustment, it should be welcomed, and I believe Lausanne leaders and participants will accept such a challenge. They are committed to a genuinely evangelical ecumenical global outreach. The road they have chosen to travel is a bumpy one filled with potholes, but they know that the journey will fail without the cooperation of fellow travelers in the faith.

EFFORTS AIMED AT A.D. 2000

There seems to be a growing prophetic urgency in the hearts of God's people as the year 2000 approaches. Responding to that urgency have been groups like Evangelization 2000. Evangelization 2000, under the leadership of Father Tom Forrest, is dedicated to rallying Catholics to the challenge of global evangelism within the next decade. It is accomplishing its agenda by joining ranks with other church efforts at worldwide evangelism. Service committees, such as the North American Renewal Service Committee, which is under the dynamic leadership of Dr. Vinson Synan, are giving birth to efforts such as *A.D. 2000*, which is a magazine geared toward networking these committees. The common denominator of all such groups is simple: they want to give a special birthday gift to Jesus Christ in the year 2000—a more Christian world.

INDIVIDUALS IN PROPHETIC LEADERSHIP

In John Paul II's recent exhortation to the lay faithful, *Christifideles Laici*, he records for all of us a compelling call to reevangelize the church. Some Christians question his position as successor to Saint Peter—I do not. Others question his theology—I do not. But no one can question his love for Jesus Christ and deep commitment to proclaiming the gospel. I believe he is the leading evangelical Christian in the world. His courage has opened doors that have long been shut. His visits to Eastern Bloc countries and Latin America prophetically preceded and affected the events that have occurred there.

Dr. Billy Graham is another prophetic leader. A beautiful exception to the problem of arrogant Western presumptions, he has long worked with native churches and, though criticized by some, was proclaiming the gospel behind the Iron Curtain long before the Berlin Wall showed any cracks. He acknowledges that God is in the midst of Eastern Orthodoxy and Roman Catholicism, not just Protestantism.

One other prophetic voice is Chuck Colson. Through his writings, ministry, talks, and other commitments, he has scaled over the walls separating believers, courageously standing with Christians of all traditions to confront the darkness of our age. He and his work embody the spirit of charity and love of Christ to all believers and nonbelievers.

His organization, Prison Fellowship Ministries, has demonstrated a prophetic and courageous ecumenism. In fact, recently Chuck asked what we at Franciscan University thought of PFM's statement of faith, and we raised some concerns about its terminology but little about its content. Chuck immediately began reworking the statement to alleviate our concerns. Why? Because he is committed to making PFM genuinely ecumenical. It always takes leaders such as Chuck who are willing to change and be misunderstood to move the rest of us on to higher ground.

Several years ago we honored Chuck with our Poverello Medal, our highest award given annually to the man, woman, or organization which most reflects the spirit of Saint Francis in his simple love for Jesus Christ. We honored Chuck for his work with PFM and his prophetic ministry in a desperate world.

Dr. James Dobson and Harald Bredesen, both also mentioned earlier, are great evangelical believers who are speaking prophetically to our time: Dr. Dobson, to the Christian family and beyond to our Western culture; Harald, to the churches, with a clarion call for their renewal and reunification.

I also believe Ralph Martin is a significant prophetic voice for our day. A Catholic layman, Ralph has long been active in renewal movements such as Cursillo and the Charismatic Renewal. He is also a founder of the Word of God community and a leader in community movements. An ardent pro-lifer, he has been arrested for saving children from abortionists. He has consistently and clearly proclaimed a message of Christian unity, and through his work in Servant Ministries, his many books, and his television and radio program "Choices We Face," he delivers a strong evangelical message of repentance and conversion.

Another prophetic voice that I deeply admire is Mother Angelica. She is a Franciscan nun with a big vision who has presided over a modern-day miracle, the Eternal Word Television Network. EWTN is a Catholic television network proclaiming the gospel twenty-four hours a day. The story of Mother, the sisters who have joined her, and the work of the network are chronicled in numerous books about her life. She demonstrates the kind of evangelical fervor, courage, and conviction for which this book calls.

Yet another voice crying in the wilderness is Pat Robertson. His Christian Broadcasting Network has brought hope to Christian people for many years. His clear teaching, personal example, and founding of Regent University have been an inspiration to Christians of all churches. For me personally, he inspires me to give my whole life to God.

Over my years at Franciscan University, I have come to know many holy men and women of faith. My experiences have only deepened my hunger for genuine evangelical cooperation. Among the keynote speakers at our annual Priests' Conference have been Dr. Vinson Synan, Reverend Bob Mumford, and Reverend Terry Fullam. In other conferences we have been blessed by the teaching of Elisabeth Elliot and Reverend Glandion Carney. Franciscan University is committed to ecumenism, and we are committed to being Catholic. These other Christian men and women are also committed to ecumenism, and like us, just as dedicated to their respective traditions. For all of us, the overriding desire that the nations be brought to Jesus Christ brings us together.

OUR FAMILY CONTINUITY

Did you notice the threads of continuity woven between all of these groups, movements, and prophetic leaders? All of them are sharply focused on Jesus Christ as personal Lord. All seek ways to share His lordship among themselves and with others. And all desire unity. They sense the urgency of our mission under the call and example of Christ, and they realize we cannot meet it as separated brethren going in separate directions.

In these movements and others, hundreds of thousands of people in the Body of Christ have found access to renewal. And as these movements grow, their fruit will become even more widespread and apparent. Their testimonies to personal encounters with the Lord Jesus verify their readiness to plan and share effective cooperative evangelistic efforts. They understand that personal evangelism must call for ongoing conversion, that renewal must begin within the Body of Christ before it can reach the darkness beyond.

Even though their practices have not always measured up to a perfect theology of community or ecumenism, the very existence of their attempts testifies to a common conviction that to belong to Christ is to belong to His Body and to do what He commanded. The groups and individuals discussed here understand that community is a necessary dimension of church life and that as a community we have a mission to equip Christians to share their faith in Jesus Christ and share His love to all. These movements and leaders call us back to the roots, back to the real meaning of the word *radical*. The root of the faith is quite simply the cross of Jesus Christ.

Let's all be radical. Let's grasp the cross together, hold it high, and move out to tell a dying world that everlasting life is available only in the One who hung on this cross almost two thousand years ago, then rose from the grave, declaring victory over death for all who trust in Him.

CHAPTER **13**

The Family for Others

Long-standing Christian tradition has celebrated the Pentecost event as the birthday of the church. On the day of Pentecost, the promise of another comforter was fulfilled and the Lord began to dwell in a new, fresh, and wonderful way among His earthly family. How? By the presence of His Holy Spirit. That Spirit transformed what had been a fearful group of disciples (including Mary, the Mother of the Lord) into an empowered church sent out as the family for others. The presence of the Holy Spirit gave that New Testament family the power to proclaim good news to a troubled generation and to live as a community of light in the midst of darkness. The simple biblical description of that early church experience is found in the Acts of the Apostles:

> They devoted themselves to the apostles' teaching and to the fellowship, to the breaking of bread and to prayer. Everyone was filled with awe, and many wonders and miraculous signs were done by the apostles. All the believers were together and had everything in common. Selling their possessions and goods, they gave to anyone as he had need. Every day they continued to meet together in the temple courts. They broke bread in their homes and ate together with glad and sincere hearts, praising God and enjoying the favor of all the people. And the Lord added to their number daily those who were being saved. (Acts 2:42–47, NIV)

They lived differently, they loved differently, and they knew that their life was no longer their own. Out of a unity forged in blood, they literally transformed the first century.

Certainly they had differences. They were human, and they were sinful. But through it all they maintained their unity, even as they spread internationally and interculturally. Still fresh in their hearts was the impassioned prayer of the Master: "May they be brought to complete unity to let the world know that you sent me" (John 17:23, NIV). Apostolic instruction, breaking bread, prayer, fellowship, community, and mission—their practice bound Christians together, helped them change the shape of their world, and caused them to reach out to others in faith and compassion.

Well, as it was in the first century, can it be in the twenty-first? Yes. An impossible dream? No. It is God's plan for us here and now. What has thwarted it? We have. In our own way, we have all contributed to the division and wounds in the Body of Christ. Through sins of commission, omission, and just plain-old petty rivalry, ignorance, and pride, we have bruised and scarred Christ's family. Nevertheless, it can be healed, but not through "sloppy agape," nondenominationalism, or false ecumenism, and certainly not through triumphalism, judgmentalism, and mean-spirited attacks on Christians by Christians.[1] The home is broken, and as always the children have suffered the most.

Many today who have suffered from the effects of dysfunctional families (those affected by divorce, alcoholism, drug abuse and addiction, compulsive behaviors, domestic violence, physical and emotional abuse, and many other wounds) have discovered the steps to freedom in a very simple formula for conversion known as the Twelve Steps. Originally formulated by Alcoholics Anonymous, these steps have had an almost miraculous impact on countless thousands. I believe the Twelve Steps are quite simply a restatement of the Christian message of honest surrender, admission of fault and need, repentance, restitution and restoration, and ongoing conversion and mission. Read them carefully with this perspective in mind.

The Twelve Steps of Alcoholics Anonymous

1. We admitted we were powerless over alcohol and that our lives had become unmanageable.
2. Came to believe that a Power greater than ourselves could restore us to sanity.
3. Made a decision to turn our will and our lives over to the care of God as we understand Him.
4. Made a searching and fearless moral inventory of ourselves.

5. Admitted to God, to ourselves, and to another human being the exact nature of our wrongs.
6. Were entirely ready to have God remove all these defects of character.
7. Humbly asked Him to remove our shortcomings.
8. Made a list of all persons we had harmed, and became willing to make amends to them all.
9. Made direct amends to such people wherever possible, except when to do so would injure them or others.
10. Continued to take personal inventory, and when we were wrong, promptly admitted it.
11. Sought through prayer and meditation to improve our conscious contact with God as we understand Him, praying only for knowledge of His will for us and the power to carry that out.
12. Having had a spiritual awakening as the result of these steps, we tried to carry this message to other alcoholics and to practice these principles in all our affairs.[2]

With some slight modifications to Steps 1 and 12, these Twelve Steps could help guide our wounded church family through a proven and effective means of healing and restoration. Here are the modifications I have in mind:

1. We admitted that we were powerless over *the divisions in the Body of Christ and that our life together* had become unmanageable.
12. Having had a spiritual awakening as the result of these steps, we tried to carry this message to other *Christians* and to practice these principles in all our affairs.

Now reread all of the steps with these modifications. Do you see how God could use our application of these steps to restore our church family to unity and wholeness?

I believe the honesty, tough love, and gutsy willingness to change evidenced in the principles set forth in these steps could have a tremendous impact on our own ecumenical efforts. How have we become affected (or perhaps infected) by the dangerous family feuds initiated and perpetuated generationally by the great divorce? How do we view Christians of other churches? Have any negative, perhaps inherited, prejudices colored our approach to family life and mission?

The application of a process at least similar to these steps to the current destructive effects of the divisions within the Christian family could have sweeping effects on our efforts at true ecumenism. We must begin somewhere, both for the sake of our own family health and for the sake of those outside of the family. So much needs to be done. The next century confronts us with a missionary challenge that can only be met through a common, cooperative evangelical agenda. We must rediscover our roots in our common family heritage and recognize that what we hold in common compels us to work together.

As I have tried to show throughout these chapters, I am not espousing a naive wish but rather a conviction which runs deep, not only in my own life, but in the lives of thousands of other believers worldwide. The current divisions among Christians, insofar as they feed mistrust, are insane. Misunderstandings, ignorance, pride, and prejudice have weakened our efforts, clouded our witness, and armed our common enemy with formidable weapons. Let's not cover up the divisions any longer with pious sounding jargon and self-justifying polemic. The disunity among us is insanity. The only One who can ultimately restore our unity (sanity) is the Lord. But we can begin to cooperate with Him by rediscovering some common ground and, in the power of His Spirit, building on it as we move ahead on a common mission.

Throughout these many pages, I have detailed aspects of our common faith and mission, but they are so important and central that I would like to summarize and reiterate them here, one last time. Read them slowly, thoughtfully, prayerfully. Allow the Spirit to witness to your spirit that these things are so, that they are vital, that they can be redemptive, that they can truly be used by Him to restore the unity of the church of Pentecost, the family of families, the Family for others.

A COMMON BOOK

The Bible is the treasure chest of our common faith. Though we may disagree in our understanding of its origin and even perhaps its content, evangelical Christians agree it is God's holy Word given as a "measuring stick," a rule of love for all of life.

A COMMON HISTORY

All of our churches, groups, traditions, communions, and fellowships spring from one root—the root of Jesse (Rom. 15:12), the root and offspring of David (Rev. 22:16)—Jesus Christ. He is our Founder, our Savior, our Head, our Lord. We are His bride, His people, His flock, His family.

We would all do well to study our family history through all the centuries with an eye toward rediscovering our common heritage. We could all rejoice in the victories, repent for the mistakes and, most importantly, grow through the lessons.

A COMMON CREED

Although our doctrines are grounded in Scripture, they have been expressed and formalized in numerous creeds. Some of these creeds are distinctively Catholic, some are definitely Protestant, and others are explicitly Orthodox. Two creeds, however, have found acceptance among almost all Christian churches: the Apostle's Creed and the Nicene Creed (see Chapter 1). These creedal formulas contain the essence of our common faith, "the faith that was once for all entrusted to the saints" (Jude 3, NIV).

A COMMON SAVIOR

Perhaps most important to remember is that we have a common Savior. There is not a Protestant Jesus, a Catholic Jesus, or an Orthodox Jesus. Certainly each church communion has cherished important distinctives in doctrine and practice arising from reflections upon Him, but He is the same, as the author of Hebrews reminds us, "yesterday and today and forever" (Heb. 13:8, NIV).

In his correction of the Corinthian Christians, Paul asks a question we should ponder: "Is Christ divided?" (1 Cor. 1:13, NIV). He cannot be and He is not. But we can be and we are. Let's not confuse our state for His. He is united and the same; we are divided and different. Different is okay, even healthy and good.

Divided is neither good nor healthy. Christ longs for us to be united again under Him.

My friend Harald Bredesen spearheads an effort called The Prince of Peace. He honored Mother Teresa with an award for her witness to the world of Christ's love, and she accepted it. A truly ecumenical coalition, including Regent University and Franciscan University, came together to plan the event. As Harald and I worked together on this award ceremony, we looked to the Lord for a Scripture passage that would express His deep longing for the unity of His people. We were drawn to Paul's exhortation to the Ephesian Christians, who in their day were struggling through some deep issues involving the coming together of both Jewish and Gentile Christians in the Body of Christ. Paul's response to their struggle has tremendous relevance for us. As you read his words, hear them speak to your heart.

> For [Christ] himself is our peace, who has made the two [Gentile and Jew] one and has destroyed the barrier, the dividing wall of hostility, by abolishing in his flesh the law with its commandments and regulations. His purpose was to create in himself one new man out of the two, thus making peace, and in this one body to reconcile both of them to God through the cross, by which he put to death their hostility. He came and preached peace to you who were far away and peace to those who were near. For through him we both have access to the Father by one Spirit. (Eph. 2:14–18, NIV)

Our common Savior can destroy the wall of ignorance and hostility that has separated us and seriously hindered our missionary efforts. And when their divisive and derisive wall finally collapses, it will unleash a flood of grace that will soak the parched and abused souls of God's people, nourishing the seeds of peace and unity that long to grow.

A COMMON MISSION

Perhaps the clearest statement of our common mission is found in the most quoted gospel passage and the verses that follow it:

> For God so loved the world that he gave his one and only Son,
> that whoever believes in him shall not perish but have eternal
> life. For God did not send his Son into the world to condemn
> the world, but to save the world through him. Whoever
> believes in him is not condemned, but whoever does not
> believe stands condemned already because he has not believed
> in the name of God's one and only Son. This is the verdict:
> Light has come into the world, but men loved darkness
> instead of light because their deeds were evil. Everyone who
> does evil hates the light, and will not come into the light for
> fear that his deeds will be exposed. But whoever lives by the
> truth comes into the light, so that it may be seen plainly that
> what he has done has been done through God. (John 3:16–21,
> NIV)

This is the heart of our common evangelical proclamation, our
kerygma. Our task is to proclaim it by our words and deeds.

To effectively carry out our mission, we need to be fully
empowered by the same Holy Spirit who has animated our family
from the day of Pentecost; we need to be fully faithful to our own
convictions, those that flow out of our common faith and those that
come from our distinctive church traditions; we need to be in communion with God's people and in submission to church authority;
we need to make room for one another, building on our commonalities while respecting our differences. The harvest is indeed plentiful and the laborers are still few. But united, we are many. United,
we can support one another to accomplish our common, divinely
commanded agenda.

Within each of our churches, we need to preach an evangelical message to awaken dry bones and rouse sleeping warriors. To
the nations who have never heard or who have turned a deaf ear to
the One who fashioned them from dust, we need to "tell the old,
old story of Jesus and His love." It's an old story that's ever new.
It's *our* story . . . *our* family history . . . and we must not rest until
we see the members of our family span the globe, locked arm-in-
arm in the unifying love of our common Lord.

AN UNCOMMON PLEA

You have heard my plea to all Christians to lay down their
weapons, scale the great wall of division, embrace each other once

more as fellow members of the same church family, and together penetrate the stronghold of our common foe with the reconciling sword of the gospel. You have heard about other individuals, groups, communities, churches, and fellowships which are fighting the good fight from a solid ecumenical base and calling for fresh recruits from every corner of the Christian camp. Encouraging? Yes. Tragic? That too, because all these voices are too few. They are still lonely cries echoing across the battlefields of secularism, relativism, atheism, New Age-ism, and all the other *isms* threatening to kill and bury believers and unbelievers alike. Our plea is still rarely voiced and even more rarely heard. It seems insane, doesn't it? Given all we have in common, the plea for peace in our family is still uncommon.

But once again, when we turn back the pages of our common history, we find how old this uncommon plea really is. Back in 1749, we discover a great evangelical Protestant hero of mine, John Wesley, writing a letter to a Catholic friend. This lengthy piece of correspondence would later become a tract which was distributed in Ireland where great bitterness existed between Catholics and Protestants. But before that, it would be placed into the hands of one Catholic, given as a vehicle to foster unity, not divisiveness, in a personal relationship. From this letter exudes the heart of a man on fire for the gospel and true ecumenism. It is too long to quote in its entirety, but if we would only hear Wesley's uncommon plea, perhaps more of us would take it as our own, and perhaps in time, it would reverberate throughout the world, carried on every tongue that confesses Jesus Christ as Lord.

1. You have heard ten thousand stories of us who are commonly called Protestants, of which, if you believe only one in a thousand, you must think very hardly of us. But this is quite contrary to our Lord's rule, 'judge not, that ye be not judged' (Matt. 7:1), and has many ill consequences, particularly this: it inclines us to think as hardly of you. Hence, we are on both sides less willing to help one another and more ready to hurt each other. Hence brotherly love is utterly destroyed and each side, looking on the other as monsters, gives way to anger, hatred, malice, to every unkind affection—which have frequently broke out in such inhuman barbarities as are scarce named even among the heathens.

2. Now can nothing be done, even allowing us on both sides to retain our own opinions, for the softening our hearts towards each other, the giving a check to this flood of unkindness and restoring at least some small degree of love among our neighbours and countrymen? Do not you wish for this? Are you not fully convinced that malice, hatred, revenge, bitterness (whether in us or in you, in our hearts or yours) are an abomination to the Lord (Prov. 15:26; 16:5)? Be our opinions right or be they wrong, these tempers are undeniably wrong. They are the broad road that leads to destruction, to the nethermost hell.

3. I do not suppose all the bitterness is on your side. I know there is too much on our side also. So much that I fear many Protestants (so-called) will be angry at me, too, for writing to you in this manner, and will say, 'Tis showing you too much favour; you deserve no such treatment at our hands.'

4. But I think you do. I think you deserve the tenderest regard I can show, were it only because the same God hath raised you and me from the dust of the earth and has made us both capable of loving and enjoying him to eternity; were it only because the Son of God has bought you and me with his own blood. How much more, if you are a person fearing God (as without question many of you are) and studying to have a conscience void of offence towards God and towards man?

5. I shall therefore endeavour, as mildly and inoffensively as I can, to remove in some measure the ground of your unkindness by plainly declaring what our belief and what our practice is: that you may see we are not altogether such monsters as perhaps you imagined us to be.

After describing the essentials of Protestant belief, Wesley made an appeal Christians of all traditions should accept. Indeed, his four closing exhortations could still serve as the basis for a genuine ecumenism and genuinely evangelical agenda.

16. Are we not thus far agreed? Let us thank God for this, and receive it as a fresh token of his love. But if God still loveth us, we ought also to love one another. We provoke one another to love and to good works. Let the points

wherein we differ stand aside: here are enough wherein
we agree, enough to be the ground of every Christian
temper and of every Christian action.

O brethren, let us not still fall out by the way. I
hope to see you in heaven. And if I practise the religion
above described, you dare not say I shall go to hell. You
cannot think so. None can persuade you to it. Your own
conscience tells you the contrary. Then if we cannot as
yet think alike in all things, at least we may love alike.
Herein we cannot possibly go amiss. For of one point
none can doubt a moment: God is love; and he that
dwelleth in love, dwelleth in God, and God in him
(1 John 4:16).

17. In the name, then, and in the strength of God, let us
resolve, *first, not to hurt one another,* to do nothing unkind
or unfriendly to each other, nothing which we would not
have done to ourselves. Rather let us endeavour after
every instance of a kind, friendly and Christian behaviour
towards each other.

Let us resolve, secondly, God being our helper, to
speak nothing harsh or unkind of each other. The sure way
to avoid this is to say all the good we can, both of and
to one another; in all our conversation, either with or
concerning each other, to use only the language of love;
to speak with all softness and tenderness, with the most
endearing expression which is consistent with truth and
sincerity.

*Let us thirdly, resolve to harbour no unkind thought,
no unfriendly temper towards each other.* Let us lay the axe
to the root of the tree (Matt. 3:10), let us examine all that
rises in our heart and suffer no disposition there which is
contrary to the tender affection. Then shall we easily
refrain from unkind actions and words, when the very
root of bitterness is cut up (Heb. 12:15).

*Let us, fourthly, endeavour to help each other on in
whatever we are agreed leads to the Kingdom.* So far as we
can, let us always rejoice to strengthen each other's hands
in God. Above all, let us each take heed unto himself
(since each must give an account of himself to God) that
he fall not short of the religion of love; that he be not
condemned in that he himself approveth. O let you and
me (whatever others do) press on to the prize of our high

calling—that, being justified by faith, we may have peace with God through our Lord Jesus Christ; that we may rejoice in God through Jesus Christ, by whom we have received the atonement (Rom. 5:1-2); that the love of God may be shed abroad in our hearts by the Holy Ghost which is given unto us (Rom. 5:5). Let us count all things but loss for the excellency of the knowledge of Jesus Christ our Lord, being ready for him to suffer the loss of all things and counting them but dung, that we may win Christ. (Phil. 3:8)[3]

One day we *will* see the true family unity all of us should desire—the unity Wesley so much wanted with his Catholic brother in Christ. Until then, we can together cry out the ancient prayer of our ancestors recorded in the last verses of our family album: "Amen. Come, Lord Jesus. The grace of the Lord Jesus be with God's people. Amen" (Rev. 22:20-21, NIV).

NOTES

1. Evangelical Catholic: A Contradiction in Terms?

1. Ignatius of Antioch, "Letter to the Smyrneane," 8:12, *Early Christian Fathers*, Cyril Richardson, ed. (Philadelphia: The Westminster Press, 1953).
2. As cited from Alan Schreck, *Catholic and Christian* (Ann Arbor, MI: Servant Books, 1984), 59.
3. Austin Flannery, O.P., ed., "Decree on Ecumenism," *Vatican Council II: The Conciliar and Post Conciliar Documents* (New York: Costello Pub., 1975), par. 3.
4. Austin Flannery, O.P., ed., "Domestic Constitution on the Church," in *Vatican Council II: The Conciliar and Post Conciliar Documents* (New York: Costello Pub., 1975), par. 1.
5. Saint Augustine of Hippo, *City of God*, 19:14–17. See also Schreck, *Catholic and Christian*, 29-39.
6. Flannery, ed., "Dogmatic Constitution on the Church," par. 14.
7. *The Encyclopedia of Religion*, Mircea Eliade, ed. (New York: MacMillan, 1987), 190.
8. *New Encyclopedia Britannica* (Chicago: William and Helen Benton, 1983), 3:133. See also *The Encyclopedia of Religion*, Mircea Eliade, ed. (New York: MacMillan, 1987), 191.
9. *The Encyclopedia of Religion*, 191.
10. Ibid., 194.
11. Ibid.
12. William Barclay, *New Testament Words* (London: SCM, 1964), 62–64.
13. Gerhard Kittel, ed., *Theological Dictionary of the New Testament* (Grand Rapids: William B. Eerdmans, 1973), 2: 770.
14. Anthony Gilles, *Living Words: A Simple Study of Key New Testament Concepts for People Who Don't Know a Word of Greek* (Cincinnati: St. Anthony Messenger, 1985), 34–35.
15. Ronald Roberson, "Can Evangelicals Be Sacramental?", *Again* 6:2 (April 1984), 4.
16. Michael Hennel, "Evangelical Spirituality," in *The Westminster Dictionary of Christian Spirituality*, ed. Gordon S. Wakefield (Philadelphia: The Westminster Press, 1983), 138.

17. Ibid.
18. Thomas Howard, *Evangelical Is Not Enough* (Nashville: Thomas Nelson, 1984), 149.

2. Over the Rainbow

1. Accurately, "because the one who is in you is greater than the one who is in the world" (1 John 4:4).
2. In fact, Stuart is the only traveling companion I had who has not found faith in Jesus Christ. At the time of the writing of this book, he was living somewhere in Japan. As far as I know, he is still pursuing answers in Eastern religions.

3. There's No Place Like Home

1. Carl F. H. Henry, "The Christian Scholar's Task," lecture given at "Oxford '88," C. S. Lewis Summer Institute (England: Oxford University, 1988).

4. Classical Revival at a Catholic College

1. Michael Scanlan, "Making and Keeping Catholic Colleges Catholic," adapted from a presentation given by Michael Scanlan at "Oxford '88," C. S. Lewis Summer Institute (England: Oxford University, 1988).

5. Returning to Our First Love

1. C. S. Lewis, *The Problem of Pain* (New York: Macmillan, 1962), 46.
2. Flannery, ed., "Dogmatic Constitution on the Church," par. 9.
3. See Alan Schreck, *Catholic and Christian* (Ann Arbor, MI: Servant Books, 1984), 49.
4. Flannery, ed., "Dogmatic Constitution on the Church," pars. 8, 9, 22, 25.
5. Thomas of Celano, "Second Life," chap. 68, in *St. Francis of Assisi: Writings of Early Biographies, English Comnibus of the Sources For the Life of St. Francis*, Marion Habig, ed., (Chicago: Franciscan Herald, 1973), 446.

6. Paul Little, *How to Give Away Your Faith* (Downers Grove, IL: InterVarsity, 1966), 35.
7. Pope Paul VI, *On Evangelization in the Modern World* (Washington D.C.: United States Catholic Conference, 1975), par. 22.
8. Charles Colson, *Against the Night* (Ann Arbor, MI: Servant, 1989), quote taken from galley proofs which were modified on pages 23 and 81 of the book.
9. Pope John Paul II, in *Existential Personalism*, by Andrew Woznicki (New Britain, CT: Mariel, 1980), 4.

6. Faith and Works: The Full Family Life

1. See Alan Schreck's *Basics of the Faith: A Catholic Catechism* (Ann Arbor, MI: Servant, 1987), ch. 10. See also his *Catholic and Christian*, ch. 9.
2. Norman Geisler, *The Roots of Evil* (Grand Rapids, MI: Zondervan, 1978), 46–47.
3. Schreck, *Basics of Faith*, 159.
4. Ibid.
5. Flannery, ed., "Dogmatic Constitution on the Church," par. 42.
6. Peter Kreeft, *Heaven, the Heart's Deepest Longing* (San Francisco: Harper & Row, 1980).
7. C. S. Lewis, *The Great Divorce* (New York: Macmillan, 1946), 72.
8. Schreck, *Catholic and Christian*, 39.
9. William Barclay, *The Daily Study Bible Series: The Letter of James and Peter* (Philadelphia: Westminster Press, 1975), 60.

7. Evangelical Counsels: Wisdom for Family Living

1. Neil Postman, *Amusing Ourselves to Death: Public Discourse in the Age of Show Business* (New York, NY: Viking, 1985), 3–4, emphasis added.
2. Ibid., 121.
3. Glandion Carney, *Heaven Within These Walls* (Ventura, CA: Regal, 1989), 45.
4. Saint Francis De Sales, *The Introduction to the Devout Life*, John K. Ryan, trans. (New York: Image Books, 1966), 122.
5. Paul K. Meagher, O.P., ed., *Encyclopedic Dictionary of Religion* (Washington: Corpus Press, 1979), 932.
6. Ibid.

7. Dallas Willard, *The Spirit of the Disciplines* (San Francisco: Harper & Row, 1988), 194–95.
8. Ibid., 205.
9. S. O'Riordan, "Chastity," *New Catholic Encyclopedia* (New York: McGraw-Hill, 1967), 516.
10. Willard, *The Spirit of the Disciplines*, 170–71.
11. Luke 3:21–23; Mark 1:35; Luke 5:16; 6:12; 9:16; Matt 14:23; 15:36; Luke 9:18, 28–29; 10:21; 11:1; John 11:41–42; Matt. 19:13; John 12:27–28; Luke 22:17–19, 32; John 14:16; Luke 24:30–31, 50–53. For more on Jesus' prayer life and teaching, see Curtis C. Mitchell's *Praying Jesus' Way* (Old Tappan, NJ: Fleming H. Revell, 1977).
12. Rom. 13:1–6; Eph. 6:1–9; Heb. 13:17.

8. Our Family Tree

1. John Woodbridge, ed., *Great Leaders of the Christian Church* (Chicago: Moody, 1988), 24.
2. Ibid., 84.
3. Ibid., 293.
4. Ibid., 288.
5. Jay P. Dolan, *Catholic Revivalism: The American Experience; 1830–1900* (Notre Dame: University of Notre Dame Press, 1978), 69–70.
6. Ellen H. Walworth, *Life Sketches of Father Walworth*, 2nd ed. (Albany: J. B. Lyon Co., 1907), 129.
7. G. K. Chesterton, *Orthodoxy* (New York: Image Books, 1959), 2.

9. The Children of the Great Divorce

1. Paul Weyrich, *The Weyrich Insider* (Dec. 6, 1989).

10. Humpty Dumpty Solutions

1. Flannery, ed., "Decree on Ecumenism," par. 11.

11. Genuine Ecumenism: The Road Back Home

1. Richard John Neuhaus, talk given at Franciscan University of

Steubenville, Spring 1989. Adapted from his *The Catholic Moment* (San Francisco: Harper & Row, 1987.)
2. David Guralnik, ed., *Webster's New World Dictionary* (New York: William Collins, 1979), 194.
3. Flannery, ed., "Decree on Ecumenism," par. 5.
4. Flannery, ed., "Decree on Ecumenism," par. 4.
5. Pope John Paul II, *The Lay Members of Christ's Faithful People* (Boston, MA: Daughters of St. Paul, 1988), par. 34.
6. T. S. Eliot, *Christianity and Culture* (New York: Harcourt Brace, 1949), 18.
7. Colson, *Against the Night*, 104–105.
8. Hans Urs Von Galthazaar, *Convergences: To the Source of Christian Mystery* (San Francisco: Ignatius, 1983), 14–15.

12. Family Examples of Ecumenism at Work

1. William Bright, "Re-Evangelization of the United States," *World Evangelization* 16:60 (July-August 1989), 9.
2. Patty Mansfield, in *Portion of My Spirit*, by Michael Scanlan, T.O.R. (St. Paul, MN: Carillon Books, 1979), 1.

13. The Family for Others

1. An excellent analysis of the sad but all-too-frequent attacks Christians make on each other can be found in Bob and Gretchen Passantino's book *Witch Hunt* (Nashville: Thomas Nelson, 1990).
2. The Twelve Steps are reprinted with the permission of A.A. World Services, Inc. Permission to reprint the Steps does not mean that A.A. has reviewed or approved the contents of this publication nor that A.A. agrees with the views expressed herein. A.A. is a program of recovery from alcoholism. Use of the Steps in connection with programs which are patterned after A.A. but which address other problems does not imply otherwise.
3. John Wesley, *Works*, vol. 10, 80–86, in *Protestants and Catholics*, by Peter Toon (Ann Arbor, MI: Servant Publications, 1984), app. 4.